W9-BWE-025

A GOD WITHIN

ALSO BY RENÉ DUBOS

So Human an Animal

A God Within

 RENÉ DUBOS

CHARLES SCRIBNER'S SONS / NEW YORK

The author acknowledges with thanks permission to quote as follows:

on pages 130 and 230 from *Western Star* by Stephen Vincent Benét.
Holt, Rinehart and Winston, Inc.
Copyright 1943 by Rosemary Carr Benét.
By permission of Brandt & Brandt.

on page 281 from *Four Quartets* by T. S. Eliot
and on page 293 from *The People, Yes* by Carl Sandburg, respectively
By permission of Harcourt Brace Jovanovich, Inc.

A—7.72 (H)

PRINTED IN THE UNITED STATES OF AMERICA

LIBRARY OF CONGRESS CATALOG CARD NUMBER 76–37224
SBN 684–12768–7 (cloth)

To JEAN

WHO ENRICHES THE WORLD

WITH THE DIRECTNESS OF HER PERCEPTION

CONTENTS

PREFACE

I WROTE the last chapter of *A God Within* while collaborating in the preparation of a report *(Only One Earth: The Care and Maintenance of Our Small Planet)* for the United Nations Conference on the Human Environment. As a member of an international team, I had to think in global terms about the earth; each part of our planet is related to every other part and each earthling belongs to the family of man. As author of *A God Within,* in contrast, I deal with the distinctive genius of each place and each person.

These two attitudes are not incompatible; in fact they are complementary. From family to clan, from clan to nation, from nation to federation, enlargements of allegiance have occurred throughout the history of mankind without weakening the earlier loves. We can develop a rational loyalty to planet earth while maintaining an emotional attachment to our prized diversity. The present book might have been entitled "In Praise of Diversity."

A GOD WITHIN

INTRODUCTION

The Hidden Aspects of Reality

Early man possessed extensive knowledge of the sky and clouds, the plants and animals, the rocks, springs, and rivers, among which he lived. He derived from his senses much factual information about nature around him, which enabled him to cope effectively with the external world. Very soon in his social evolution, however, perhaps at the time of becoming *Homo sapiens,* he began to search for a reality different in kind from that which he could see, touch, hear, smell, or otherwise apprehend directly. His awareness of the external world came to transcend his concrete experiences of the objects and creatures he dealt with—as if he perceived in them a form of existence deeper than that revealed by outward appearances. He imagined, though probably not consciously, a Thing behind or within the thing, a Force responsible for the visible movement. This immaterial Thing or Force he regarded as a god—calling it by whatever name he used to denote the principle he thought to be hidden within external reality. Even in modern times, the people of tribes that have remained in a Stone Age culture imagine deities everywhere around them and tend to regard gods and goddesses as more real than concrete objects and creatures. The conceptual environment of primitive man commonly affects his life more profoundly than his external environment. And this is also true of modern man.

The preclassical and classical Greeks symbolized the hidden aspects of man's nature, in particular the forces that motivate him to perform memorable deeds, by the word *entheos* —a god within. From *entheos* is derived "enthusiasm," one of the most beautiful words in any language.[1] Man today may no longer believe in the divine origin of inspiration, but there are few who do not retain the ancient and almost mystical faith that enthusiasm is the source of creativity. Whatever their religious or philosophical allegiance, all men know that there would be little chance of improving the world if it were not for the faith derived from the god within; the poet would be silent if it were not for his Muse.

In the original Greek sense, the word enthusiasm means far more than deep interest, ardent zeal, or twinkling eyes. It implies the "divine madness," the mania that Socrates regarded as the mainspring of all worthwhile creations. As Plato worded it in *Phaedrus*, "In reality the greatest of blessings come to us through madness, when it is sent as a gift of the gods . . . madness, which comes from god, is superior to sanity, which is of human origin."[2]

The Greek meaning of enthusiasm also suggests that logic and clear thinking do not account entirely for the creative manifestations of human life. Indeed, scientists as well as artists, administrators as well as reformers, have acknowledged that their most valuable ideas and achievements emerged—spontaneously, as it were—from the subconscious chiaroscuro region of their minds, in the form of unprocessed ore that had only to be refined and shaped by conscious processes.

Even René Descartes, champion of the purest form of

rationalism, reported that his famous method originated during a dreamlike state over which he had no control. *"X novembris 1619, cum plenus forem Enthousiasmo, et mirabilis scientiae fundamenta reperirem."* (10 November 1619, when I was full of enthusiasm, and I discovered the fundamental principles of a wonderful knowledge.)[3] Subconscious inspiration, then, rather than orderly methodic thought was primarily responsible for the *Discours sur la Méthode.*

Ideals and commitments are thus commonly the expressions of *entheos,* the god within each of us, which accounts for the emergence and governance of our thoughts and actions. Scientifically explained, the god within is the manifestation of the attributes and attitudes we each derive from our hereditary endowment and our experiential past—the biological forces which generate the energy and provide the direction for our lives. This explanation is obviously incomplete, since it does not take free will into account, but at least it points to the mechanisms by which the responses we make to surroundings and events determine the characteristics that make each one of us a unique, unprecedented, and unrepeatable person.

Cities, landscapes, regions, and places in general also derive their uniqueness from hidden forces. The traveler can instantly perceive the atmosphere of London in a pub, or that of Paris on the *terrasse* of a café. He need only cross the frontier between Italy and Switzerland to be aware that he has moved into another culture. But no simple explanation can account for the origin of the differences between one city or one country and another. There is more to the uniqueness of a place than the geology, topography, and climate of the land, or the genetics, economics, and politics of its population.

Ancient people avoided this dilemma by identifying each place with a particular deity that personified its distinctive qualities. Although this interpretation of local differences still has a picturesque value, even for us, we do not take it seriously because we no longer believe in dryads, nymphs, and genii. And yet, rationalists that we are, and scornful of any thought that there is a ghost in the machine, we still respond emotionally to such phrases as "the genius of New England" or "the spirit of the Far West." Numerous books are still being written on the Florentine genius, and it was not long ago that the English writer Lawrence Durrell entitled a collection of travel essays *Spirit of Place*.[4] The widespread acceptance of the words genius and spirit to denote the distinctive characteristics of a given region or city implies the tacit acknowledgment that each place possesses a set of attributes that determines the uniqueness of its landscape and its people.

When applied to a place or a person, the word "nature" is as vague but also as rich in complex connotations as genius or spirit. According to dictionaries, one of the meanings of nature is "the essential character or constitution of something" or "the intrinsic characteristics and qualities of a person or thing." The word nature so defined provides a factual explanation for what the ancients called genius or spirit. It denotes not only the geographic, social, or human appearances but also, and especially, all the forces hidden beneath the surface of reality. For the people of the Greco-Roman classical age, no account of a place or of man's role in it was complete without the evocation of mysteries in which heroes and gods were the chief actors.

Places and persons acquire their distinctiveness from the interplay between their inherent characteristics and the external forces that act upon them. Since places and persons continuously evolve as they age and as conditions change, one might expect that, with time, they would be transformed beyond recognition, but this is not the case. Distinctiveness persists despite change. Italy and Switzerland, Paris and London, have retained their respective identities through many social, cultural, and technological revolutions. The facial traits of an adult or even of an old person can be recognized in portraits made during childhood. One of the most striking manifestations of the god within is indeed the persistence of distinctive traits.

Viable human institutions also develop an inner life, which makes each acquire an identity and retain it in the midst of change. From the beginning of the United States as an independent country, two visions of utopia were in contention. The Hamiltonian Federalists emphasized elitism and a mercantile policy, whereas the Jeffersonian Republicans favored populism and pastoral ways of life. Political parties have changed their labels, philosophies, and allegiances in the course of time, but the struggle between these two contrasting tendencies has continued, progressively involving new economic forces and demographic groups. This struggle has largely determined the shape of American political and social history and has also provided American literature with some of its unique and most important themes.[5]

Another characteristic of the American socio-political scene derives from English influences during the colonial period. The countries influenced by Anglo-Saxon law on the one hand and the countries of continental Europe on the other have functioned according to different political philosophies, even though they belong to the same Western culture. In Great Britain and then in North America, political doctrines have emphasized constitutional government based on the division of political power; Adam Smith's free market system fits in this political philosophy. The present efforts in the United States to reestablish community control in several aspects of social life belong to the town hall tradition. In contrast, continental Europe has usually favored a greater concentration of power in the central government—whether monarchy or republic—and stricter control of commerce as a form of mercantilism.

A startling illustration of persistence in modern Japan of sociocultural traits almost inconceivable in Western technological societies was provided in an article in the *Wall Street Journal*. The article refers to an ancient Japanese belief in the possibility of some form of reprisal from the dead if their souls are treated disrespectfully. Japanese tailors go so far, the account states, as to gather annually for a religious ceremony to honor needles worn out that year and thrown away. Now that Japan has become a great industrial power, a similar concern is directed toward the effects of modern technology. Shotaro Kamiya, president of the Toyota automobile company, is reported as stating: "I have been feeling very sorry for the persons who died in traffic accidents and who might have perished on the roads in vehicles made in our factories."[6] He thus decided to build in the hills near the company's plant a large shrine, containing a statue of the Buddhist deity of mercy, and dedicated to the repose of the persons killed in his firm's vehicles. The president of an American or European automobile company would certainly have expressed his sorrow in a more prosaic manner.

When social continuity is merely an expression of narrow-minded conservatism, it is obviously a source of cultural weakness. In many cases, however, continuity plays a creative role by enabling social forces to achieve cultural identity through long-range effects. The countries of Western Europe may be similar in geography, climate, and population structure; yet each has its own identity, derived from the impact of regional forces continued over many centuries. Washington, D.C., and

Ottawa are contrasting capital cities, not so much because the United States and Canada differ in geographic character and economic wealth as because they embody different social and cultural traditions.

Social continuity accounts for the fact that national traits are rarely completely destroyed by political revolutions. Throwing the rascals out of office is always much easier than really changing the social framework. Communist Russia has adopted internal and international policies that are strangely similar to those of the Czarist regime. Many aspects of English life have remained essentially the same under Tory, Liberal, and Labor administrations.

The endurance of an evolving system is a reflection of dynamic stability in the various phases of its development. Once a complex system has begun to move in a certain direction, the very transformations it undergoes set up, almost automatically, limits to the range of possible moves it can make in response to changing conditions. The channeling of response at each step of development has long been recognized for the human and animal embryo, in which certain developmental processes are triggered at critical junctures; each triggering in turn brings about a particular set of changes that cannot be reversed and that generate consecutive patterns which at each step impose a direction on further development. In all living systems, whether they are embryos, landscapes, or cultures, organization limits the possibilities of reorganization.

Normal development is thus a self-directing process in which form and function emerge and evolve together, to a large extent along patterns derived from the past. Since the system as a whole tends to shape itself, its arrangement can rarely be imposed from the outside. Order emerges continuously from interrelationships inherent in the system's own structure, constantly creating a fundamental pattern that survives as long as the whole survives.

In this book I present examples to show that the inner structure of a given system—man, society, or place—exerts a governing influence on its further development. In nature, inanimate objects also have an inner structure which imposes a pattern on the changes they undergo even when they are transformed into artifacts by man. Carvers and sculptors have long recognized that the structure of the wood, stone, or ivory inevitably influences the artist's creation.

In China, the ancient jade cutters spent a great deal of time studying the piece of rough stone before they decided on its finished shape—flower, fruit, insect, or bird. In the National Palace Museum of Taipei, one of Ch'ing's finest jade pieces is a Chinese cabbage in realistic colors, with two grasshoppers on the dark upper parts of the leaves, the whole being carved from a single stone.

From time immemorial, African sculptors in wood have made it a practice carefully to select the particular fragments of tree limbs or of trunks to be used for a certain purpose. The sculptor takes into consideration not only the soundness of the wood but also its innate structure and patterns, because he feels that the block to be carved contains a spirit and therefore is already endowed with a power of its own even before it is shaped. Understanding the spirit of the wood constitutes an essential part of the wood carver's skill. Michelangelo expressed a similar feeling about marble in one of his best-known sonnets:

> The best of artists has that thought alone
> Which is contained within the marble shell;

> The sculptor's hand can only break the spell
> To free the figures slumbering in the stone.[7]

Students of Eskimo culture have found that these people also attempt to recognize the spirit they assume to be present in natural objects and use technical skill less for their own gratification than for helping the spirit to emerge into the open. Ivory carving has long been practiced among the Avilik Eskimos. Before their skill was commercialized, they rarely tried to impose a pattern on nature, or their own personalities on matter. Rather they practiced carving as a normal activity of everyday life which helped them to establish more intimate relationships with the people, animals, and objects around them.

As the carver held the raw fragment of ivory in his hand, he turned it gently this way and that way, whispering to it, "Who are you? Who hides in you?" The carver rarely set out consciously to shape a particular form. Instead of compelling the fragment of ivory to become a man, a child, a wolf, a seal, a baby walrus, or some other preconceived object, he tried subconsciously to discover the structural characteristics and patterns inherent in the material itself. He continuously let his hand be guided by the inner structure of the ivory as it revealed itself to the knife. The form of the human being or of the animal did not have to be created; it was there from the beginning and only had to be released.

A witness has described the way the very process of handling the fragment of ivory helped the carver to become aware of the form hidden in it and of what he could do to help the form step forth alive:

> Ohnainewk held a baby walrus tooth in his palm, turned it slightly, and there, unmistakably! the form of an

animal almost burst through the surface. As he cut lightly here, indented there, he spoke softly, diffidently; he was not passive, yet his act of will was limited, respectful: respectful to the form that was given.

Here is a seal still in a tooth; now it is out, revealed more clearly.

"Ringed seal, one carves it
Hiding now
Ringed seal, one carves it
Moving now
Ringed seal comes to me."[8]

Poetical creation presents similarities to the view of reality held by primitive people and to the practices of carvers and sculptors. The very idea of an organic form implies that there exists a peculiarity to each aspect of creation. The role of the poet is to discover and reveal this fundamental structure. Form is the expression of content. A person, a place, a fragment of matter are the manifestations of inner forces and patterns which may remain hidden until unmasked, released, or developed by willed creative acts or fortunate circumstances.

The respectful attitude of Eskimo carvers toward ivory symbolizes an ideal for modern man's relation to the external world. Instead of imposing our will on nature for the sake of exploitation, we should attempt to discover the qualities inherent in each particular place so as to foster their development. Human life should grow, not quantitatively through the conquest of nature, but qualitatively in cooperation with nature. Mankind, however, is at present committed to a policy of conquest. Although it has been claimed that man's domination of nature originated with the Judeo-Christian tradition, this attitude can in fact be traced far back into prehistory through the evolution of tools.

The first tools used by man were probably sharp stones, shells, or animal teeth—all objects with a naturally occurring cutting edge; these objects were selected for suitability rather than shaped to purpose. Natural stones that were used as tools are called eoliths or dawn stones; they still play a role in the life of some Australian aborigines and of the few other peoples who have retained a primitive way of life.

Gradually stones and other objects were deliberately shaped for cutting. The first objects produced by human agency were probably made of flint by flaking. The flake could be used as a scraper, and the core of the stone as an ax. Continuous refinement of skill, going hand in hand with choice of better material, led progressively over hundreds of thousands of years to the handsome and efficient tools of the Neolithic period. But, sophisticated in design and ornamented with complex carving as they were, late Neolithic tools continued to take advantage of the characteristics inherent in the raw material. They still related man to nature.

After half a million years of experience with stone, men learned to work with bronze and iron. With these metals, the morphological characteristics of the raw material no longer had relevance to the form and use of the tool; only the physical characteristics were of importance in the process of fashioning. Man had entered the technological age and taken a long step toward segregating himself from nature.

Technology is giving man immense power over the cosmos, but in its present form it is depriving him of the sustenance he could derive from direct contact with nature. According to the Greek legend, the giant Antaeus retained his strength only while in direct contact with the earth; for this reason he was readily overpowered by Hercules when his two feet were off the ground. Because man is still of the earth, he too loses attributes essential to his survival when he allows the technological way of life to dissociate him completely from the natural environment.

Man's bondage to nature does not imply, however, that the quality of human life is linked inexorably to an unchangeable order of things. Human nature and external nature possess multiple potentialities that man can discover and use according to his fancy. Even the Eskimo carver has probably more creative freedom than was suggested, since it is he who recognizes the structures hidden in the fragments of ivory and selects the ones to be brought out. There exists in the human mind a prefiguration of reality, an interior imagery of nature, that the English poet Gerard Manley Hopkins called the "inscape."[9] To a large extent, this inscape determines the manner in which man transforms objects and landscapes into creations that are true both to their nature and to his own nature.

If more were known of nature and of man, many hidden aspects of the natural world could be brought to light and incorporated into human life. Such creative incorporation could improve environmental and human quality. The surface of the earth can be profoundly altered without desecrating it or decreasing its fitness for life; man also can be changed in ways that would enrich his humanness.

The continued growth of civilization depends upon the discovery of the hidden qualities in human and external nature and upon their integration into new viable social structures. The real test of scientific and technological prowess will be our success, first in discovering hidden qualities and then in manipulating them in ways that will enlarge human life within the constraints imposed by the unchangeable aspects of man's nature and of the natural order of things.

J. Robert Oppenheimer, discussing complementarity, referred to it as an order which means that the parts fit into the whole and that the whole requires the parts. The ultimate justification for this philosophy is that the cosmos is a gigantic organism evolving according to laws which are valid everywhere and therefore generate a universal harmony. The fundamental law of ecology, it is often said, is that everything is relevant to everything else. Throughout history, men have tried to express this law in the great religions and even in certain religious heresies. The medieval Brotherhood of the Free Spirit is said to have believed that "God was immanent in everything and that once one had experienced this God-presence in himself, he became a Free Spirit; he was again living in the Garden of Eden."[10]

The common mortal, unfortunately, can apprehend creation only in the form of restricted systems. Awareness of this limitation led the American entomologist Stephen Forbes, as far back as 1887, to recognize the necessity of dealing with more restricted natural situations, the microcosms that are now called ecosystems: "A lake . . . forms a little world within itself—a microcosm within which all the elemental forces are at work and the play of life goes on in full, but on so small a scale as to bring it within the *mental grasp.*"* [11]

The various microcosms, or ecosystems, with which man deals are thus his own mental creations; indeed they derive their size and shape from the characteristics and limitations of his senses and conceptual apparatus. The "spirit" or "genius" of a place, of a creature, or of an object, is the perception of some facet of nature by the god within the human observer.

*Italics within quotations throughout this book, unless otherwise noted, are introduced by me for purposes of emphasis.—R.D.

CHAPTER 1

Worlds Within a World

We are all born with a gift of wonder. Some of us retain the child's belief that creation is fabulous. A lifetime commitment to the majestic abstractions of modern science has not weakened my sense of marvel at the seemingly miraculous appearance of commonplace happenings. The explosive emergence of a particular type of wild mushroom at the appropriate time and place after a soaking rain still appears to me a phenomenal event. So does the arrival of land turtles on my lawn in the Hudson River Highlands the very week that wild strawberries are ripe enough for them to eat. As a young scientist interested in wine fermentation, I learned with delight that among the many kinds of yeast which exist in nature the proper yeast spontaneously appears on the grape just before harvest time.[1] Yeast cannot be found on the vine during winter, spring, and early summer, but it is extremely abundant on the grapes at the time they ripen, ready to initiate fermentation as soon as the grape juice has been loaded into the vats. Then the yeast disappears from the vineyard after the harvest not to reappear until the next summer, as if brought in by a wine god. William James had good reason to quote with glee: "the Universe is wild—game-flavored as a hawk's wing. Nature is miracle all."[2]

I should not speak of miracles, since I know that there is order in creation and that the world of matter and the world of life are governed by the same universal laws. All material objects, different as they appear to be, are built out of the same fundamental particles and forces. All living creatures—microbes, plants, animals, and men—derive a fundamental unity from their common origin in some primordial protoplasm that presumably emerged from matter more than three billion years ago and has continued to differentiate and evolve ever since. But these grand abstract views of creation do not describe the world to which I respond. What I experience is not abstract universality but rather that each rock looks and feels different from any other rock; each region or season has a quality of light all its own; each person's smile at a particular moment constitutes a unique event in the history of mankind.

My inclination is to emphasize particulars rather than universals, differences rather than similarities. I find it important, of course, that men and apes have many characteristics in common, but I find it even more intriguing that they are obviously so different. And I am much more interested in what a particular person has to say than in the fact that all normal persons are able to speak. As years go by, I notice with increasing pleasure and astonishment that children I knew and places where I lived half a century ago are still readily recognizable despite the changes brought about by social upheavals and the ravages of time. Paradoxically, the dullest persons and cities acquire interest from the fact that they retain their own type of dullness while aging and developing.

Descriptions, however detailed and objective they may be, rarely convey to me the uniqueness of a person or a place. Nothing can substitute for the living experiences during which the person or the place becomes part of my own life. If a chill descends on me when I read or hear the word "humanity," it is because this abstract concept does not evoke the vital warmth that can be generated only by the presence of a real person. The living quality of the human encounter demands something akin to the I-Thou relationship defined by the Jewish religious scholar Martin Buber (1878–1965). If I soon become restless during theoretical discussions about "the environment," it is because this bland term does not convey the sensual impact of a real place. The environment is not a pervasive something out there but rather implies the responses of the whole being to the stimuli received from the place.

The very small French village in which I grew up was then and has remained to this day outside the mainstream of the modern world. Even though it is located only thirty miles north of Paris, its name, Hénonville, is not on any map. Yet limited as village life was, it provided a rich variety of experiences which are still alive in my memory and which are indeed incarnated in my whole organic being. As is probably the case for all children, I was bewitched not only by the persons and places I actually knew but perhaps just as much by the persons and places I imagined during hours of daydreaming. This enchantment, using the word in its strong etymological sense, has conditioned my whole life. It continues to color all my feelings and has certainly influenced everything I express in this book.

Except for very short trips, I never left Hénonville until the age of thirteen. My early remembrances are therefore of a world which I could directly see, hear, smell, and touch. There was the one-room school house which also served as city hall for the 450 inhabitants; a thirteenth-century church with lichen-covered walls in the center of the village; farms with numerous domestic animals; hills so accessible that the highest of them was the site of the cemetery; small woodlands here and there; muddy ponds crowded with frogs, eel, and carp; immense fields of wheat, alfalfa, and sugar beets, separated by narrow country roads leading on to other small villages a few miles away.

The sensual experiences I derived from the familiar scenes of village life were soon supplemented by imaginings derived from pictures in elementary school books. These generated in my mind a dream world, just as vivid as my external world but of a very different quality. I thus became acquainted in imagination with the strange people who inhabited the strange places shown in my schoolbooks: thoughtful Caucasians with blond hair, wise Orientals with yellow skin, black people and red people with powerful bodies and threatening faces. Only the direct experiences of later life made me realize that the knowledge derived from pictures and literary descriptions is never sufficient to communicate the real impact of a place or a person. I had to travel before I could really know the sensual and emotional quality of arid deserts and wet estuaries, of torrential streams and endless oceans, of tropical forests and inaccessible mountains, and of the real people who lived and functioned in these real places.

My view of mankind became more precise, but also more fanciful, when I discovered in advanced textbooks the portraits of historical personages, each with a description relating achievements to facial characteristics, familial background, place of origin, and period of civilization. History then seemed easy to understand from the personalities of its heroes as revealed in these portraits: Charlemagne's imperial majesty, Saint Louis's royal sanctity, Voltaire's diabolic cleverness, Rousseau's romantic vision, Byron's poetic frenzy, Bismarck's political realism, and somewhat later Woodrow Wilson's social idealism. Heredity, education, place, and time were sufficient

—so it appeared—to explain all personality characteristics and all historical events.

I now realize that motivation and free will are more important than behavioral determinism in shaping the course of human life and that accidents play a large role in history. On the whole, however, I have not moved far beyond the primitive biological concepts of my youth. In fact, I doubt that science has added much of practical importance to our ancestors' empirical knowledge of human behavior. We have learned a great deal about the composition and the functions of the body and have begun to relate feeling and thinking to some processes in the brain, but the aspects of life which are uniquely human have so far eluded identification with anatomical structures and physiological mechanisms. The attitudes and activities which set man apart from other animals can be apprehended only by observing the responses of real persons to surroundings and events. This approach may appear hopelessly complex, but there is no hope that a simpler one will serve. Although the biological machine can be analyzed piece by piece, humanness cannot be understood by reducing man to something less than human and ignoring the complexities which make for the unique richness of his life.

We come into contact with the world through the sensations we perceive with our whole organic being, but there is much more than that to our view of the world. In each of us sensations are converted into very personal conceptual structures by mental processes which involve our genetic and experiential past and are therefore different from everybody else's mental processes. Each person has a unique picture of the world, largely of his own creation. Paraphrasing Alfred North Whitehead, the English-born mathematician turned

American philosopher (1861–1947), it can be said that when we praise the rose for its scent, the bird for its song, the sun for its radiance, the moon for its glow, nature gets credit which should go to ourselves. In reality, nature is "soundless, scentless, colorless, merely the hurrying of material, endless, meaningless."[3] We, not nature, create from the jumble of external physical phenomena the sounds, scents, colors, and meanings which make up our emotional and intellectual lives.

Man, being a social animal, could not long survive if his own private world were not integrated to some extent at least with the public world. In each particular situation, natural forces and historical influences generate patterns of behavior and of taste which are shared by most of the persons exposed, especially early in life, to the same forces and influences. Nations and social groups are the outcome of the clumsy efforts made by mankind to create institutions within which persons of different but compatible individualities can live and function together. Thought, tolerance, and objective knowledge help us to establish contacts with the rest of mankind and thus to escape from the tragic solitude of absolute privacy. But despite our individual and collective efforts at universality each one of us lives, as it were, in a private world of his own.

Like individual human beings, landscapes and civilizations display distinctive characteristics. While they change in the course of time, they retain a uniqueness derived in large part from the set of conditions under which they emerged and also from the factors which influenced their subsequent evolution. The phrases *"genius loci"* and "spirit of place" symbolize the forces or structures generally hidden beneath the surface of things which determine the uniqueness of each place.

A superficial uniformity has of course been impressed on most parts of the world by technologic civilization—its jet aircraft, travel agencies, canned foods, television programs. All human beings, furthermore, are threatened directly or indirectly by nuclear warfare, shortages of raw materials, protein hunger, mass poisoning, radiation, and pollutants. It is therefore imperative that the spaceship earth be considered as a unit by statesmen, technologists, and sociologists and that it be managed as an integrated ecological system. This necessity, however, does not imply that this planet is becoming "One World." The global view of the earth is essential for the scholars who study the problems of the world as a whole, and it may be convenient for some members of the international jet set. But it means little for those human beings, the immense majority of us, whose daily life is dominated by local issues and by the concrete problems of day-to-day existence. Despite the increasing mobility of populations and the standardization of modern cosmopolitan technology, most normal people function almost exclusively in a limited segment of the world, as limited socially as it is geographically. Local problems are for them of far greater magnitude and urgency than the global problems of the spaceship earth.

Local characteristics, furthermore, persist despite changes, and they impose a pattern of their own on ways of life introduced from the outside. The game of golf is played according to the same rules all over the world, but the attitude of the golfer is not the same in Scotland, where the game originated and where sheep may still be pastured on the course, as it is in those exclusive golf clubs of the United States where the greens are artificially created and maintained, and where access is only by automated carts. A Japanese publication has stated that golf is now played in Japan with an "avidity probably unequaled anywhere in the world." Standard golf equipment is naturally used on Japanese courses according to international rules, but "the attitude of the players toward the game, the things they say (and don't say) to each other, plus the ritual bath, drinks, food, and the awarding of prizes after the round (everyone gets a prize)—all these features and more mark the experience as distinctively Japanese."[4]

The names of countries, regions, and cities thus denote landscapes and human attitudes with a distinct and lasting personality. Despite the tremendous, and one might have thought unifying, impacts of the industrial, agricultural, and social revolutions, which have affected almost simultaneously all parts of Europe and America, New England continues to differ from England, Mississippi from the Middle West, Southern California from South Carolina or South Dakota. When changes occur in a place or a culture, they take place within a historical continuity that assures the persistence of the original characteristics, even though often in a greatly modified form. Each place has a spirit of its own which progressively shapes its physical appearance and the genius of its people.

The globe-trotter whizzes past the rice paddies and bazaars of Asia, the provincial towns and vineyards of Europe, the cornfields and giant office buildings of North America, without recognizing the inner forces that give uniqueness to each one of these environments and which govern their activities. The tourist goes sightseeing in New York, London, Paris, Moscow, Calcutta, Timbuctoo, without experiencing the intimate organic life of these cities, let alone understanding the hidden peculiarities of their metabolism which are responsible for the continuity of their physical and human characteristics.

People who are rooted in a place—as most people are because they do not have the opportunity and rarely have the desire to move far away from their homes—may be less conscious of its distinctive characteristics than the scholar, or even than the sightseer or globe-trotter. But precisely because they are geographically stable, they become an organic part of the place and contribute to the persistence of its character. They incarnate its spirit.

Wherever I go, I find that the land, the ways of life, and the reactions of people are much like what I remember them to have been from my early experiences, or what I had imagined them to be from my early readings. After almost forty years of absence, I found myself instantly at home when I returned in the 1960s to certain villages of France and Italy in which I had lived and worked during my youth before I settled in America. And when I first visited Tahiti, Australia, Taiwan, and Hong Kong a few years ago, I had no difficulty in relating to the landscapes and people of these countries because they had so much in common with the pictures I had formed years ago from the accounts of explorers and novelists. The sway of palm trees in the languorous South Pacific skies will survive invasions by jet aircraft and international tourists, just as the bewitching charm of Paris and Rome still comes through the noise and fumes of motor cars.

The transportation industry itself has retained a national flavor. The glamorous steamships of the 1930s were microcosms of their homelands. They displayed for the traveler the most enticing expressions of life in their respective countries in the way of decor, food, entertainment, behavior, and even misbehavior. The *Majestic* and the *Mauretania*, the *Île de France* and the *Normandie*, the *Bremen* and the *Europa* were truly England, France, and Germany afloat.[5]

Admittedly, crossing the oceans in a jet plane provides little time for an effective display of national characteristics. All great airlines use the same kind of aircraft; their pilots, ground crews, and cabin personnel operate according to the same international regulations; the food served in flight is good —but international. Airports, however, retain an intense national character. The John F. Kennedy Airport is unmistakably

American, Heathrow English, Orly French, Fiumicino (formerly Leonardo da Vinci) Italian, and Kingsford Smith Australian. The human atmosphere in these great international air-traffic centers is so pervasively national that the phrase "a cup of coffee" calls forth a beverage peculiar to each one of them. Different is the way of sitting at the bar, the tone and topic of conversation with the waiter, the manner of flirting with the waitress, the style of approach to the taxi driver, and, I presume, the proper way of spending a few hours with a call girl.

Food stuffs also change character to fit local tastes when they migrate from one region to another. I know that the Roquefort cheese served in the Causse country where it is produced differs from what is sent under the same name to most American restaurants. The leaves of tea and tobacco become transformed into products with as many aromas and colors as there are civilizations. The formula used for the preparation of Coca Cola, I understand, is not quite the same in New York as it is in New Orleans, in Vermont as in Virginia.

Speeches and books about One World are thus of no avail against persistence of place. The more I travel and function among different groups of people, the more I believe in the validity of the ancient Basque proverb, *"Chaque pays a sa loi, chaque maison sa coutume"* (Each country has its system of laws, each house its customs). The expressions home, *foyer, casa, Heim,* and at home, *chez soi, a casa, zu hause* have meanings so peculiar to each country and social group that they cannot be directly transferred from one language to another.

I have lived and worked in several countries and have repeatedly traveled from one continent to another. Out of this experience I have become convinced that, far from becoming uniform, peoples and places are continuing to differentiate, as they have since the time of the great dispersals during the Old

Stone Age. I am happy that there are on earth many worlds, instead of One World, because diversity enriches human life and facilitates the emergence of new cultures and new values. I truly believe that if we can learn to practice tolerance, the many worlds of the earth, each proud of its genius, are more likely to generate a real and creative peace than could a homogenized and anonymous One World.

As far back as one can read into the human mind—at least beginning with the Sumerian texts five thousand years ago—there have been men trying to discover or imagine some universal basis for matter and for life. The striving for unity seems to be one of the fundamental urges of mankind. This striving may be at the basis of the complex systems of symbiosis—in other words, of biological partnership—which are ubiquitous in nature among unrelated species. It may contribute also to the spontaneous and deeply moving expressions of tribal and national unity often referred to as mob behavior—the spontaneous formation of large groups protesting against objectionable social situations, or rejoicing at the time of great collective achievements, or marking with grief the death of a hero.

The striving for unity may indeed have deep biological roots in the very first forms of life. As I have mentioned, all living things are probably derived from the same kind of primordial protoplasm, the progeny of which has been differentiating ever since into the innumerable types of organisms which have populated the earth. Furthermore, when cells from different animal species are placed in contact, they can be made to unite by the artifice of certain complicated laboratory manipulations. It is thus possible to produce experimentally hybrid cells which are half mouse and half man, or half mouse and half kangaroo, as the case may be. Some of these hybrid cells are capable of multiplying, and when they do they retain part of the hereditary material from both animal species of which they are the offspring. This peculiar ability of different types of cells to unite under special circumstances would seem to suggest that there persists throughout the living world an affinity capable of reassembling the elements of different forms of life which had become differentiated eons ago in the course of organic evolution. Dr. Lewis Thomas of Yale Medical School has gone so far as to suggest that were it not for the formidable arsenal of forces that has generated the countless different expressions of biological individuality in the course of evolution, "we might have ended up as a mass of invariant, interliving, undifferentiated life, missing all the fun."[6]

Even more powerful than the urge for unity, however, are the forces for differentiation which are at work everywhere on earth and which account for the overwhelming variety of the inanimate and organic worlds. Our planet owes its exciting diversity to the fact that each person and each place exhibit uniqueness of characteristics and of fate. There are unquestionably universal laws applicable to all forms of matter and of life, but there are also forces which cause each individual person and each individual place to become a unique expression of these laws. The phrase "a god within" symbolizes for me the forces that create private worlds out of the universal stuff of the cosmos and thus enable life to express itself in countless individualities.

CHAPTER 2

A Theology of the Earth

How drab and gray, unappealing and insignificant, this planet would be without the radiance of life.

The earth is one of the nine planets in the solar system, third in distance from the sun, fifth in size, and with a radius of less than four thousand miles—a mere speck in space. Judged in these terms, it is a trivial astronomical object, one of the smallest among the celestial bodies that gravitate through the boundless universe. But while the physical measurements worked out by astronomers give a quantitative picture of the earth, they do not give a true picture because they do not take biological characteristics into consideration.

Hegel pointed out more than a century ago that *Richtigkeit,* correctness, is not the same thing as *Wahrheit,* the truth. It is correct to define the earth by quantitative studies, but the more interesting and significant truth about it transcends measurements concerning its size, motions, and place in the cosmos. The earth is unique in the solar system because it possesses qualities derived from the myriad forms of life it harbors. Being a living organism, it is more varied, more changeable, more unpredictable, than inanimate matter, and also more delicate.

The early aviators, flying at relatively low altitudes and

low speeds, had the opportunity to discern the bones of the earth beneath its covering of living flesh. They could recognize that the covering of vegetation is in many places so tenuous as to appear to be but a little moss in the crevices, which could readily be destroyed. But they realized also that this covering, thin and fragile as it is, creates the green of the forest, the brilliance of flowers, the varieties of blue in atmosphere and ocean, and most remarkably the phosphorescence of human thought.

It was worth the many billions of dollars spent on the manned space program to obtain further evidence that the earth is unique in the solar system by virtue of the sensuous appeal it derives from its green and blue mantle, and of the intellectual vibration it derives from man. The Apollo missions may not have yet discovered much of theoretical interest and practical importance concerning outer space, but they have enabled us to see with our own eyes that the surface of the moon is pockmarked, dusty, gray, and drab. The photographs taken from the Mariner spacecrafts have furthermore destroyed any illusion about the existence of Martians and their canals. The soft glow of the moon and the exciting redness of Mars are not attributes inherent in these lifeless bodies but the qualities bestowed on them by human eyes, looking at them through the atmosphere of the earth. In contrast, the accounts of the astronauts have helped us to experience on a cosmic scale how colorful, warm, inviting, and diversified the earth is against the bleakness and coldness of outer space. These unique qualities originate exclusively from the activities of living things.

All ancient civilizations have expressed, each in its own way, wonderment at the beauty of the earth. Aristotle tried to imagine how men who had spent all their lives under luxurious conditions but in caves would respond when given for the first time the chance to behold sky, clouds, and seas. Surely, he writes, "These men would think that gods exist and that all the marvels of the world are their handicrafts" (*Politics*, I, 8). One of the least attractive aspects of technological civilization is a progressive loss in this concern for the beauty of the earth. Scientists, as men, have as much natural appreciation for the sensual qualities of the earth as other men. In their professional capacity, however, they tend to be less charmed by the uniqueness of the planet than by the fact that it moves through space according to the same physical laws that govern other planets. It is not unlikely that this downgrading of the earth to the level of a minor celestial object has played some part in the devaluation of nature and of human life. And yet the earth transcended the nature of a mere astronomical object when it began to harbor life, more than three billion years ago. The visual evidence provided by space travel now gives larger significance to Aristotle's image. Although the earth is but a tiny island in the midst of vast reaches of alien space, it derives unique distinction from being—alone in the solar system—like a magic garden blooming with by myriads of different living things which have prepared the way for self-reflecting human beings.

When the earth was formed from the sun about four and a half billion years ago, the atmosphere consisted chiefly of gases, including hydrogen, ammonia, and methane, but no free oxygen; the burning surface was exposed to fierce ultraviolet radiation and had no water. Such an environment was obviously incompatible with the existence of any form of life, let alone human life.

The various other planets of the solar system had at first a structure not unlike that of the earth. They underwent profound changes with different courses and at different rates, depending upon their relative size and position with regard to the sun. But only on earth did these changes result in conditions that eventually permitted the emergence of life.

During the first two billion years of the earth's existence, hydrogen progressively escaped from the atmosphere, carbon dioxide and water were released from the crust through intense volcanic activity; some of the chemical ingredients now present in all living cells were produced by solar radiation acting on the components of the primordial atmosphere. By the end of that period, the oceans had been formed, and sugars, purines, pyrimidines, amino acids, and other organic substances produced from the atmosphere's components by the solar irradiation had begun to accumulate in the surface waters. And then, by unknown processes, self-reproducing protoplasma became organized from these simple organic materials. Life had begun, and from then on living things increased in complexity and diversity through evolutionary processes. Eventually, the earth's atmosphere came to consist chiefly of nitrogen gas, to which was added the free oxygen released from carbon dioxide by the photosynthetic activities of primitive organisms.

It is probable that for an immense period of time life could exist only beneath the ocean's surface, where it was protected against excessive ultraviolet radiation emanating from the sun. As the water was rich in nutrients, one may assume that once life had started, oceans soon teemed with primitive organisms. Progressively, these organisms evolved into more complex forms as the conditions changed. What is certain in any case is that blue-green algae very similar to the ones that exist now have been found in Pre-Cambrian deposits which are two billion years old. Such algae have been and remain to this day among the most effective producers of the oxygen which is essential for the existence of animals and men.

Life as we know it has thus emerged and evolved in response to the consecutive occurrence of a multiplicity of different conditions: certain gases escaped from the primordial atmosphere; they were replaced by a nitrogen-oxygen mixture; liquid water accumulated on the land surface; and a proper temperature range came to prevail. While it is certain that the earth is the only part of the solar system to have achieved this state of compatibility with life, similar conditions may exist elsewhere in the cosmos. This, however, is a matter for speculation, unsupported by factual knowledge.

The emergence of life requires such an extraordinary combination of circumstances that it constitutes an event with a very low order of probability—so low indeed that it may have occurred only once. Certain scientists, however, believe that, since there may be many planets in other systems which have had an evolutionary development similar to that of the earth, life must have emerged repeatedly. According to them, "we are not alone" in space.[1] Whether this is true or not, one must agree with the physicist and theologian William Pollard of the Oak Ridge Associated University that there may not be

> . . . another place like the earth within a thousand light years of us. If so, the earth with its vistas of breathtaking beauty, its azure seas, beaches, mighty mountains, and soft blanket of forest and steppe is a veritable wonderland in the universe. It is a gem of rare and magic beauty hung in a trackless space filled with lethal radiations and accompanied in its journey by sister planets which are either viciously hot or dreadfully cold, arid, and lifeless chunks of raw rock. Earth is choice, precious, and sacred beyond all comparison or measure.[2]

The adjective "sacred" may be surprising in a description of the characteristics of this planet, and yet it expresses an attitude which has deep roots in the human past and still persists now. The very fact that the word "desecration" is commonly used to lament the damage men are causing to the environment indicates that many of us have a feeling that the earth has sanctity, that man's relation to it has a sacred quality.

In common usage, the meaning of the word "nature" is extremely limited. It does not refer to the earth as shaped by cosmic forces, but almost exclusively to the living forms on which men depend and to the earth's atmosphere and surface, which are the creations of life. The interdependence between man and the other forms of life is so complete that the word nature usually has biological connotations, even when referring to inanimate substances. In practice, we do not live *on* the planet earth but *with* the life it harbors and *within* the environment that life creates.

For example, the oxygen we breathe is a product of life. As I have mentioned, it was being released into the atmosphere in a free form by primitive organisms that lived more than two billion years ago. It is still being produced by most members of the plant kingdom, by the microscopic algae of ocean plankton as well as by the most gigantic trees. Microbes and plants are thus absolutely necessary for the existence of animals and men, not only because they produce food but also because they literally create a breathable atmosphere.

Like the atmosphere, the present surface of the earth is also a creation of life. Everywhere, under natural conditions, the topsoil is alive with insects, grubs, earthworms, and microbes, which find shelter in it, feed from it, and in so doing transform it chemically and physically. This is true whether the soil supports forests, prairies, tundras, grasslands, farmlands, gardens, or parks. Organic gardeners have legitimate scientific reasons to claim that earthworms contribute as much as fertilizers to the fertility of the soil. In fact, the microbial forms of life which are invisible to the naked eye are at least as important as earthworms and insects. Every speck of humus contains billions of living microbes, belonging to countless different varieties, each specialized in the decomposition and transformation of one or another type of organic debris derived from animals, plants, or other microbes. The expert can often detect the activities of microbes in the soil simply by handling and smelling it when warm and humid weather increases the intensity of microbial life. Surprising as it may seem, soil microbes account for a large percentage of the total mass of the living stuff of the earth.

Experience shows that under usual conditions the remnants of animals and plants do not accumulate in nature. Very rapidly they are consumed by microbes and thereby taken through a chain of chemical alterations which break them down step by step into simpler and simpler compounds. The microbes themselves eventually die, and their bodies are also transformed by microbial action. In this manner the constituents of all living things are returned to nature after death. Reduced to simpler forms, they are available for the creation of new microbial and plant life, which is eventually consumed by animals and men. Microbes thus constitute indispensable links in the chain that binds inanimate matter to life.

The eternal movement from life to dead organic substances, then to microbial bodies, and finally to simple chemical molecules which are converted back into plant and animal life again, is a physical manifestation of the myth of eternal return. During the late Roman Republic, the Epicurean philosopher Lucretius untiringly reiterated in his poem *De Rerum Natura* (On the Nature of Things) that nothing arises except as a result of the death of something else, that nature remains always young and whole in spite of death at work everywhere, and that all living forms are but transient aspects of a permanent substance. It is literally true that all things come from dust and to dust return, but to a dust eternally fertile. Throughout the living world and particularly in the soil, all organisms constantly enact the famous phrase of Lucretius's poem: "Like runners in a race, they hand on the torch of life."

The soil is thus a truly living organism because its chemical composition and its texture at each particular site are constantly regenerated from the primeval rock by the activities of living things. Every site, furthermore, accommodates a multiplicity of different kinds of organisms, each of which occupies a localized, special niche that it modifies to a form even more suitable for its needs. Social bees have an environment that differs from that of solitary bees living in the very same field, in part because the two do not use the same kind of resources, and even more because the social bees create their own microclimate inside the beehive. The soil under an oak forest differs from what would have developed in the same rock formation under a pine forest, because these two species of trees have different root systems. As pine needles accumulate, furthermore, they produce a surface layer different from the humus into which oak leaves are transformed when they die and decompose. In addition, the quality of light under an oak tree is different from what it is under a pine tree. All living things thus create microenvironments which enrich the diversity of the earth's surface.

In nature, most changes elicited by the interplay between a particular species of organism and its total environment are in the long run beneficial to both. The changes that result from these reciprocal effects account for the immense diversity of places and living things on earth. They also explain the exquisite fitness and interdependence between all aspects of creation so commonly encountered in undisturbed environments.

Fitness and interdependence, however, are not static properties. Slowly, but inexorably, all aspects of the earth are changing and this requires of living things that they also change in order to maintain their compatibility with environmental conditions. The ability to evolve is therefore an essential attribute of life; evolutionary changes constantly alter the manifestations of fitness and interdependence. These changes, furthermore, progressively result in the production of new forms of life from old forms, thus increasing in a continuous manner the diversity of biological systems and of their activities. Diversity accounts in large part for the self-repairing processes which tend to occur spontaneously when accidents disturb the natural order of things—hence the adaptability and resilience of the living earth. It accounts also for the adaptability, resilience, and richness of human life.

When man emerged in his present biological form during the Stone Age, he must have been fitted for the conditions prevailing around him. Since fitness in the biological sense implies suitable interrelationships between the organism and the total environment, there is scientific justification for claiming, as did the Harvard physiologist L. J. Henderson (1878–1942) in *The Fitness of the Environment*, that the environment was ready for man when he appeared on earth.[3] Half a century earlier, Walt Whitman had concerned himself with a similar problem but from the point of view of the poet and humanist; for him, the "primal sanities" of nature were the qualities of the earth that make for a rich human life.

Whitman's "primal sanities" and Henderson's "fitness" refer to the conditions under which man evolved and to which his biological constitution is still adapted. But while man's biological nature has remained much the same since the Stone Age, his surroundings and ways of life have changed profoundly. Civilization is often in conflict with "primal sanities" and "fitness," as evidenced by the present ecological crisis. This conflict accounts for the unfortunate fact that the science of human ecology, which should be concerned with all aspects of the relationships between man and the rest of creation, has come to be identified almost exclusively with the problems of disease and alienation resulting from environmental insults. Yet there is much more to human ecology than this one-sided view of the relationships between man and the external world.

Man is still of the earth, earthy. The earth is literally our mother, not only because we depend on her for nurture and shelter but even more because the human species has been shaped by her in the womb of evolution. Each person, furthermore, is conditioned by the stimuli he receives from nature during his own existence.

If men were to colonize the moon or Mars—even with abundant supplies of oxygen, water, and food, as well as adequate protection against heat, cold, and radiation—they would not long retain their humanness, because they would be deprived of those stimuli which only earth can provide. Similarly, we shall progressively lose our humanness even on earth if we continue to pour filth into the atmosphere; to befoul soil, lakes, and rivers; to disfigure landscapes with junkpiles; to destroy the wild plants and animals that do not contribute to monetary values; and thus to transform the globe into an environment alien to our evolutionary past. The quality of human life is inextricably interwoven with the kinds and variety of stimuli man receives from the earth and the life it harbors, because human nature is shaped biologically and mentally by external nature.

Admittedly, certain human populations have functioned successfully and developed worthwhile cultures in forbidding environments, such as the frozen tundras or the Sahara. But even the most desolate parts of the Arctic or the Sahara offer a much wider range of sensations than does the moon. Eskimo life derives exciting drama from ice, snow, and water, from spectacular seasonal changes, and from the migration of caribou and other animals. The nomadic Tuaregs have to cope with blinding and burning sand, but they also experience the delights of oases. Being exposed to a variety of environmental stresses and having to function among them is far different from living in a spacesuit or a confining space capsule, however large it may be, in which all aspects of the environment are controlled and which eliminate extraneous stimuli almost completely.

Participation in nature's endless whims provides the vital contact with the cosmic forces which is essential for sanity. In *The Desert Year*, the American drama critic turned naturalist Joseph Wood Krutch (1893–1970) pointed out that normal human beings are not likely to fare well in areas lacking visible forms of life. For example, they rarely elect to stay long in the deserts of the American Southwest, as if this kind of scenery, magnificent as it is, were fundamentally alien to mankind.

> Wherever, as in this region of wind-eroded stone, living things are no longer common enough or conspicuous enough to seem more than trivial accidents, man feels something like terror. . . . This is a country where the inanimate dominates and in which not only man but the very plants themselves seem intruders. We may look at it as we look at the moon, but we feel rejected. It is neither for us nor for our kind.[4]

Men seek contact with other living things probably because their own species has evolved in constant association with them and has retained from the evolutionary past a biological need for this association.

Human nature has been so deeply influenced by the conditions under which it evolved that the mind is in some ways like a mirror of the cosmos. Some of the early Church fathers had a vision of this relationship, as illustrated by Origen's exhortation to man: "Thou art a second world in miniature, the sun and the moon are within thee, and also the stars."[5] Nearly two thousand years later, the British biologist Julian Huxley reformulated Origen's thought in modern terms and enlarged it to include his own concepts of psychosocial evolution:

> The human type became a microcosm which, through its capacity for self-awareness, was able to incorporate increasing amounts of the macrocosm into itself, to organize them in new and richer ways, and then with their aid to exert new and more powerful influences on the macrocosm.[6]

Sir Julian's statement implies two different but complementary attitudes toward the earth. The fact that man incorporates part of the universe in his being provides a scientific basis for the feeling of reverence toward the earth. But the fact that he can act on the external world often makes him behave as if he were foreign to the earth and her master—an attitude which has become almost universal during the past two centuries.

The phrase "conquest of nature" is certainly one of the most objectionable and misleading expressions of Western languages. It reflects the illusion that all natural forces can be entirely controlled, and it expresses the criminal conceit that nature is to be considered primarily as a source of raw materials and energy for human purposes. This view of man's relationship to nature is philosophically untenable and destructive. A relationship to the earth based only on its use for economic enrichment is bound to result not only in its degradation but also in the devaluation of human life. This is a perversion which, if not soon corrected, will become a fatal disease of technological societies.

The gods of early man were intimately connected with the earth and belief in them generated veneration and respect for it. But respect does not imply a passive attitude; early man obviously manipulated the earth and used its resources. Primitive religion in fact was always linked with magic, which was an attempt to manage nature and life through the occult influences that were assumed to lurk in the invisible world. There is a fundamental difference between religion and magic. In the words of the Polish-born American anthropologist Bronislaw Malinowski (1884–1942), "Religion refers to the fundamental issues of human life, while magic turns round specific concrete and detailed problems."[7] Our salvation depends upon our ability to create a religion of nature and a substitute for magic suited to the needs and knowledge of modern man.

The problems of poverty, disease, and environmental decay cannot be solved merely by the use of more and more scientific technology. Technological fixes usually turn out to be a jumble of procedures that have unpredictable consequences and are often in conflict with natural forces. Indeed, technological magic is not much better than primitive magic in dealing with the fundamental issues of human existence, and, in addition, it is much more destructive. In contrast, better knowledge of man's relationships to the earth may enable us to be even more protective of the natural world than were our primitive forebears; informed reason is likely to be a better guide for the management of nature than was superstition or fear. We do know scientifically that the part of the earth on which we live is not dead material but a complex living organism with which we are interdependent; we also know that we have already used a large percentage of the resources that have accumulated in the course of its geological past. The supply of natural resources, in fact, presents a situation in which the practical selfish interests of mankind are best served by an ethical attitude.

For most of its geological history, the earth had no stores of fossil fuels or of concentrated mineral ores. These materials, which are the life blood of modern technology, accumulated slowly during millions upon millions of years; their supply will not be renewed once they have been exhausted. They must therefore be husbanded with care—for immediate reasons and also for the sake of the future. The natural resources that we now gouge out of the earth so thoughtlessly and recklessly certainly should not be squandered by a few generations of greedy men.

From the beginning of time and all over the world, man's relationship to nature has transcended the simple direct experience of objective reality. Primitive people are inclined to endow creatures, places, and even objects with mysterious powers; they see gods or goddesses everywhere. Eventually, man came to believe that the appearances of reality were the local or specialized expressions of a universal force; from belief in gods he moved up to belief in God. Both polytheism and monotheism are losing their ancient power in the modern world, and for this reason it is commonly assumed that the present age is irreligious. But we may instead be moving to a higher level of religion. Science is at present evolving from the description of concrete objects and events to the study of relationships as observed in complex systems. We may be about to recapture an experience of harmony, an intimation of the divine, from our scientific knowledge of the processes through which the earth became prepared for human life, and of the mechanisms through which man relates to the universe as a whole. A truly ecological view of the world has religious overtones.

The earth, as I have said, came to constitute a home suitable for man only after it had become a living organism. The sensuous qualities of its blue atmosphere and green mantle are not inherent in its physical nature; they are the creations of the countless microbes, plants, and animals that it has nurtured and that have transformed its drab inanimate matter into a colorful living substance. Men can exist, function, enjoy the universe, and dream dreams only because the various forms of life have created and continue to maintain the very special environmental conditions that set the earth apart from other planets and generate its fitness for life—for life in general and for human life in particular.

Man is dependent on other living things and like them must be adapted to his surroundings in order to achieve biological and mental health. Human ecology, however, involves more than interdependence and fitness as these are usually conceived. Human beings are influenced not only by the natural forces of their environment but also and probably even more by the social and psychological surroundings they select or create. Indeed, what they become is largely determined by the quality of their experiences. Henry Beston wrote in *The Outermost House*:

> Nature is part of our humanity, and without some awareness and experience of that divine mystery man ceases to

> be man. When the Pleiades, and the wind in the grass, are no longer a part of the human spirit, a part of very flesh and bone, man becomes, as it were, a kind of cosmic outlaw, having neither the completeness and integrity of the animal nor the birthright of a true humanity.[8]

These words convey one aspect of the ecological attitude that must be cultivated to develop a scientific theology of the earth.

But there are other aspects, based on the fact that man is rarely a passive witness of natural events. He manipulates the world around him and thus sets in motion forces that shape his environment, his life, and his civilizations. In this sense, man makes himself, and the quality of his achievements reflects his visions and aspirations. Human ecology naturally operates within the laws of nature, but it is always influenced by conscious choices and anticipations of the future.

The relationships that link mankind to other living organisms and to the earth's physical forces thus pertain to science but also transcend science. They involve a deep sense of engagement with nature and with all processes central to life. They generate a spirit of sacredness and of overriding ecological wisdom which is so universal and timeless that it was incorporated in most ancient cultures. One can recognize the manifestations of this sacredness and wisdom in many archaic myths and ceremonials, in the rites of preclassical Greeks, in Sung landscape paintings, in the agricultural practices of preindustrial peoples.[9] One can read it in Marcus Aurelius's statement that "all living things are interwoven each with the other; the tie is sacred, and nothing, or next to nothing, is alien to ought else." In our time, the philosophical writings of Whitehead have reintroduced in a highly intellectualized form the practical and poetical quality of ecological thought.

Human ecology inevitably considers relationships within

systems from the point of view of man's privileged place in nature. Placing man at the pinnacle of creation seems at first sight incompatible with orthodox ecological teachings. Professional ecologists, indeed, are prone to resent the disturbing influence of human intervention in natural systems. If properly conceived, however, anthropocentrism is an attitude very different from the crude belief that man is the only value to be considered in managing the world and that the rest of nature can be thoughtlessly sacrificed to his welfare and whims. An enlightened anthropocentrism acknowledges that, in the long run, the world's good always coincides with man's own most meaningful good. Man can manipulate nature to his best interests only if he first loves her for her own sake.[10]

While the living earth still nurtures and shapes man, he now possesses the power to change it and to determine its fate, thereby determining his own fate. Earth and man are thus two complementary components of a system, which might be called cybernetic, since each shapes the other in a continuous act of creation. The biblical injunction that man was put in the Garden of Eden "to dress it and to keep it" (Genesis 2:15) is an early warning that we are responsible for our environment. To strive for environmental quality might be considered as an eleventh commandment, concerned of course with the external world, but also encompassing the quality of life. An ethical attitude in the scientific study of nature readily leads to a theology of the earth.

CHAPTER 3

Deep Are the Roots

Most of the hundred billion human beings who have walked the earth since the appearance of *Homo sapiens* lived in ignorance not only of industry but also of agriculture. As recently as six thousand years ago, a large percentage of the world's population was still nonagricultural, living exclusively from hunting and the gathering of wild plants. This does not imply, however, that life for early man was as nasty, brutish, and short as used to be assumed. In modern times, even the Australian aborigines and the Bushmen in the Kalahari Desert are relatively well-fed. At no great expense of effort and time they obtain a fairly well balanced diet from the animals and plants of those inauspicious areas. Paleolithic hunters occupied habitats more favorable than the Australian and Kalahari deserts, and it has been calculated that some thirty hours of hunting and gathering a week sufficed to provide them with a great abundance and variety of food. Early man, living near the migration routes of bison, reindeer, and other large animals, had thus leisure time for an intense social life and for developing the art of the Ice Age.

The human species emerged in a subtropical environment, but its evolution was completed during the Ice Age. Man was thus shaped not by a stable sluggish climate as prevailed during the reptilian times, but rather by the highly challenging conditions of the tremendous winter resulting from the presence of the glacial ice over much of the earth. The selection of certain human types associated with climatic factors and with the hunting and gathering ways of life was probably much the same over all the inhabited parts of the world and this uniformity accounts even today for the unity of mankind. The effects of selection pressures were so profound, indeed, that the human species has not changed significantly for at least fifty thousand years. The continuous migrations of Stone Age men all over the planet, and their experiences with climatic upheavals, naturally resulted in an immense variety of genetic types, but genetic variation was never profound. We are still so like our Stone Age ancestors in fundamental needs and bodily structure that the best relics scientists have of early man are modern men. The distant evolutionary past has significance even for our emotional and intellectual life. Reindeer hunters living in the southwest of France fifteen thousand years ago expressed symbolically in their paintings and engravings preoccupations which are still meaningful to us. The performance of rituals, and the designing of ornaments were probably aspects of their lives as important as was the making of the weapons they used for hunting. If we could really understand the symbols used by Cro-Magnon man in his artistic efforts, this would reveal more than his tools do, not only about his culture but also about present-day human nature.

Our immense proficiency in managing beasts and forests, mountains and waters, space and time has changed our relations to external nature but has not significantly affected our own physical and mental being. Many problems of civilized life have their origin in the fact that we function in the technological world with a biology and psychology dating from the Stone Age. The dead weight of the social institutions inherited from the historical past is probably less of a handicap in the present world than are the reflexes, rhythms, physiological functions, and neural circuits inherited from our evolutionary past.

The dissociation between man's biological nature and his total environment becomes especially profound when the rate of change accelerates, as it did during the agricultural and urban revolutions of the Neolithic and Bronze ages, and again during the industrial revolution of the past two centuries. Biological mechanisms of evolution are so slow that they cannot possibly keep pace with such changes in the ways of life and in the surroundings.

Human life in highly technicized societies thus presents a paradox which may spell a bright future for our species, or its demise. On the one hand, the external manifestations of human existence change continuously and at an increasing rate under the influence of social and technological innovations. On the other hand, man's anatomical structures, physiological processes, and psychological urges remain in phase with the cosmic conditions that prevailed when *Homo sapiens* acquired his biological identity. Paul the Apostle was using words which could be interpreted in modern evolutionary terms when he stated: "Observe, the spiritual does not come first, the animal body comes first, and then the spiritual. The first man was made 'of the dust of the earth': the second man is from heaven" (I Corinthians 15:46–47; New English Bible). But Paul does not seem to have fully realized that the "animal body" persisted even after it had given rise to the spiritual. Nor has the modern world gone far toward understanding, let alone managing successfully, the dual nature of man.

Among the most obvious and stable of the ancient links of man with the world of nature are the daily, seasonal, and lunar rhythms exhibited by most functions of his body and mind. These rhythms clearly reflect the governing influence that cosmic forces exerted in the distant past on all aspects of human evolution.

Many important bodily functions of animals exhibit seasonal changes which persist even when temperature and humidity are kept constant, as is commonly done under laboratory conditions. The chemical and hormonal processes by which the body utilizes sugar differ predictably from season to season. The migration and mating drives, the color and quality of the fur in mammals, the plumage and song in birds are but a few of the many traits which remain linked to the seasons even when environmental conditions are artificially maintained constant. The chemical changes in the sex glands set in motion by the environment in early spring are of special importance because they initiate the processes of courtship display, and nest building at the proper time. The search for a mate and the care of the young thus involve patterns of behavior that are related to cosmic forces. And the same applies to man, even in the most urbanized and technicized societies.

During the first warm days of spring, all normal human beings perceive that nature is at work in their bodies and their minds, just as it is in plants and beasts. The new burst of life which brings forth the tender green shoots of vegetation and causes birds to start singing and nesting also makes men, women, and children feel the need to expend their energy and express their biological feelings in wanderlust and various forms of play, Maypole dances, college pranks, Mardi Gras festivities, games of love, and marriage celebrations.

The behavioral patterns associated with the seasons cannot be entirely accounted for by changes in temperature or in the luminosity of sky. They have their seat in the genetic constitution and originate from a time in the evolutionary past when man lived in such direct contact with nature that he could survive only if his bodily functions and his mental responses were precisely geared to the seasonal rhythms of nature and the availability of resources. In some primitive form, the rites of spring have probably existed since mankind's beginnings. The more civilization developed, the less man remained directly dependent on nature; yet changes in his ways of life did not markedly alter his fundamental needs and rhythms. In the most sophisticated cities, carnival is still celebrated when the sap begins running up the trees, just as it was thousands of years ago.

In man, as in other animals, blood pressure, hormonal activities, and other physiological functions are governed by cosmic influences. A temperature of 55 degrees Fahrenheit seems chilly in July but balmy in December, because the fundamental processes of the human body are different in summer from what they are in winter. The seasonal differences persist irrespective of the way of life, type of clothing, and use of air conditioning. Although the mechanisms responsible for these biological rhythms are poorly understood, it can be safely assumed that, in the course of evolutionary development, man acquired a number of adaptations which enabled him to withstand the food shortages and other stresses common in the winter season. These adaptive mechanisms became inscribed in the genetic code and persist unchanged, although they serve no useful purpose under the conditions of modern life. Functioning in the technological environment with a biological equipment developed in the Stone Age may indeed be responsible for some of the diseases of the modern world.

In addition to the biological rhythms determined by the seasonal movements of the earth around the sun, there are others (daily rhythms) which are linked to the daily rotation of the earth on its axis and probably still others associated with the movements of the moon around the earth.

The very word "lunatic" indicates an ancient belief that the moon affects human behavior. Many reports of behavioral disturbances in insane asylums and other institutions seem to substantiate this belief. Recent statistical studies suggest, furthermore, that the various phases of the moon are correlated with differences in birth rates.[1] In 1966, birth rates were unusually high exactly nine months after the power blackout in the Northeastern States. Commentators naturally traced the increase in numbers of conceptions to increased sexual activity during the darkness caused by the lack of electricity. They failed to notice, however, that on the night of the blackout there was a full moon in a bright, clear sky—a situation which has been claimed to be associated with higher conception rates in animal species as well as in man.

While the biological effects of the lunar rhythms are still questionable, the effects of the daily rhythms are well defined and of great practical importance. In one particular experiment, hourly recordings of oral temperature were made on the same two days of each month from January to November on a man living in a subantarctic environment. His temperature was consistently higher in the spring and summer than in the fall and winter, thus reflecting the seasonal fluctuations mentioned earlier. In addition, whatever the season, his temperature was higher in the afternoon than at night—evidence of a daily rhythm. Daily fluctuations occur in practically all other bodily characteristics that have been studied, ranging from chemical composition of the blood to secretion of hormones.

The daily fluctuations of bodily and mental characteristics affect many practical aspects of human life. The response to a given drug, for example, is markedly influenced by the time of day at which the drug is administered. Even our outlook on common events differs at night from what it is in bright daylight. The change in hormone levels according to the hour of the day certainly accounts in part for these differences in mood and gives a biological justification to Napoleon's saying that there is no brave soldier at three o'clock in the morning.

The daily biological rhythms of man are not immutably set. They can be altered by changes in the physical environment and in living habits, but such alterations commonly result in physiological disturbances which, though transient, may be profound. For example, changing from day to night work shifts or moving from one longitude to another by airplane usually causes discomfort. During a thirty-hour trip by propeller plane from the continental United States to Japan and Korea in the 1940s, the amounts of adrenal steroid hormones secreted by the passengers were measured at frequent intervals of time. Hormone secretion remained synchronized with U.S. standard time throughout the trip but changed progressively after arrival in Asia. It did not become fully synchronized with Asian time, however, until nine to ten days after arrival. Thus, for more than a week, the passengers had to function with hormone levels and body temperatures completely out of step with local time. Their biological state and psychological reactions at night were what they should have been at midday, and vice versa. Similar observations have been made on passengers traveling from America to Europe, but in this case the adjustments in hormone secretion and body temperature occurred more rapidly, in four to five days, probably because the longitudinal displacement was smaller. The physiological disturbances resulting from rapid changes of longitude have naturally become more striking with jet travel, and one can anticipate that they would be even more disturbing at supersonic speeds.

Experienced world travelers know that saving time during transit over long distances commonly has to be bought at the cost of discomfort and decreased efficiency upon arrival. From the practical point of view, it would naturally be desirable for persons who plan to participate in a sporting event or attend a conference in another part of the world to take steps for minimizing the physiological disturbances caused by changes in longitude. Unfortunately, there is as yet no convincing evidence that this can be achieved, either by adopting before departure a sleep-wakefulness pattern adapted to the new location, or by using drugs for accelerating physiological readjustments. Adequate time for adaptation after arrival remains the only certain method for overcoming the biological and psychological effects of the longitudinal shock.

Some of the needs, tastes, and habits of modern man have their origin in the fact that the biological cradle of *Homo sapiens* was on the plateaus of East Africa, in a subtropical climate with alternating rainy and dry seasons resulting in corresponding growing and resting periods of vegetation. Man thus emerged in a type of climate similar to that of the California or Mediterranean coasts. Most human beings feel comfortable in such a semitropical climate and try to imitate it in their dwellings. The explorer Vilhjalmur Stefansson, who spent two years among the Eskimos, asserted that the insulating power of their parkas and igloos enabled them to live most of the time in a very warm environment, even during the Arctic winter. As he repeatedly stated in *The Friendly Arctic*, during winter, the Eskimos lived in homes that were stationary tropics; when they went out of doors, they carried tropical warmth with them inside their clothes.[2]

Modern air conditioning now makes it possible to create everywhere on earth, and even in space capsules, artificial environments having a semitropical temperature at all times of the year. However, since early man was exposed to marked daily and seasonal fluctuations of temperature throughout his evolutionary development, maintaining the temperature of our dwellings and working places at a constant temperature of 72 to 75 degrees Fahrenheit may be biologically unsound. A truly desirable formula of air conditioning should probably be programmed for daily and seasonal fluctuations.

The human species had its early homes in regions of springs and streams, hills and valleys, rock shelters in cliffs, with a varied vegetation of trees, shrubs, and herbs, but no dense forests. This description fits not only the plateaus of East Africa but also the Dordogne Valley in southwestern France where Cro-Magnon man lived. The best-known Upper Paleolithic sites of this part of France were situated in and above valleys which served as migration routes for reindeer herds. In Mesopotamia also, the rock shelters and caves that were occupied by ancient man overlook broad valleys and are rich in bones of plains-dwelling animals.

Many themes of mythology and of classical art unfold in pastoral landscapes and under climatic conditions which are pleasant to us, probably because they resemble the savanna-like country in which *Homo sapiens* completed his biological evolution. Throughout history and in many parts of the world, bucolic paintings have depicted pastures with clumps of large trees under which shepherds tend their flocks and young people play at games of love. Pastoral life is obviously associated with some of the most pleasant memories of mankind; the biblical Eden symbolizes the earthly paradise we have lost.

Few are the parts of the world which provide conditions as pleasant biologically as are the semitropical, savannalike landscapes symbolized by the words Eden or Arcadia. But all civilizations have created a variety of parks and gardens inspired from imaginary pastoral scenes, themselves derived from the type of country in which man lived a thousand centuries ago. To a large extent, the art of living consists in trying to recapture ancient biological satisfactions in a modern context.

Along with preferences for certain types of climates and landscapes, we have inherited from our Stone Age ancestors patterns of behavior and of social organization which provide a biological basis for modern life.

Paleolithic hunters, and probably for a long time Neolithic farmers, lived in small bands that occupied a limited territory and had only limited contacts with other human groups. Such living conditions must have favored the development of a sense of loyalty to the members of the band but also of territoriality and of hostility toward strangers. These attitudes are common among animals and are reflected in our own behavior. The word for "stranger" still has pejorative overtones in European languages.

According to statements made by anthropologists during a symposium on "Man the Hunter" in 1966, primitive nuclear units were usually limited to some fifty persons and tribal groups to some five hundred persons.[3] It is probable that these "mystic" numbers had their origin in very early hunting practices. For hundreds of thousands of years, the precursors of *Homo sapiens* gained their livelihood by hunting together in small groups and sharing the products of their cooperative efforts. Before the days of bow and arrow, many men had to work together to trap and kill large game, but on the other hand, in the absence of crops, population density had to remain low. The practicalities of life before the invention of weapons and of agriculture thus probably played a large role in determining the minimum and maximum size of the social group and must have influenced thereby the development of the human brain. Even in modern society, the numbers of human beings with whom an individual deals on a really personal basis have not been significantly increased by the development of elaborate means of communication—telephones, radio, television, and other forms of mass media. The range of meaningful relationships is determined less by social conventions or technological inventions than by biological limitations.

Social conflicts are also conditioned by the distant past. Although much has been written concerning man the killer, evidence for a killing instinct is most questionable. Admittedly, the fact that the consumption of game was important for man's survival during the Early Stone Age makes it probable that the skills involved in hunting were then a source of pleasurable experiences. The Stone Age hunter, furthermore, could not afford to be sorry for the game he killed, any more than a cat is sorry for its victim. Even such a devotee of Zen Buddhism as the American poet Gary Snyder could write that "the hawk, the swoop, and the hare are one,"[4] and so are of course the cat, the pounce, and the mouse. Evolution has built a link between biology, behavior, and psychology, and this is reflected in the efforts made throughout history to maintain hunting as a noble sport.

Killing is a behavioral trait common to all predator animal species. This does not justify the assumption, however, that aggressiveness per se is a fundamental instinct which drives man to kill man. Early man was very sparse in numbers and most of his efforts must have been directed to food getting rather than to engaging in conflict with his own kind. Judging from the people who still live today in a Stone Age culture, the kind of "mutual aid" that the Russian anarchist Prince Kropotkin (1842–1921) observed among animals in the wild is a more characteristic attitude of primitive human life than is destructive conflict. From the beginning, human behavior was characterized by long-continued care of the young and by other altruistic qualities. Furthermore, mankind seems to have been remarkably peaceful for thousands of years during the early Neolithic period that preceded the establishment of cities and of social power structures. Even during modern times, several primitive tribes exhibit little evidence of violent conflicts. Biological aggressiveness commonly finds ample outlet in hunting, ritualized conflict, and in the patterns of retributive justice. In their intragroup relationships, the Australian aborigines seem to have successfully channeled most of their aggressiveness into socially useful behavior. Even between groups, conflict is often limited by cultural canons such as equality of chance and limitations on permissible casualties.

At a meeting held in May 1970 under the auspices of UNESCO, specialists on aggression unanimously rejected the theory of instinctive human aggressiveness. People act violently because they have been taught to do so, or made to do so, and not because they were born aggressive. To kill is not an instinct, but a socially acquired trait.

In animal populations as in present-day primitive human societies, competition is commonly resolved through ritualized conflicts that tend to avoid mortal wounds. After a short struggle one of the antagonists accepts defeat and leaves the field to the one that appears to be the stronger. Some historical practices, such as jousting among medieval knights, have been seen as forms of human ritualized conflict. It has even been suggested that international sport competitions and the space race between the United States and the Soviet Union might constitute a modern form of ritualized conflict that could eventually serve as a substitute for war.

Man's distant past probably conditions even his reaction to crowding. From time immemorial, human beings have been tolerant of high population density, at least if one judges from the large numbers of animal bones and human artifacts found in the immediate vicinity of certain caves or other sites used by early man. The Neolithic settlements, the fortified medieval towns, the Pueblo villages of the Rio Grande, the Hopi villages in Arizona, had small populations in comparison with those of modern cities, but their geographical areas were so restricted that their population density must have been great. Imperial Rome was also densely populated, as was Teotihuacan, the giant prehistoric city in the Valley of Mexico which had 125,000 to 200,000 inhabitants crowded into one-story apartment compounds.[5]

Large American cities give the impression of being painfully crowded even though the number of people per square mile in urban America is smaller than in most other urbanized parts of the world. Crowding in technological societies means not only people but their automobiles, radios, telephones, television sets—all the mechanical equipment of their everyday life with the various forms of pollution that it entails. The American city is traumatic not so much because of high population density as because the impact of each inhabitant is multiplied by the amount of technological power at his command. Each year more electric power is used for more air conditioners and other gadgets, all of which generate heat, thus increasing the demand for air conditioners which in turn call for more electric power in a truly vicious circle. The city dweller is exposed to so much technological overload that he confuses people with machines and pollution; yet he is starved for companionship with his fellow men. All persons who were in New York City during the great blackout of 1965 have commented on the warmth of the human feelings brought to the surface by the experience. Similarly, whenever Fifth Avenue and other arteries were closed to vehicular traffic during 1970, the lively crowds in the street did not create a traumatic environment, but rather the exhilaration that comes when large numbers of people share the same pleasurable experiences. The same density of people in the subway would have been no fun. The trauma of crowding in modern cities derives much less from human contacts than from technological impact.

More important than population density in any given area is the origin of its inhabitants. Until recent times, cities consisted in very large part of people who, irrespective of their distant origins and economic or social class, were familiar with one another because they had grown up in fairly close contact. The necessity of sharing many experiences of daily life compelled them to develop protective social mechanisms which reduced violent social conflicts. Of necessity, the servants lived near their masters; few were the tradesmen and businessmen who could retreat to the suburbs; the church parish contained both rich and poor. Now, in contrast, massive and sudden migrations are bringing unknown people into established communities, especially in American cities. Evolution has not prepared mankind for this experience; whatever the color of his skin, the stranger is still regarded as a potential threat. In New York City, for example, the successive immigrations of Irish, Jews, and Italians in the nineteenth century, then of Southern blacks and of Puerto Ricans in the twentieth century, have elicited, each in its turn, similar kinds of so-called racial tensions. The ubiquitous hostility to the newcomer—whatever his religion or skin pigmentation—derives in part at least from the apprehension the stranger engendered in the Stone Age.

Even in the ordinary events of daily life, we exhibit physiological responses very similar to those of our Stone Age ancestors when suddenly they faced a threat, such as a dangerous animal or a human being whom they regarded as a potential competitor. The survival of early man often depended upon his ability to mobilize body mechanisms that enabled him to fight effectively or to flee rapidly. The fight-and-flight response with all its hormonal and biochemical accompaniments still occurs when modern man experiences a threat, even an imaginary one. He reacts as if he were in danger of being physically attacked when he finds himself in a difficult social situation, in his job, for example, or at a dinner party. The cave man who survives under the skin of the sophisticated city dweller is ready to fight whenever a threatening gesture is made on the social scene. But since the response now rarely has a physical outlet, it results in tensions which have a deleterious effect on health.

Man's tendency to symbolize all his experiences and then to react to the symbols as if they were actual stimuli can also be traced far back in prehistory. Extensive evidence of man's early symbolic life can be found in the schematic designs that ornament Paleolithic weapons and tools, as well as in the rituals that took place in the depths of the Paleolithic caverns. Whatever their precise significance, the statues of women and the carvings and paintings of men, animals, and plants created during the Early Stone Age indicate that early man had the ability and the need to express in a symbolic form his thoughts about reproduction, hunting, and his relation to the cosmos.

Early man may have used artistic representation to gain power over what he represented. Furthermore, he must have painted and drawn, carved and modeled because this helped him to explore, and better grasp the world around him. Representative art gave him control over things, not only in the crude sense of magic power, but also in the deeper sense of an integration between the external world and the self. At least a hundred thousand years ago, Neanderthal man buried his dead with offerings in a crouched position oriented from east to west, and in some cases on beds of wildflowers. Some form of ultimate concern may thus be coeval with mankind. The need to symbolize death and the afterlife may constitute one of the attributes that set man completely apart from the animal kingdom.

Now as in the past, human beings respond not only to the objective characteristics of a given situation, but at least as much or even more to the symbols it represents for them. This transposition explains in part why certain human groups seem to accept conditions that others find intolerable. The attitude of a slum dweller may not be the same in Harlem or in the Watts section of Los Angeles as in the shanty towns of Hong Kong or Rio de Janeiro. Living conditions in the slums of North America are no worse and probably better than they are in the shanty towns that surround most Asian and Latin American cities. But in Harlem and Watts the slum is a symbol of segregation, whereas the shanty town is regarded as a step from agrarian poverty to city life with its potentialities. In one case, the slum means despair and in the other hope. Objectivity is misleading when it does not take subjective feelings into account.

The survival of the distant past manifests itself in very specific ways. We build wood fires in backyard patios or in steam-heated city apartments because fire—the hearth—is one of the great realities around which human life has been organized for ages. We keep plants and animals around us as if to maintain contact with our own origins. We travel far on weekends to lose ourselves momentarily in nature and experience again the wilderness from which our ancestors emerged a hundred centuries ago. The appeal of small islands may be that they evoke a world of which we can perceive the limits, as was the case during the stable era of the Stone Age. When we can afford it, we go back to hunting, first using guns, then bows and arrows, and any day we may start using spears armed with points fashioned from stones with our own hands, not out of necessity, but to re-establish one more link with our Stone Age past.

The distant past—how deeply we are imprinted with it! The astronauts' descriptions and excellent photographs have informed us that the surface of the moon is pockmarked, dusty, gray, and lifeless. But the moon is still "the white wonder of the skies, so rounded, so velvety, moving so serene. . . . In her so-called deadness there is enormous potency still, and power even over our lives. The Moon! Artemis! The great goddess of the splendid past of men!"[6]

People were immensely excited by the first lunar landing but had become almost blasé by the time of later Apollo missions. In contrast, there is increasing interest in African safaris, archeological digs all over the world, and efforts to discover eternal wisdom in prehistoric remnants or in ancient astrology. Childish as many contemporary expressions of the counterculture may be, they express modern man's desire to recapture a richer mode of response to the enigma of existence; they constitute an acknowledgment that the secrets of life can often be reached not so much by what we learn as by what we half remember with the biological memory of the human species. Only by probing into the dark and misty areas where zoology, prehistory, and anthropology meet, can we ever understand how man transcended his animal origin.

The persistence of traits inherited from the evolutionary past accounts for the difficulty in understanding fully our own attitudes and our responses to life situations. When the French philosopher Blaise Pascal wrote in the seventeenth century that the heart has its reasons which reason does not know, he acknowledged that many determinants of behavior do not originate from conscious reason and are beyond its control. There are woven into the fabric of human nature physiological and behavioral imperatives that no system of education can erase. Some of these became established during evolutionary development and are shared by all members of the human species; others arose from experiences so ancient that their origins are obscure.

Gary Snyder evokes the power of these immemorial behavioral traits in his description of Kumbh Mela, the festival of the Pitcher celebrated along the Ganges during spring. Men with long hair and beards, carrying conch horns and tridents, march, chanting in low voices, all stopping and then starting together: "A sudden sense of archaic tradition. Not just two or three thousand years, but fifty thousand years. A tribe of bushman shamans on the move. Or marching up out of some Pleistocene stratum under the hills."[7] And despite the constant threat of cholera, millions of men attend the festival of the Pitcher every year, as if they were part of a procession that started hundreds of centuries ago from some Stone Age sanctuary.

Certain immemorial folk traditions have origins that can be readily traced to peculiarities of the local environment, as illustrated by the psychologist Erik H. Erikson in "Observations on the Yurok: Childhood and World Image." The Yurok Indians live on lagoons and at the mouths of small streams in a forested area some two hundred miles north of San Francisco. They are a secluded and steadfast tribe, occupying valleys hidden from the rest of the world by mountains and giant trees. Scarcity of food during much of the year has led them to practice cautious hoarding and to develop puritanical self-control in all phases of their social behavior, especially in the training of their children. However, Yurok life has an undercurrent of subdued prayerful expectation for the period once a year when fantastic numbers of salmon "come home" in the Klamath River. At that time, the Yurok become carnal and indulgent, as if all the puritanical bonds of their society were broken. The red salmon steaks, available everywhere in abundance, seem to create in the exultant tribe an orgiastic mood which is the equivalent of carnival or Mardi Gras in countries of Greco-Roman civilization.[8]

Until the sixteenth century, it was commonly believed even by the most sophisticated scholars that individual characteristics were under astrological influences. For example, persons born under the signs of Jupiter, Saturn, or Mercury were expected to exhibit respectively a jovial, saturnian, or mercurial temperament. As long as physicians remained under the spell of ancient Greek medical science it was generally believed that the sanguine, phlegmatic, bilious, and choleric qualities of human beings could be respectively traced to the effects of blood, phlegm, yellow bile, and black bile.

We have moved far from this ancient biology, but our views of temperament still rest on many unproven assumptions. Instead of believing in astrological influences we now accept the idea that the whole hereditary endowment is transmitted from one generation to the next by chemical mechanisms located in the cell nucleus. Instead of accounting for temperament by a combination of the four body humors, we state in complex jargon that the traits by which a person is known, including his behavior, result from the influence of environmental factors on the phenotypic expressions of his genetic endowment. Our scientific philosophy of man states in a narrow deterministic way that developmental and behavioral characteristics are the consequences of the interplay between heredity and environment. Yet, few scientists really believe, deep in their hearts, that the orthodox concepts of determinism are sufficient to account for human life. Before dealing with this thorny question, I shall consider briefly some of the obvious problems, and others not so obvious, posed by man's responses to his environment.

In his essay "On the Uses of Great Men," Ralph Waldo Emerson (1803-1882) expressed succinctly the biological truth that physical, mental, and behavioral traits are profoundly affected by surroundings and events. As he wrote, "There are vices and follies incident to whole populations and ages. Men resemble their contemporaries even more than their progenitors."[9]

We resemble our progenitors because we derive from them our genetic constitution. But we usually resemble our contemporaries even more, because we share the same environment, and therefore are exposed to the same conditions during critical phases of life. It is well known that during the past few decades the maturation of young people has greatly accelerated in all the countries that have adopted the ways of Western civilization. Children are taller than they were a century ago; they achieve sexual maturity three to four years earlier and they become larger adults than were their ancestors. This change in growth pattern is just as striking among Orientals as among Occidentals. The Japanese used to be thought of as a small race, but now many of their teenagers are almost as tall as Americans of the same age, not because of any change in the genetic constitution of the Japanese people, but because of the new ways of life in postwar Japan.

In addition to body size and age of sexual maturity, many other biological and psychological traits of man are profoundly affected by the modern urban and technological environment. Furthermore, these effects in turn influence man's behavior and the forms of his civilization. As the Japanese grow taller and heavier, changes will have to be made in the size and design of their furniture, houses, school buildings, playgrounds, and means of transportation. One may also anticipate alterations in the landscaping of their gardens, in the management of their scenery, and even in their ceremonial life. The traditional Nippon culture is likely to be profoundly altered by the effects that the modern ways of life will increasingly exert on the biology and psychology of the Japanese people, and these alterations in turn will further change the conditions under which Japanese people will develop in the future.

As commonly used, the word environment refers almost exclusively to the physical forces intercepted by the sense organs and to the social forces created by the community. But man's biology and behavior are influenced by many other factors which are not the less powerful for being unrecognized.

The effects of the environment which are not perceived by the sense organs are often elusive and for this reason not considered important. As an example, the effects caused by the waves of the electromagnetic spectrum other than light-wave length, or the biological rhythms geared on the daily, lunar, and seasonal cycles, are commonly overlooked. The perceived environment constitutes therefore only a limited part of the total physicochemical environment.

Each living thing, furthermore, inhabits a perceptual world of its own. A dog, sniffing the breezes or the traces of a rabbit on the earth, lives in a world that a man or a frog can hardly perceive. An insect searching for a mate, a salmon crossing oceans toward its spawning ground, or a bird exploring the soil or a tree trunk to extract an insect from it, uses clues that are meaningless for other animal species. Much of behavior is thus influenced by stimuli which make the perceptual environment differ from species to species and indeed from one individual organism to another.

Responses to the environment involve in addition many factors that were almost universally ignored a few decades ago. Animals have been shown to receive information through many unfamiliar ways, such as ultrasound waves for bats, infrared waves for moths and pit vipers, and the substances known as pheromones (or exohormones) which many organisms excrete into the external environment. Recent discoveries indicate that human beings are sensitive to radio waves and magnetic fields and that their autonomous nervous system, blood-clotting mechanism, blood pressure, and other physiologic processes are affected by changes in the weather. It is legitimate to assume that human beings, like other organisms, also use exohormones for certain types of subconscious communications. Parapsychologists have indeed suggested that extrasensory perceptions should really be regarded as "crypto-sensory responses." Various channels of communication, so elusive that they were once dismissed as nonexistent and indeed thought to be impossible, thus enable us unconsciously to acquire valuable information from the physical and biological environment and from our fellow men.

Although we perceive more of the external world than we realize, we ignore certain aspects of it which are obvious to our most immediate neighbors. The phrase, "perceptual environment" thus has highly subjective overtones. The perception of racial or national characteristics differs from one social group to the other; the statement common among Caucasians that all Chinese look more or less alike certainly has its counterpart among Orientals with regard to Caucasians. The perception of social inequalities and inequities also differs from person to person and from time to time. Social justice may be a universal concept, but in practice the awareness and exercise of it are conditioned by highly personal experiences.

In addition to the aspects of the total environment that

are outside of us, in the external world, there are others that exist only in the individual mind and therefore constitute a person's private conceptual environment. The environment of a primitive population living on a Micronesian atoll includes of course the sea, the land, and the sky, but it also includes a host of spirits that lurk everywhere. Although the spirits of the Micronesian conceptual environment do not have concrete existence, they nevertheless affect profoundly the inhabitants of the atoll. They become malevolent when not properly treated and elicit behavioral responses that may be more dangerous than wounds inflicted by sharks or poisonous eels.

Nor is the conceptual environment of less importance in industrial societies. Whether sophisticated and learned, or primitive and ignorant, every human being lives in a conceptual environment of his own which conditions all his ethical and social attitudes, such as his opinions concerning the nature of progress, his view of man's place in the cosmic order of things, the attributes that he associates with the word God. Both the philosopher Alfred North Whitehead and the theologian Harvey Cox have made it clear that the concept of deity, and the names by which it is designated, have evolved with man's view of the cosmos.[10] It is because the perceptual and conceptual environments are so highly personal that each one of us lives in a private world of his own. As civilization becomes more complex and exacting, moreover, the conceptual environment acquires greater and greater importance because it acts as a mediator in all aspects of the interplay between man and the rest of creation.

The effective environment of a given person thus must be differentiated from the obvious environmental forces measured by the orthodox natural and social sciences. Man's behavior and the evolution of his societies are profoundly conditioned by the responses he makes to his perceptual and conceptual environments which include much less and also much more than what can be detected by objective observations and measurements. I have chosen the word "response" instead of "reaction" to indicate that the interplay between man and environment is not merely a passive affair but commonly implies on his part the exercise of free will.

At every moment of life, the biological and psychological characteristics of a given person are thus the expressions of past experiences which have become incorporated in his body and mind. Of particular importance are the responses made by the organism during the early formative stages of development, because they affect biological and psychological characteristics throughout the whole life span. Anatomical structures, adult body size, physiological functions, and longevity, as well as learning ability and behavioral patterns, are lastingly affected by the environmental conditions which impinge on the organism during prenatal and early postnatal life.[11] Many aspects of the total environment—perceptual and conceptual—have been shown to play a role in this early conditioning. Nutrition, infection, temperature, humidity, type of housing, intensity and variety of stimuli, degree of crowding, various types of social associations or deprivation, memories, aspirations, and imaginary experiences are among the environmental factors of early life that affect biological and mental characteristics, profoundly and lastingly.

The experiences of early life are of special importance because man's body and brain are incompletely developed at the time of birth and therefore achieve their full expression while being exposed and responding to environmental stimuli. The human brain is three times as large at six years of age as it is at birth, and its fundamental architecture develops during this early period through an elaborate sprouting of dendrites.

Language, imagination, consciousness, and the sense of self-identity also reach a high level of development at that time. Some of the most important developmental processes thus occur in response to early experiences, but, whatever the nature of the environment, all expressions of human nature have their roots deep in the past.

CHAPTER 4

Individuality, Personality, and Collectivity

Urban agglomerations are often likened to anthills or beehives. They harbor human beings who seem to function like social insects, huge numbers of them playing identical roles in the community and returning to their appointed cells morning and evening, as if they were but interchangeable units in a complex colony. Scholars have contributed to this collective, anonymous view of mankind by emphasizing in their studies those attributes shared by all human beings. They have discovered generalizations which apply to biological man, social man, political man, economic man, man in the abstract. But in the real world, no two human beings are alike, and all prize their individuality above everything else. The man of flesh and bone, portrayed by the Spanish philosopher Miguel de Unamuno (1864-1936), cares little for universality; he cherishes his uniqueness.[1]

All members of the human species share the same fundamental anatomic structures, physiologic needs, and mental attributes, but the similarities go much further. Whatever the pigmentation of the skin and the thickness of the lips, a smile is a smile everywhere. The facial expressions and behavioral patterns expressing love, anger, surprise, and fear are common to all races of men. The candid camera has proved that the responses of young women to flirting are almost identical in Samoa, Papua, France, Japan, Africa, and among South American Indians.

> The flirting girl at first smiles at the person to whom attention is directed and lifts her eyebrows with a quick, jerky movement upward so that the eye slit is briefly enlarged. This most probably inborn greeting with the eyes is quite typical. Flirting men show the same movement of the eyebrow, which can also be observed during a friendly greeting between members of the same sex. After this initial, obvious turning toward the person, in the flirt there follows a turning away. The head is turned to the side, sometimes bent toward the ground, the gaze is lowered, and the eyelids are dropped. Frequently, but not always, the girl may cover her face with a hand and she may laugh or smile in embarrassment. She continues to look at the partner out of the corners of her eyes and sometimes vacillates between looking at and an embarrassed looking away.[2]

Civilizations differ from period to period and from place to place, but they are all based on the same biological drives and fixed action patterns. Poems of love or sorrow, monuments celebrating worship or triumph, are universally meaningful. A Chinese lullaby or one from a Western country will be just as soothing to either an Occidental or an Oriental child. Cosmetics for heightening the lines of the eyes have been found in Neolithic remains and have been used in one form or another by all people at all times, as have masks, kingly robes, and hieratic arts.

Irrespective of origin, people are therefore much more alike than they are different, but in spite of this uniformity we never forget that we differ in geographical and national backgrounds, in religious and philosophical allegiances, and most importantly in the mysterious combination of qualities and defects which makes each one of us a unique specimen of the human species. Even identical twins differ from each other; despite the adjective indentical, they do not need social security cards or records of their voices and gestures to be aware of their individual distinctiveness.

Each person, furthermore, retains his distinctive characteristics as he grows older and when he moves from one place to another. The ancient Greeks had this permanency in mind when they scoffed at the wrongdoer who protested that he should not be punished for what he had done because—as the Greek philosopher Heraclitus had demonstrated—he was now a different person. Everyone is today and will be tomorrow only a slightly modified expression of what he was yesterday or at any time in the past. In the midst of change, we exhibit a sameness and continuity which other people recognize. The way a person walks or engages in a conversation is commonly sufficient to identify him from among thousands of strangers, even after years of absence; Ulysses was immediately recognized by his dog when he returned from his travels. This uniqueness and permanency of individual characteristics are essential components of self-awareness.

In common usage, the word "man" sometimes refers to the human species as a whole, and sometimes to a particular person. This dual meaning symbolizes a paradox inherent in the human condition. We believe in the unity and universality of mankind, but most of our daily life has to do with the existential diversity of its individual members. In this chapter I emphasize uniqueness rather than biological unity, the self rather than society, what each person elects to be and to do rather than the collective attributes and activities of mankind.

Most scientific studies of human development and behavior deal with man as if he were the passive product of genetic and environmental forces—a biological automaton. This deterministic approach is justified by the facts that each child is born with a particular body and a particular nervous system; that each mother has her own style of motherhood which is the result of her own life in a given society at a given moment of history; and that surroundings affect all phases of development. As Erikson points out, however, even such an inescapable constellation of constitutional and environmental determinants leaves a good deal of leeway as to what the child can become when he grows into an adult.

> While it is quite clear, then, what *must* happen to keep the body alive (the minimum supply necessary) and what *must not* happen, lest he die or be severely stunted (the maximum frustration possible), there is increasing leeway in regard to what *may* happen; and different cultures make extensive use of their prerogative to decide what they consider workable and insist on calling necessary. Some people think that a baby, lest he scratch his own eyes out, must necessarily be swaddled completely for the better part of the day throughout the greater part of the first year; but also that he should be rocked or fed whenever he whimpers. Others think that he should feel the freedom of his kicking limbs as early as possible, but should "of course" be forced to wait for his meals until he, literally, gets blue in the face.. . . What then is "good for the child," what *may* happen to him, depends on what he is supposed to become, and where [italics Erikson's].[3]

What the child becomes, furthermore, depends a great deal upon his own willful and creative activities. The existence of free will, at any age of life, probably can never be demonstrated scientifically; science implies determinism. In practice, however, all human beings, including the most deterministic philosophers and experimenters, believe that they have some measure of freedom in their decisions or at least in their choices; freedom posits free will. The American Nobel laureate in physics Arthur Compton is reported to have stated that, if Newton's laws were incompatible with his freedom to raise his left arm when he had a fancy to do so, then Newton's laws had to be changed. That even animals have free will seems to be accepted by many scientists if one judges from the "law of animal behavior" inscribed in two famous biological laboratories, one in Europe and one in the United States: "Under precisely controlled conditions, an animal does as it damn pleases."[4]

Free will is usually regarded as a primary datum of experience, but nothing is known of the mechanisms through which it intervenes in life processes. One reason for this ignorance may simply be that the experimental method as now practiced deals only with reproducible phenomena and therefore must ignore the unpredictable manifestations of free will. In fact, the experimenter does his best to mask and even obliterate these unpredictable manifestations through the statistical treatment of his findings. The experimental methods of biology are useful only for deterministic processes, and this imposes limitations on the use of science in the study of human life, and of other forms of life as well.

From the very first day of life, the child perceives his environment, stores information about it, and develops patterns of response that become a permanent part of his organic being. Even in this early phase, awareness of environment is not entirely passive, since it is an expression of the biological urge to explore—a curiosity that is universal in its general manifestations but takes forms peculiar to each organism. Very soon, the responses to environmental stimuli become conscious and are converted into creative processes; the child behaves as if he were selectively exploring the world around him with some kind of purpose in mind.

Children differ, of course, and each tends to select the environmental conditions best suited to his innate endowment. Increasingly, furthermore, the child tries to create a world, external and conceptual, in which to discover himself. Play can be regarded as the chief method children use for securing the kinds of sensations and perceptions out of which they construct their private reality. In other words, the child is a selector of environment before he becomes a solver of problems.

From approximately the age of five, almost every child uses consciously the environmental information and patterns of responses he has already acquired, to imagine a world of his own in which he can act out his thoughts; his individuality thus develops along the lines determined by his imagination. I am using here the word "imagine" in the strong etymological sense given it by Shelley in his essay "In Defence of Poetry." When Shelley wrote, "We want the creative faculty to imagine that which we know," he meant "to create an image" out of what we know. Much of subsequent life consists in the unfolding of the patterns which we create for ourselves in our conceptual world early in life.

The view that individuality develops progressively through the incarnation of past experiences is not as obvious as it sounds. Most ancient and medieval biographies describe heroes as if they had no past and were born with primary ideal qualities. Saint Augustine did much to change this naive interpretation of behavior by stating explicitly in his *Confessions* that a person could imprison himself in a second nature by his past actions. Since the past of human beings is highly influential at any time in their lives, it follows, according to Saint Augustine, that they differ from one another to the extent that their wills have shaped them through unique constellations of choices and experiences.

Throughout life, the person retains some freedom in selecting his occupations, associations, and surroundings and thereby in shaping his further development. The feeling of identity emerges and becomes sharper as a consequence of complex adjustments that begin during infancy and continue throughout childhood, adolescence, and adulthood. As Erikson puts it: "The process of identity formation emerges as an *evolving* configuration . . . gradually established by successive ego syntheses and resyntheses throughout childhood—integrating constitutional givens, idiosyncratic libidinal needs, favored capacities, significant identifications, effective defenses, successful sublimations, and consistent roles."[5] Each phase of adaptation generates a crisis, calling for adaptive mechanisms to harmonize libidinal forces with the new demands made by society.

Seen from a developmental point of view, the events of childhood continue to be reflected in all stages of life, not because early experiences rigidly determine the future, but because they condition all subsequent responses. Individuality is thus "becoming" rather than "being," a continuously evolving structure made up of inherited and acquired characteristics that are integrated at each step into an organic whole. The fundamental pattern of integrated structure is enduring and remains an effective guide to development long after the conditions that have brought it into being have disappeared.

The persistence of individuality cannot yet be explained

in biological terms. Even though nerve cells do not multiply after birth, they keep growing at a rate matching the fastest proliferating cells of the adult body, and yet amidst all this flux, the mind retains a sense of identity throughout life. This stability implies the existence of a pattern of neural organization that is essentially independent of metabolic changes.

Since the unique mental structure of a person is in part his own creation, it follows that his responses to surroundings and events can acquire during his development an increasing degree of independence from his evolutionary past and from the culture in which he was born. Irrespective of theories concerning the ultimate nature of free will, this independence accounts for man's ability to make choices and take decisions, thereby influencing his future. Free will, however, can operate only if there is first a motive, and this in turn implies the existence of some belief to provide a basis for choice. Individuality thus becomes more complex and also better defined as a person continues to develop. Adult man is *par excellence* the creature who can eliminate, choose, organize, and thereby create.

Whereas the child is chiefly playful and experimental, the adult focuses on specific and conscious experiences. He practices selective inattention to the objects for which he has no immediate use and develops a kind of tunnel vision that helps him to move toward selected goals. This focusing on a limited range of experiences and goals is largely responsible for one's individual evolution and gives a deep and almost tragic significance to a statement made by Albert Camus in his novel *La Chûte: "Après un certain âge tout homme est responsable de son visage."*[6] An almost identical statement appears as the very last entry in George Orwell's notebooks, a few months before his death: "At 50, everyone has the face he deserves."[7] There could not be any more absolute affirmation of belief in personal responsibility for the quality of one's own life and character.

The choices that a person makes concerning his activities and environment affect not only his own future but also the development of young people exposed during their formative years to the conditions resulting from these choices. Each individual decision thus influences the social group as a whole. In this sense man makes himself, individually and socially, through a continuous series of willful acts that are governed by his value judgments and his anticipations of the future.

The words "individuality" and "personality" are used almost interchangeably, though they are completely unlike in etymology. The interest of this etymological difference is that it points to biological and social forces which play a large role in shaping the characteristics of human beings. The meanings of the words individuality and personality need to be sharpened in order to set forth the complementary roles in human life of environmental influences and of deliberate choices.

The characteristics by which we know a person depend of course upon the uniqueness of his genetic endowment; except in the case of identical twins, no two human beings possess the same array of genes. Furthermore, as mentioned earlier, practically all life situations leave a permanent imprint on the developing person. Between the genes and the person's characteristics there intervene the complex processes of development and senescence which are affected by social, economic, cultural, and other environmental factors.

Even though early environmental influences cannot readily be recaptured by conscious memory, they are of special importance for development because they create the patterns on which all subsequent life experiences are organized. As the body and mind progressively evolve, structures, feelings, thoughts, and actions become integrated into an organic whole.

The word "individuality" has the same root as "indivisible"; it implies an organization so well integrated that health and even viability are threatened if the various constituents of the system are separated. Organic integration and stability of interrelationships between structures and functions account for the uniqueness and permanency of the organism.

The Latin word *"persona"* seems to be derived from an Etruscan word meaning mask. In archaic societies, a mask (or a costume) was placed on a human being to symbolize his place and function in the social group. Considered from this point of view, "personality" therefore denotes roles and attitudes deliberately acquired rather than the unavoidable expression of biological forces. In many cases, the personality expresses what the human being believes himself to be, rather than what he really is. However, even though the *persona* may be fiction, it always conditions social relationships, as is indicated by such phrases as "be yourself" or "this is not worthy of you." More importantly, the self-selection of a *persona* is an essential step in development, because, as the Irish poet William Butler Yeats stated it, "If we cannot imagine ourselves as different from what we are and assume that second self, we cannot impose a discipline upon ourselves. . . . Active virtue is therefore consciously dramatic, the wearing of a mask."[8]

Since personality is an attribute added on to, or assumed by, the organism, it may be removed or lost when the role or attitude that it symbolizes is no longer appropriate or needed. In primitive societies, and perhaps even more in our own, political or environmental disturbances commonly cause sudden changes of personality. The word personality seems more suitable for human beings than for animals precisely because it implies values, rather than biological constitution.

The development of the plastic arts illustrates how man's ability to choose and to decide enables him to make use of his biological individuality in order to generate his personality as an artist. The statues, paintings, carvings, and other artifacts made by Early Stone Age Man provide evidence that the biological attributes for artistic expression are very ancient and perhaps originated with *Homo sapiens.* Acuity of perception and representational skill have not shown any detectable improvement since the Stone Age. They are qualities which are biological in essence and which have always been unevenly distributed among people regardless of their level of civilization.

The biological ability to perceive and to represent, however, is not by itself sufficient to create works of art. The bower birds of Australia compose attractive patterns with colored pebbles in front of their nests, but their behavior is completely instinctive; if one of the pebbles is removed from the design, the bird automatically replaces it with another one of the same color. Certain apes, when provided with pigments, brushes, and canvases, can compose pictures in which colors are attractively arranged, and they will attempt to correct their composition if some parts of it are altered by the human experimenter. But there is no evidence that bower birds or apes can use their biological skills for conceptual expression.

In contrast, human beings do not react passively to the environment as if they were mechanical intermediaries in stimulus-response couplets. Like animals, they perceive their environment and develop their pictorial skills through their biological attributes, but the truly artistic response is an expressive and creative behavior for self-actualization. The famous phrase by the French painter Jean-Baptiste Corot (1796–1875), *"Un tableau, c'est un paysage vu à travers un temperament"* (A painting is a landscape seen through a particular temperament), is an inadequate description of landscape painting, because it fails to convey its creative spirit. The great painter not only represents a scene as he sees it and feels its atmosphere; consciously or unconsciously, he creates a mood for the sake of a message. Whether the human body is represented to convey religious mysticism, voluptuous experiences, or loneliness in a crowd, the choice involves human values which transcend the biological.

The artistic act thus illustrates the role of choice in utilizing the biological endowment of mankind for the creation of culture. Through the complex feedbacks that operate in all living systems, mankind is in turn modified by culture. Civilized man is what he is today because he has been doing intellectual and technological things for several millennia. Similarly, the kind of person a human being becomes is determined in large part by the kind of activities he elects to emphasize.

Although the attributes of the organism that I have designated by the words individuality and personality have different origins, in practice they constantly interplay and merge into each other. The integrated biological characteristics which constitute individuality affect in a decisive manner the acquisition or selection by a particular human being of his place and role in the social group and thus contribute to the development of his personality. On the other hand, the acquisition of personality, whether deliberately assumed or given by society, exposes the person to certain environments and experiences which influence his further development, thereby causing irreversible changes in his biological individuality.

This constant interplay between individuality and personality is the mechanism of existential expression at every moment of life.

The measure of man is his ability to overcome the constraints of determinism so that he can select or create his persona instead of passively accepting his biological individuality. "Man becomes truly human only at the time of decision," wrote the German-born American theologian Paul Tillich (1886–1965). This kind of freedom is the finest and final criterion of humanness.

Michel de Montaigne owes his perennial appeal to the urbane manner in which he accepts the constraints of the external world and acknowledges his own limitations, yet manages to create his personality out of these constraints and limitations. He urges us to remain provincial because this is natural and to enjoy our biological nature which is *"merveilleusement corporelle."*[9] But acceptance of the world as it is does not prevent him from taking an active attitude toward life by discovering what is irrefutably authentic about his own nature and expressing his real self. "There is no one who, if he listens to himself, does not discover in himself a pattern all his own, a ruling pattern which struggles against education." To live according to this pattern gives us the opportunity to create "our great and glorious masterpiece." Indeed, "to compose our character is our duty."[10]

Much of modern literature is concerned, if not with our duty to compose our character, at least with our right to affirm our chosen personality. For example:

José Ortega y Gasset: "Living is precisely the inexorable necessity to make oneself determinate, *to enter into an exclusive destiny,* to accept it—that is, to resolve to *be it.* We have, whether we like it or not, to realize our 'personage,' our vocation, our vital program, our 'entelechy'—there is no lack of names for the terrible reality which is our authentic I (ego)."[11]

André Gide: "What could have been said by someone other than you, do not say it; what could have been done by someone other than you, do not do it; of yourself, be interested only in those aspects that do not exist except in you; patiently or impatiently create out of yourself the most unique and irreplaceable of beings."[12]

Paul Tillich: "Individualism is the self-affirmation of the individual self as individual self without regard to its participation in its world."[13]

To create and affirm one's personality seems to be one of the strongest human imperatives, but it often generates attitudes which are antisocial and also self-destructive. Feodor Dostoevski has dramatized this conflict in *Notes from Underground*: "Man only exists for the purpose of proving to himself that he is a man and not an organ-stop! He will prove it even if it means physical suffering, even if it means turning his back on civilization."[14]

And Friedrich Nietzsche was even more nihilistic when he wrote, in *Thus Spake Zarathustra*, "This is my way. What is yours? As for *the* way, it does not exist."

Even under the most favorable conditions, the maintenance of a healthy personality requires constant effort, because we all harbor many conflicting tendencies and depend for our survival on complex social relationships. Every perceptive adult knows he is part beast and part saint, a mixture of folly and reason, love and hate, courage and cowardice. He can be at the same time believer and doubter, idealist and skeptic, altruistic citizen and selfish hedonist. The coexistence of these conflicting traits naturally causes tension but is nevertheless compatible with sanity. In a mysterious way, the search for identity and the pursuit of self-selected goals harmonize opposites and facilitate the integration of discordant human traits into some sort of working accord.

Since man is always part of a social structure, his integration into an organic wholeness involves not only his own biological and mental attributes, but also their interplay with the other members of his social group. Sanity is thus a perilous balance between the personal and social forces that constantly push and pull and that threaten to upset even the healthiest person, especially when he encounters a situation which is new to him. Swerving and swaying beyond a narrow margin of safety may cause him to slip and lose his equilibrium. Life is a juggling act on a tight rope.

Man, the juggler, commonly resents the limitations and controls that society imposes on his performance; but he cannot avoid them entirely. Human life would not be possible without social constraints. The social imperatives that limit the expressions of personality are probably what Nietzsche had in mind when he wrote that the ultimate ethic is biological and that we need a "transvaluation of values." Abraham's willingness to sacrifice his son symbolizes the biological law that the welfare of the group is more important than the life of its individual members. Obedience to the dictates of the group may at times take precedence over love.

Tillich's statement that individualism is the affirmation of the individual self "without regard to its participation in the world" is thus biologically untenable. No population could long survive without an integration of its component parts into a coherent structure. Just as the expressions of the body and the brain are influenced by the environment in which the organism develops, so the range of personality characteristics is limited by the constraints imposed by the total social milieu.

In appearance, Thoreau was free to escape from the bustling nineteenth century by spending much of his life in the woods beside Walden Pond. But neither he nor any of the other Concord transcendentalists could have prevented the nineteenth century from bustling around them and therefore from influencing them.

Here again Montaigne points to an urbane solution by suggesting that the better part of wisdom is to tolerate the tastes and conventions of one's contemporaries, but in a gentle spirit of skepticism: "He who asked the Delphic Oracle how it was proper to serve God received only this answer: according to the laws and customs of your country." The ultimate expression of this tolerance is the common French saying, *"Tout comprendre c'est tout pardonner"* (To understand is to forgive).[15] Understanding and forgiving are complementary human attitudes. To understand implies the belief that behavior is governed by deterministic laws; to forgive is an act of compassion which transcends determinism.

Each one of us is born with the innate biological equipment for a thousand different kinds of lives. From the day of birth, however, our development is channeled in certain directions by the physical and especially the social environment. This inevitable self-limitation is one major aspect of the tragic sense of life. It is made even more distressing by the fact that in order to achieve anything worthwhile man must function as a unity. The creation of this unity requires painful rejections and choices. We acquire our individuality from the spontaneous play of natural forces. In contrast, we compose our personality through the exhilarating but often painful process of selecting from the options available to us those that can best be accommodated within the time and place of our lives—the social frame.

CHAPTER 5

Of Places, Persons, and Nations

When I summon to memory experiences from my distant past, the images that emerge bring back to life not only the persons with whom I associated, but even more the places in which I functioned. I see myself as a little boy, pushing a wheelbarrow full of wild carrots through tall grasses and along quiet streets in the fields and villages of the Île de France, always within sight of a church steeple; my adolescent daydreams of adventure are associated with the parks of Paris and the rocky shores of the Riviera; I think of myself as a young adult reading scientific books in the Pincian Gardens in Rome, then among trees and lawns in the Hudson River Valley, or working long hours in New York and Boston laboratories.

I remember the mood of places better than their precise features, because places evoke for me life situations rather than geographical sites. When I first visited the region around Waterloo in Belgium, I did not see it as a small and dull plain; I experienced it as the stage for the last stand of Napoleon's Imperial Guard and as the landscape for Victor Hugo's poem that I had learned in school: "*Waterloo, Waterloo, Waterloo, morne plaine. . . .*"

In daily life persons are usually more important than places. Man is primarily a social animal who functioned in highly integrated hunting groups as far back as the Early Stone Age. He depended then on close association with the members of his group, even before he had achieved awareness of his individuality, let alone of his humanity. Like other human beings, I too have depended at every stage of my life, and continue to depend, upon countless men and women. Yet I am always prejudiced in favor of those who believe that landscapes profoundly affect human development.

In real life as well as in literature, persons exist as functions of the place in which they live. Dostoevski's hero in *Notes from Underground* symbolizes a type of rebellion against the Establishment which is universal, but he expresses it in a very Russian way.[1] The Protestants in Monpellier, Nîmes, and other cities of Southern France take their stand against the pope at least as earnestly as the Lutherans in Stockholm or the Presbyterians in Belfast, but they do it in a Mediterranean way, with bodily gestures and movements of the fingers and arms as much as with arguments and prayer.

An extreme and truly fascinating manifestation of the relationship between place and mind has been recently reported by the Russian psychologist A.R. Luria in *The Mind of a Mnemonist*.[2] Dr. Luria describes in detail a patient with a phenomenal retentive memory, who remembered figures, words, or sentences not as abstract symbols but only in close associations with specific places and life experiences. He could make his pulse race just by imagining himself walking to the railroad station to catch a train. In the memory of this person, words and figures were always linked to visual and other sensual perceptions. As pointed out by Dr. Luria, his patient's mind was retentive, because it was "speculative" in the etymological sense of the word: it functioned chiefly through visual images. The Russian word for speculative is *umozritelny,* which literally means "seen with the mind." Most of us, indeed, think through the agency of the sensual images that we derive from the world around us.

In the course of our daily life, we constantly respond to buildings, landscapes, trees, clouds, stars, and other elements of the non-human universe as much as we do to social experiences. We are shaped by these responses. The openness of vast plains or seashores makes the body and the mind different from what they would have become in the subdued light of forest clearings or mountain valleys. Folklores as well as the sophisticated forms of literature take it for granted that individuality is molded by the features of the place in which the person develops. Few persons have as precise a memory of these features or of the sensual perceptions associated with them as did Dr. Luria's mnemonist, but all of us reflect in our individuality the worlds we have experienced. A person born and raised in Florence cannot help being conditioned by churches, palaces, and parks, their sights, sounds, and smells. Even if the Florentine is not consciously aware of these experiences they nevertheless become part of his being and make him lastingly different from what he would have become in London, Paris, Barcelona, or New York.

Lawrence Durrell presents in its most extreme form the view that human beings are expressions of their landscapes rather than of their genes: "I believe you could exterminate the French at a blow and resettle the country with Tartars and within two generations discover, to your astonishment, that the national characteristics were back at norm—the restless metaphysical curiosity, the tenderness for good living and the passionate individualism: even though their noses were now flat." Durrell is just as dogmatic concerning what would happen "if one fed a group of Chinese *in China* exclusively on an American diet. I don't see them growing a speck larger myself. They might get fat and rosy on the diet, but I believe the landscape, in pursuit of its own mysterious purposes, would simply cut them down to the required size suitable to home-grown Chinamen."[3]

Durrell of course made these pronouncements tongue in cheek; he knew well that the spirit of place involves many factors other than the landscape. The patterns of behavior and taste that characterize racial, regional, and national groups are influenced by the ways of life as much as by physical surroundings, by cultural history as much as by natural history. These qualifications, however, may not be as significant as they sound, because all cultures have deep resonances with the qualities of the nature from which they derive inspiration and sustenance. Even if I had been born with yellow skin and a flat nose, instead of a Caucasian face, I could probably have become a typical French country boy of the early twentieth century, pushing a wheelbarrow loaded with wild carrots to feed the rabbits in a French home. But my life would have been very different if the Île de France where I was raised had been populated for the past thousand years with Tartars, who would have created a culture without Gothic churches, Descartes's rationalism, La Fontaine's fables, Impressionist painting, Baudelaire's poetry, and Debussy's musical rendering of seas, clouds, and arabesques.

The same year that Durrell presented a caricature of the environmentalist point of view in *Spirit of Place*, another British author, the famous biologist C.D. Darlington, presented an interpretation of history based on human genetics. In a book entitled *The Evolution of Man and Society*, Darlington defends the view that all important human characteristics and patterns of behavior are determined by heredity, and that all historical events have been influenced by the genetic peculiarities of the individual persons and social groups involved. Darlington considers it important for European history that the genes of William the Conqueror spread through a large percentage of European nobility and that General de Gaulle derived some of his genes from the Catholic gentry of Ireland. Darlington also believes that each social group eventually achieves a certain genetic homogeneity, because its members tend to intermarry and therefore share a similar array of genes. Genetic homogeneity would result from interbreeding and from the fact that the selection pressures peculiar to the ways of life of a given social group determine the direction of its evolutionary trends.

According to Darlington, "A social class is a group of people who breed together because they work together, and who work together because they breed together. This is true equally of servile and of ruling classes. In the Old World, all ruling classes began as military groups who attached to themselves other classes of loyal helpers."[4] In the United States, the Establishment is now in the process of becoming "genetically related," because "it is being connected with particular schools and universities" just as occurred in England long ago. The phrase "genetically related" as used by Darlington refers in a precise manner to the possession by a certain human group of certain genes or arrays of genes.

Darlington claims also that, during the Late Stone Age, mankind became progressively differentiated into two categories of people, whose contrasting occupations eventually caused them to differ genetically. Herdsmen depended entirely on livestock and were almost constantly on the move, shifting their pasturage with the seasons, whereas primitive farmers increasingly came to depend on cultivated crops for their livelihood and therefore had to settle on permanent sites. These two different ways of life would have resulted in different human types, which are represented in the biblical legend by Abel the stockbreeder and Cain the cultivator. Abel and Cain symbolize a conflict between the farmer and the stockman which has continued throughout history. The struggles between the English farmers and the Welsh drovers during the Middle Ages, and between the farming Kikuyu and the grazing Masai in modern East Africa, are only two of the countless manifestations of this age-old conflict. Even the Civil War in the United States could be seen to have its origin in a conflict between different genetic stocks. The South was dominated by men of Cavalier ancestry, with feudal and military traditions, whereas the North was populated by technically inventive and economically aggressive people descended from peasants and artisans.

Granted the importance of heredity in all aspects of human life, it would seem that—Darlington notwithstanding—social forces, environmental conditions, and historical accidents have played an even greater role in historical events. Even the differences between prehistoric herdsmen and crop-growers may have been due more to social than to genetic factors.

The primitive hunter necessarily saw himself as part of his natural surroundings and usually placed the community decision above his own self-interest. In contrast, the primitive farmer functioned in an environment which he manipulated; his life put a premium on competition, savings, and ownership, class structures and hierarchies. These contrasting attitudes were probably the expressions of social ethos rather than the result of genetic determinism. In fact, several modern tribes of mobile herdsmen are late offshoots of agricultural people who turned from peasant life to herding only after circumstances forced them to migrate into steppes and desert areas. In Melanesia, populations which had once achieved a stable agricultural life have returned to a hunter-gatherer economy as a result of warfare and other outside pressures. The American biologist D. Carleton Gajdusek has reported:

> The Guayaki Indians of South America, who still today roam as hunters through the forests of Paraguay without clothing or shelter, were, some 300 years ago, farmers settled around Jesuit missions. In the backwaters of the Upper Amazon, there are communities of unclothed hunter-gatherers and primitive agriculturalists, which have their origins in the literate and eminently civilized "conquistadors."[5]

There are of course many well-documented cases of social change in the opposite direction. Several New Guinea tribes which were still leading a Stone Age warrior life half a century ago have moved into the technological world in one generation. In his biography *Kiki—Ten Thousand Years in a Lifetime,* Alfred Moari Kiki has described his boyhood in a Stone Age New Guinean society, then his training as a pathologist, and finally his role as leader of the political Pangu party which is demanding immediate self-rule for New Guineans.[6]

Except for the Pueblos of the Rio Grande, American Indians belonged to the hunter-herdsman tradition. The Caughnawaga Mohawks in Canada did not have permanent agricultural fields but grew crops wherever they made camps. They regarded hunting and war as the most important male activities, had little hierarchical organization, and elected a leader only for their hunting parties. After these Mohawks had been forced to settle on a reservation south of Montreal, it was accidentally discovered that they had the skills required for work at great heights on skyscrapers. Although they are now extensively engaged in this specialized kind of construction work, they have retained many of their ancient ways of life. When they go to the city on a construction job, they choose a leader as their forefathers did for a hunting party; then they return to the reservation when the job is completed, just as their ancestors did after a long hunt. They have thus been able to maintain their hunting ethos while participating in the technological ethos of North America.

For Darlington what is involved here is not a social ethos, but rather genetic preadaptation with regard to skills and behavior. And yet it is well known that the biological and mental characteristics of a person or a group can be culturally determined. A Mohawk raised among Pueblo Indians in the valley of the Rio Grande would probably exhibit little evidence of so-called genetic preadaptation for work on skyscrapers.

The propensity of human beings for cultural adaptation does not mean that they have unlimited abilities or that anyone can do everything. The range of potentialities of a particular person is predetermined by his genetic constitution. But equally important is the fact that superimposed on genetic uniqueness, there is environmental uniqueness during development. As stated by the English geneticist J.M. Thoday, "Unique genotype and unique environment are interacting in the development of each individual in unique ways, and though we must classify individuals into groups for scientific, administrative or educational purposes, we ignore this uniqueness to our great loss and at our peril."[7]

The biological uniqueness generated by the interplay between heredity and environment is further enhanced by the exercise of free will. Choices, however, are never entirely free, because they must be made within the framework of a given culture. Furthermore, the genetic endowment is so malleable that it can usually be shaped to fit almost any type of human situation—whether it be a hunting, farming, urban, or technological culture. The plasticity of man's nervous system enables him to make a wide range of behavioral adjustments without having to depend on the slow process of biological evolution. This accounts for the fact that a great diversity of adaptive social states can exist side by side—for example, Navajo hogan settlements and Hopi compact villages in the American Southwest; mud-walled houses and thatched dwellings in the western Sudan; Eskimo snow houses along the central Arctic shore and houses made of driftwood timber and sod in other parts of the Arctic. Genetic preadaptation, if it exists at all, plays a very small part in the design of human societies.

The innate endowment of any normal human being is so rich and diversified that his behavior would be virtually ungovernable and his experience shapeless in the absence of constraining and guiding cultural patterns. Human behavior would be a chaos of pointless acts and exploding emotions if it were not that even the most fundamental and universal aspects of life are shaped by culture. Food habits range all the way from pure vegetarianism in certain African tribes to the almost complete absence of vegetables and fruits in the Eskimo diet. The only foods of the Kikuyu are cereals supplemented with some fruits and roots, whereas the diet of their neighbors the Masai consists of milk, raw blood, and meat. As to sexual habits, Gary Snyder has described the eroticism of China and Japan as a dark shadowy thing in a cave of brocades, the eroticism of Greece as nakedness in full blast of sunlight, the eroticism of India as hips and breasts, agile limbs on stone floors with intricate design.[8]

Landscapes and climates have effects on behavior which transcend matters of comfort and health. Sanitation may be deplorable in Greece and plumbing defective in the South of France, but this counts for little compared with the fact that the scenery, the skies, and the waters of the Mediterranean world engender tastes and attitudes which persist through life. This shaping of behavior by regional influences had been clearly recognized by the Greeks 2500 years ago. In his essay "Of Airs, Waters, and Places," the physician Hippocrates (c. 460–c. 370 B.C.) explicitly states that the physical and mental characteristics of the various populations of Europe and Asia, as well as their military prowess and political institutions, are determined by the topography of the land, the quality of the air and the water, and the abundance and nature of the food.[9]

Every age has found it necessary to reformulate, with contemporary examples, the knowledge that human life is conditioned by the remembrance of things past. In our times, for example, the American writer James Baldwin has expressed with poignancy the influences of the slum environment on the black population:

> We cannot escape our origins, however hard we try, those origins which contain the key—could we but find it —to all that we later become.
>
> It means something to live where one sees space and sky or to live where one sees nothing but rubble or nothing but high buildings.
>
> We take our shape . . . within and against that cage of reality bequeathed us at our birth.[10]

For slum dwellers, Baldwin's "cage of reality" means rubble and rats, misery and hopelessness. In prosperous communities many young people also find themselves in a cage which, although comfortable, is humanly paralyzing because devoid of worthwhile stimuli. In fact, the important factors of the environment are not only its physical characteristics but also the attitudes and memories of the social group. To quote Baldwin again:

> The man does not remember the hand that struck him, the darkness that frightened him, as a child; nevertheless, the hand and the darkness remain with him, indivisible from him forever, part of the passion that drives him wherever he thinks to take flight.
>
> A culture was not a community basket-weaving project, nor yet an act of God, was something neither desirable nor undesirable in itself, being inevitable, being nothing more or less than the recorded and visible effects on a body of people of the vicissitudes with which they have been forced to deal.
>
> A tradition expresses, after all, nothing more than the long and painful experience of a people; it comes out of the battle waged to maintain their integrity, or to put it more simply, out of their struggle to survive.[11]

As used in ordinary speech, the phrase "a people" refers to biological unity based on blood relationships. In practice, however, human societies are based chiefly on shared experiences and community of fate. For the Jewish people, according to Martin Buber, the allegiance to the Eternal God is the great unifying principle which enabled Israel to persist as a social entity, even when deprived of a territorial home.[12]

The transmission of the attitudes and beliefs which create social identity is facilitated by a long childhood. Even primitive societies used child training in many intuitive ways for the purpose of achieving some form of mature identity. The more civilized the social group, furthermore, the longer childhood is likely to be, and the more complex the social imprinting. The educational programs of all modern societies and of American society in particular have as their stated goal the development of the individual and of his ability to choose and to act independently of social pressures. Schools, however, are largely designed to substitute for the social conditioning that used to be provided by the family, the church, and other institutions. Whenever societies organize a formal system of education, they see to it that the child is exposed to those aspects of the national culture which are regarded as most valuable for social coherence and survival. Regardless of rhetorical statements, the objective of most schools, including graduate schools, is social conditioning rather than development of the individual.

Human institutions and events are of course influenced by many forces other than social conditioning. In history, as distinct from science, decisions by particular men acting through their free will are the most likely initial causes of important movements. At their beginnings, all great religions, philosophies, empires, social revolutions, and artistic doctrines are identified with a few heroes. Once started, however, a movement acquires a life of its own; it soon generates institutions which, like all living forms, tenaciously resist change and cling to their identity. When a social system has started to evolve, its very operations, as I stated earlier, automatically set up limits to the range of possible moves it can make at the next critical point. In order to maintain the internal stability essential to their health, moreover, all social systems must strive to weather the destructive maelstrom that beats on them from the outside. They survive only by developing social mechanisms which buffer environmental impacts.

The resistance of social entities to change probably accounts for the origin and continued existence of nations. Geology, topography, and climate differ from one region to another to such an extent that physical factors cannot possibly explain national characteristics, except in the case of very small nations. There are writers who claim that such designations as the "United States," "Russia," "Britain," or "France," are so much abstract journalistic palaver, because national characteristics of the land or the people either do not exist or are so ill defined and changeable as to be unimportant. Other writers, in contrast, affirm that nations are mystical entities, with a divine origin. It has been stated, for example, that "every nation has a guiding spiritual characteristic, its genius, which it acknowledges as its prince or god."[13] Here again the Eternal God of Israel comes to mind. But what is certain in any case is that so-called blood relationships are biologically meaningless and historically nonexistent.[14] A Jew appropriately named Disraeli symbolized Victorian England, and the second president of the French Republic was named MacMahon.

In his essay "The English People" George Orwell asks rhetorically: "Do such things as national cultures really exist?"[15] To which he answers that this is one of those questions in which scientific arguments are on one side and instinctive knowledge on the other. As I have said, there is no reason to believe that all members of a nation share some mystical quality derived from blood relationships or from the land on which they live. But, just the same, common sense leaves no doubt that a distinctive array of intellectual and behavioral attributes is associated with the adjectives "American," "British," "French," "German," "Greek," "Italian," or "Spanish," even more than with the adjectives "Nordic" and "Mediterranean." Likewise, the words "Chinese" and "Japanese" denote attitudes that have remained different for many centuries regardless of social regime and military conquest. Nations exist not as geological, climatic, or racial entities, but as human experiences. The American social critic Max Lerner was not entirely facetious when he illustrated the use of the two words "permitted" and "forbidden" in different European countries. "In England, everything that is not forbidden is permitted. In Germany everything is forbidden unless it is permitted. In France everything is permitted even if it is forbidden. And in Russia everything is forbidden even if it is permitted."[16]

Modern historical knowledge has confirmed that groups of people whom the accidents of history force to live together in a certain place tend to develop a body of shared ideas, values, and beliefs, which progressively becomes their ideal and guide. The culture they develop constitutes a whole which shapes itself as a continuously evolving national spirit. Order is not imposed on the national genius from the outside; it evolves spontaneously as a structure of interrelationships generated by the constant interplay of its various elements. In this light, national characteristics are the expressions, not of race or other biological properties, but of human choices based on the collective acceptance of certain conventions and traditions—and perhaps especially of myths. In "The English People," Orwell asserted that "myths which are believed in tend to become true because they set up a type of 'persona' which the average person will do his best to resemble." For example, the behavior of the British population during the Second World War "was partly due to the existence of the national 'persona'—that is to their preconceived idea of themselves."[17] Nations need heroes to symbolize their genius and serve as models of behavior.

The tastes, attitudes, and behavioral patterns which characterize the people of a particular nation endure because they are acquired during the formative years of childhood and early adulthood. This does not mean, however, that they are unchangeable. The ascetic and warlike Moslems who conquered southern Spain in the eighth century progressively lost their military stamina as they adopted the Andalusian ways of life; there is little in common between Mohammed's tent and the Alhambra in Granada, yet the spread in time is only a few centuries. The uncouth and redoubtable Norman barons of the early medieval period built huge fortresses to dominate the French countryside, but their castles were infiltrated by troubadours from the south who brought with them the cult of woman and the courts of love, thereby creating the somewhat effeminate atmosphere of late Gothic life.

Spectacular changes have occurred also in the scientific and technological proficiencies of nations. When Thomas Sprat, Bishop of Rochester, attempted in 1667 to formulate the psychological attributes of the perfect man of science, he endowed him with

> the different Excellences of several Countries. First, he should have the Industry, Activity and inquisitive Humour of the Dutch, French, Scotch and English, in laying the Ground Work, the Heap of Experiments; and then he should have added the cold, circumspect, and wary disposition of the Italians and Spaniards, in meditating upon them before he brings them fully into Speculation.[18]

Bishop Sprat's opinions should serve as a warning that national psychology can change in three hundred years and even in a much shorter time. The spectacular achievements of Russia in space, of Italy in the production of automobiles, and of Japan in electronics could hardly have been predicted from the technological development of these countries half a century ago.

It is not surprising that national characteristics change with time; what is remarkable is that some of them last for centuries despite social revolutions and foreign conquest. It has been said that the German and British characters are much the same today as when Tacitus first described them two thousand years ago. Similarly, even though the adjectives French, Greek, Italian, Spanish have meanings so elusive as to defy definition, they refer to objective qualities which have survived the upheavals of the modern era. There is a homeostasis of nations as there is a homeostasis of biological species and individual organisms.

The descriptions of American life written by European travelers since the seventeenth century reveal that certain behavioral traits which are now regarded as characteristic of the twentieth-century United States were already apparent during the colonial period and were fully established from the beginning of industrialization. The writings of the Frenchman Alexis de Tocqueville and the Englishman Viscount James Bryce are rich sources of material on this subject, but there are many others, fully as revealing.

William Chambers was a Scottish journalist who visited the United States in 1854 and reported his impressions in *Chambers's Edinburgh Journal.*[19] He had been interested by what he had seen, but like countless European visitors before and after him, he noted with scorn the hurry and bustle everywhere, the casual readiness to greet and accost, and the goblet with ice placed before every diner, whether he wanted it or not. He was amused by the homage accorded to women, who seemed to be elevated to the rank of divinities, but he was shocked by the rubbish on Broadway and also criticized the fact that no one walked who could afford to drive around in a carriage.

The comparison of Americans to "millions of squirrels running in millions of cages," has been made popular by D.H. Lawrence but this image had already been used in 1891 by Lord Bryce in his *Social Institutions of the United States:*

> The United States is more unrestful than Europe, more unrestful than any country we know of has yet been. . . . In America it is unusually hard for any one to withdraw his mind from the endless variety of external impressions and interests which daily life presents, and which impinge on the mind, I will not say to vex it, but to keep it constantly vibrating to their touch. Life is that of the squirrel in his revolving cage, never still even when it does not seem to change. . . . The ceaseless stir and movement, the constant presence of newspapers, the eagerness which looks through every pair of eyes, even that active intelligence and sense of public duty, strongest in the best minds, which make a citizen feel that he ought to know what is passing in the wider world as well as in his own—all these render life more exciting to the average man than it is in Europe, but chase away from it the opportunities for repose and meditation.[20]

The eagerness for information noted by Bryce had early given rise in America to a passion for lectures and conferences. New England provided such avid audiences for lecturers in early colonial times that Governor John Winthrop of Massachusetts expressed alarm over the fad in his journal for 1639: "There were so many lecturers now in the country, and many persons would usually resort to two or three in a week, to the great neglect of their affairs and the damage of the public."[21] The Boston ferries were so crowded on lecture days that emergency legislation was introduced into the Great and General

Court, but the voice of the people promptly killed any attempt at regulation. The demand for lecturers—on any topic—continues into our time; Emil Lengyel, a Hungarian who was himself much in demand as a platform performer after the First World War, concluded from his own success that Americans like to do their thinking collectively.[22]

Very early, foreign travelers detected in America an optimistic mood different from the skepticism and even despair in which many Europeans had been bred. Michel Guillaume Jean de Crèvecoeur, a Frenchman who had settled on a farm in New York State, exemplified this optimistic attitude when he predicted in 1801 to a European visitor that the "wild and savage" country would be completely transformed within ten years. "Our humble log houses will be replaced by fine dwellings. Our fields will be fenced in, and the stumps will have disappeared."[23] De Crèvecoeur was right but what he could not have foreseen was that the desire for change would continue to dominate American life even after the wilderness had been subdued. The Americans *"love* their country not *as it is,* but as *it will be,"* a traveler noted in the 1830s; "they do not love the land of their fathers; but they are sincerely attached to that which their children are destined to inherit."[24] This attitude is a far cry from the delight in the particular place and the particular moment symbolized by the Mandarin tea ceremonial and expressed in Henri Matisse's paintings.

The tendency to think of the present as a springboard from which to jump into a future assumed to be more enjoyable has been a weakness of American life. One of its consequences has been a tendency to neglect the immediate surroundings and to be concerned with distant goals rather than direct experiences, with process rather than with product, as if today were not worth living. Mark Twain once remarked that American life emphasizes the manner of handling experiences and materials rather than the experience or materials themselves.[25]

The impoverishment of life resulting from the sacrifice of perceptions to action was recognized at the beginning of the nineteenth century by Daniel Drake, the first Midwestern physician to achieve national stature. In a series of essays and books beginning in 1810, Drake described his impressions of American life in southern Ohio, Kentucky, and the Middle West.

> We are a migrating but not a traveling people. We think of our country only as abounding in residences; and pass from one to another, without inspecting anything between them. Thus, even migration bestows on us none of the benefits of travel. In our transits, all things are sacrificed to speed. We are not satisfied unless we add night to day; and when we awake in the morning, congratulate ourselves that we are a hundred miles nearer the point of attraction; although we may have passed through scenes and objects the most interesting, without having beheld the least or the greatest of them. Thus while we are wanderers, we remain ignorant of the relations and true character of all among which we roam; or know them only in connexion with hemp or cotton planting, commerce, land speculation, or the practice of law and medicine.[26]

Drake's description of his contemporaries as a "migrating people . . . wanderers . . . ignorant of the relations and true character" of the places among which they roam still has a familiar ring today. It calls to mind airplane passengers watching moving pictures while flying in sight of the desert or the Rockies.

Emerson once stated that "the views of nature held by any people determine all their institutions,"[27] and this statement is also true when reversed, because the ways of life always influence attitudes toward nature. In the imagination of eighteenth-century Europeans, the New World was a pastoral paradise, gentle in climate and with picturesque but amenable sceneries—the land of the good, healthy, and happy savage described by the early explorers of the southern countries. What the immigrants experienced, however, was dismay and fear on their first encounter with their new country. The American continent overwhelmed them by its sheer size, its geographical and climatic extremes. The creation of an environment better adapted to the European ways of life was the first task of the immigrants. American civilization has been torn ever since by the contradiction between pastoral myth and technological fact. Even now most Americans believe, as did their predecessors, that they must "conquer" nature rather than adapt themselves to the natural environment; they tend to put their faith in machines and technological fixes rather than in the complexities of ecological systems and in the slow processes of nature. This conquering attitude, which has dominated man's relationship to nature from the beginning of American history, has contributed to material progress and to the technological and economic supremacy of the United States, but it has also been responsible for enormous damage to the environment.

Alexis de Tocqueville had been disturbed, for example, by the fact that the planners responsible for the new city of Washington had "rooted up the trees for ten miles around, lest they should interfere with the *future* citizens of this imaginary metropolis." Tocqueville noted also that Americans built a few monuments on the largest scale but also a vast number of trivial buildings, as if built-in obsolescence had already been a practice in the early nineteenth century.[28]

Octavio Paz, a Mexican student of the New World culture, believes that the attitude of North Americans and South Americans toward nature has its basis, not in their reactions to the physical characteristics of the New Continent, but in their European origins. Whereas Europeans are the involuntary products of European history, Americans, he claims, are a "premeditated creation" of European utopias. "For many centuries, Europeans did not know they were European and only when Europe was a historical reality did they suddenly realize . . . that they pertained to something vaster than their native cities." In Europe, reality preceded the nation, whereas in America the nation began as an ideal. "The name engendered the reality. The American continent had not yet been wholly discovered when it had already been baptized."[29]

Differences between Latin Americans and North Americans come from the fact that the former are children of the Counter Reformation, whereas the latter are "children of Luther and the Industrial Revolution. Therefore they breathe easily in the rarefied atmosphere of the future. And for the same reason they are not in close touch with reality. The so-called realism of the Anglo-American is pragmatism—an operation that consists in lightening the compact materiality of things in order to change them into process. Reality ceases to be a substance and is transferred into a series of acts. Nothing is permanent because action is the favored form that reality assumes." From its very beginning, Paz continues, "America knew what it would be. . . . For more than three centuries, the word 'American' designated a man who was defined not by what he had done, but by what he would do."[30]

North Americans have always tended to assume that the world was beginning afresh with them. Belief in the goodness of man and in the possibility of recreating heaven on earth was at the core of their philosophy, just as belief in a kind of superiority inherited from the Latin genius has long been a French credo. Americans developed early a deep concern for the common man and the confidence that he could be trusted to set things right in time and to use wisely the enormous resources of the unspoiled continent. This confidence was the basis of Thomas Jefferson's belief in "the unquestionable republicanism of the American people" which was eventually idealized in Abraham Lincoln's "government of the people, by the people, and for the people."

Trust in the perfectibility of human life (rather than of man himself) is a leitmotiv of American literature. Walt Whitman believed that it was the grand mission of America to create the land of healthy and free men. For Thomas Wolfe, "The essence of all faith for people of my belief is that man's life can be, and will be, better."[31] This euphoric attitude prevailed even among the sharpest critics of American civilization. Sinclair Lewis was at heart a typical American reformer who shared the vision of his hero Cass Timberlane that America would become the "fabulous great land of the year 2000 A.D., a new Athens, stark and clean, a new land for a new kind of people."[32] The ordeals of the second half of the twentieth century have hardly darkened this vision. The common man of America, conditioned by his national culture, still believes with Thomas Wolfe that "the true fulfillment of our spirit, of our people, of our land, is yet to come."[33]

This belief has recently found a new expression in the concern for environmental quality, so typical of the American tradition in its missionary spirit and in its faith that, without abandoning any technological advantage, men can return the environment to its pristine state or *re-form* it according to their ideals.

Statements concerning the universal characteristics of mankind do not throw much light on national characteristics because, in the words of D.H. Lawrence, "Human nature is always made to some pattern or other. The wild Australian aborigines are absolutely bound up tight, tighter than a China girl's foot, in their few savage conventions."[34]

If Christian missionaries found it difficult to civilize the American Indians, it is not, as was claimed by the nineteenth-century American historian Hubert H. Bancroft, because "savages cannot be civilized under the tuition of superior races."[35] Economic factors accounted in large part for the resistance of Indians to acculturation, and even more important was the persistence of their familial and communal life. Wherever the Indian family and community were destroyed by the white man or profoundly distorted by his ways of life, Indian customs and beliefs were rapidly replaced by those of the conquerors —Spanish, English, or French. In contrast, cultural assimilation failed where the Indian forms of family life and of local community persisted, as in several parts of the Southwest. Under these conditions, the Indian family continued to indoctrinate children in the traditional culture, and the Indian form of local community acted as a regulator of change. These conservative forces minimized the social impact of the white man by slowing the incorporation of his cultures into the ancient ways of life.

All over the world, countless young people are now trying to disengage themselves from the type of life created by Western civilization during the past century. The new rebels are concerned with living in the *now* rather than with anticipations of the future; they emphasize *being* rather than "becoming something else in the perpetual game of nature," as Emerson called it.[36] At their best, the present countercultures represent values that are universal, yet many of their expressions have characteristics that are distinctively national. The dreamy attitudes of the mid-twentieth-century *Wandervogel* in Germany are strangely reminiscent of nineteenth-century

German romanticism; the white bicycles of the Amsterdam *provos* have the sensible, practical quality of Dutch life; the barricades thrown up by the rebellious French students in 1968 seem to be later models of those erected by the Paris bourgeois revolutionaries in 1830 and 1848. The youth movement of the 1960s in the United States calls to mind a modernized Wild West life style with glamorized motorcycles instead of horses with elaborate trappings, and pot instead of fire water.

The universality of mankind expresses itself in the rich diversity of persons and cultures because each member of the human species incarnates the genius of the place in which he develops. This biological truth is so complex that it almost defies scientific statement, let alone analysis. Fortunately, it was translated into simple words that are meaningful for everyone by Kwang-na, an eighty-year-old woman, famous as a doctor among the !Kung Bushmen of the Kalahari Desert:

> There are different kinds of people in the world; first there are black people, they raise cattle and crops, and have their own kind of medicine which is based on sorcery. Then there are white people, and these people have trucks, and motor vehicles, and they have their own kind of medicine which is contained in sharp needles. Then there are the red people, us Bushmen; we don't have trucks or cattle, but we have the mongongo nut, but we also have our own kind of medicine and that is the kind of healing I do . . . and so you see these are the different kinds of people with the different ways of life, but inside we are all the same. The blood that is inside our bodies is the same color . . . we are really only one people.[37]

CHAPTER 6

Persistence of Place

Surprising as it may seem to the bulldozer generations, the really profound changes in the landscapes of the earth occurred several thousand years ago. They were the work of the few million men who, during more than two hundred generations, worked with the simple tools and techniques of the Neolithic and Bronze ages. It may be true that more factories and highways have been built during recent decades than in all ages past, and it is certain that technology now enables more men than at any time before to move farther and faster. But these achievements may not have consequences either as profound or as lasting as was the conversion of wilderness into agricultural lands during the very early phases of civilization.

The valleys of the Euphrates and the Nile were unpromising swamps and reed jungles teeming with wild beasts before Neolithic man disciplined the banks of the rivers and introduced irrigation. This was a tremendous enterprise carried out largely through brute physical force: "The swamps had to be drained by channels, the violence of flood-waters to be restrained by banks, the thickets to be cleared away, the wild beasts lurking in them to be exterminated."[1] As a corrective for modern technological conceit it is well to remember that by 2000 B.C. the irrigation civilizations of the eastern Mediterranean area had invented basket work, fabrics, and pottery, harnessed the force of oxen and the wind, developed wheeled vehicles and sailboats, learned to use most of the nonferrous metals, and so on. The arch, the solar calendar, writing, numeral notations, and most of the fundamental social institutions around which our own life is now organized date from this most productive era in human history. When the Egyptians introduced the plow, 7000 years ago, they provided mankind with the single technological innovation which has had the most profound and lasting influence on the surface of the earth.

Until Neolithic times the temperate regions all over the world were covered with forests, and they would still be if it were not for human intervention. In Europe, the use of fire and the maintenance of livestock by more than a hundred generations of peasants had almost completed the creation of agricultural lands by the early Middle Ages. In North America also, the fires set by pre-agricultural Indians played a large role in replacing the original forest by the prairie. Wherever man settled in the temperate zone, he converted the primeval forest into pastoral scenery.

The destructive impact of human activities on the land was first publicized more than a century ago by the American lawyer turned conservationist George Perkins Marsh (1801–1882) in his book *Man and Nature,* revised as *The Earth as Modified by Human Action: A New Edition of "Man and Nature."*[2] Marsh made it clear that everywhere human interventions have left an indelible mark on nature. "Not a sod has been turned, not a mattock struck into the ground, without leaving its enduring record of the human toils and aspirations that accompany the act."[3] Although the alterations of nature brought about by early human activities have thus had lasting consequences, not all of these have been desirable. Fire and livestock enabled man to break the great forest barriers of northern Europe and thereby to create rich and beautiful farmlands, but the final result of these and other techniques of deforestation was destructive and produced eroded land in many other parts of the world. As indicated by T'ang and Sung poetry, the now barren hills of central and northern China were once richly forested. There is convincing evidence that most of the deserts in the Near East and in Asia were caused by overgrazing some 4000 years ago. In *Critias,* Plato described the effects of deforestation on the Greek landscape. "Deluges washed the soil down from the mountains and it was lost because the land dropped abruptly into the sea." As a result, Attica became a "skeleton of a body wasted by disease." Long ago, Plato continues, there were abundant forests in the mountains which provided fodder for the animals and storage for water, which could then issue forth in springs and rivers. "The water was not lost, as it is today, by running off a barren ground to the sea." The extent of these forests, many of which had been cut down, was revealed in the traces still remaining and by the sanctuaries which were situated at the former sources of springs and rivers.[4]

It is probable that, as mentioned earlier, the hunter-gatherers of the Early Stone Age found it possible to obtain enough food by only a few hours of daily work. Since the Neolithic Era and until the present century, however, most men have been dependent upon exacting agricultural labor for their survival. They have devoted the largest percentage of their time, energy, and skills to clearing forests, tending domestic animals, tilling the soil, building walls with the stones they removed from the land. Landscapes which appear to us natural and ageless because they have hardly changed during historical times in reality are man-made. They are the engravings of societies older than written history.

Judging from archaeological evidence, early men shunned deep forests and marshy lowlands, settling by preference in open landscapes and hills. Civilization probably began on areas of limestone and chalk for the simple reason that well-drained soils were healthier and easier to cultivate than were alluvial plains. The influence of geological and topographical factors on the evolution of human settlements appears clearly from the prehistory of Great Britain. This is discussed by the English biologist Jacquetta Hawkes in *A Land*[5] and particularly by the English geographer Cyril Fox in *The Personality of Great Britain.*[6] The pervious chalk uplands of Britain were occupied very early in the Stone Age and have never been abandoned. Recent aerial photographs have revealed that Bronze Age people also lived in some valleys, such as the gravel terraces of the river Trent. It would seem, however, that although the impervious areas of deep clay soil in the lower Thames valley were potentially fertile, they were not heavily settled by the ancient Celtic people, probably because they were unhealthy and difficult to till. Later the Romans and then the Saxons introduced power technology capable of uprooting the dense oakwood forests which at the time of their arrival still covered the heavy clay soils of the Thames valley. Civilization then shifted from the Salisbury plain to the lower Thames valley as the latter area progressively became deforested.

The agricultural techniques employed by successive invaders have thus played as important a role as have the geology and topography of the land in determining the occupation of the different areas of Great Britain by Celtic, Roman, Saxon, and Norman populations. Similar historical forces, operating over many centuries, have affected other human settlements all over the world. Despite social upheavals, however, many population groups have maintained a remarkable geographical stability for which there is no simple biological explanation. Dialects and tribal customs of Celtic origin still persist in areas of Great Britain and France where Celtic people were originally entrenched more than two thousand years ago. Although people of Celtic origin are concentrated in granitic regions, and people of Anglo-Saxon origin occupy the much richer alluvial plains, the reason for this correlation is not biological, as has sometimes been claimed, but simply the expression of historical accidents.

The activities of modern man rarely obliterate the marks left on the land by the work of his distant ancestors. In western Europe aerial photographs have confirmed the evidence derived from ancient documents that much of the farmland was initially created by the Neolithic settlers who cleared the forests and broke the sod thousands of years ago. Many roads are also of very ancient origin.[7] As early as the Stone Age channels of exchange had been opened from one part of Europe to another, and even to Asia. An immensely extended road system ran from Siberia through the Russian and German plains, crossing the Seine over the island which was to become Paris, the Loire valley near Poitiers, the Pyrenees at Ronceveaux, then spreading through Spain and perhaps reaching into North Africa. Early agricultural settlements developed local roads linking field to field, field to village, and village to village, thus progressively forming networks which grouped several villages into larger regional units. Ancient roads were of the type now designated as "spatial," because their course was determined chiefly by the contour of the land and other topographical considerations.[8] In the course of time, the networks were joined into complex national systems, but these retained the essential patterns determined by their spatial origin, even when profoundly transformed by modern highway technology. In contrast, the Roman system of highways followed courses very different from those of the Neolithic and Bronze age spatial roads, because they were designed, not for local communication, but for linking together the various parts of the Roman Empire.

The long-range trend in the evolution of roads was much the same in North America as in Europe. The trails opened by the buffaloes and the Indians became the traders' "traces" which widened into roads, then into turnpikes. An erratic cow path in what was then called New Amsterdam became Broadway, which still meanders through the gridiron pattern of New York City and now continues along the Hudson into Yonkers. The Old Albany Post Road, which was opened around 1670 for stagecoach traffic between New York and Albany, barely changed its course when it was converted into the much-traveled automobile highway 9 in the twentieth century; one of the relays built for the horsedrawn coaches of the eighteenth century is now the nationally famous restaurant The Bird and Bottle. Most of the early trading posts were located along the early trails on the sites of Indian villages endowed with certain natural advantages. Many of those which commanded the water systems of the country have grown into such cities as Albany, Pittsburgh, Detroit, Chicago, Saint Louis, Kansas City, all of which became in the course of time important centers of railroad and air transportation. The progressive evolution of trails into highways and railroads, and of trading posts into commercial and industrial cities, gives historical justification to the motto that used to advertise the New York Central railway system along the Hudson and Mohawk valleys to the Great Lakes area and Chicago: "The Indians discovered it, the White Man used it, New York Central developed it."

The techniques used for opening both the ancient spatial roads and the Roman highways profoundly affected the local botany and the land. These effects are so lasting that differences in vegetation can be detected by aerial photography, thus providing botanical evidence of the original course of the road or highway even where it has been altered by shortcuts and bridges.

Although primitive man began to develop roads very early in his social evolution, this does not mean that he was an aimless wanderer. The freely drifting human horde is an unfounded myth; early man always became identified with a well-defined territory. Great human migrations of course took place during the Paleolithic and Neolithic periods. For example, small bands of men from Asia progressively spread over the American continents on repeated occasions. But primitive people rarely moved far from their bases except when compelled by circumstances—such as crowding, threats from a stronger group, or the need to create a new settlement because of exhaustion of the land. Certain modes of life may also have made long displacements necessary, as with hunters who followed big game or herdsmen who followed the seasonal migrations of their cattle. On the whole, however, men tended to remain within a fairly familiar territory of which they knew the resources and where they had ready access to water and shelter. Great mobility did not become a common human trait until historical times; even today, in fact, most of the world's people are born and die within a radius of a few miles.

Because of the relative stability of populations, local styles developed in very early times. On the North American continent, for example, the sandals made by primitive people many thousand years ago differed in design and workmanship within a given geographical region according to the settlement. Customs, beliefs, and ceremonials also became differentiated, as illustrated by the local characteristics in styles of carving, painting, engraving, sculpture, and in the design of tools and weapons.

Numerous monuments, places of worship, and trading centers which have their origin deep in the past also have persisted into the present day, despite political, religious, and economic upheavals. The immense alignments of Carnac in France still awe the visitor with their Stone Age mystery. In England, Stonehenge and Avebury, which date from approximately 1900–1700 B.C., survived the Saxon invaders, the anti-pagan Christians, and—most surprisingly—the eighteenth-century "stone breakers" who made it a practice to collect building stones from ancient sites. Canterbury Cathedral, which was built on the site of a pre-Saxon monument, became a Christian shrine which has remained a focus of English life ever since. The same can be said, of course, for all the important religious and ceremonial sites of Asia and Europe—the hallowed places which in French are appropriately designated *hauts lieux* of civilization. The sanctity of place is as old as man's association with the caves of Altamira and Lascaux. Christianity never displaced completely the religion of nature; rather it built its own temples on sites where worship had been practiced from time immemorial.

The persistence of the *hauts lieux* is not an accidental fact of history; it derives from the dynamic ethos of the places themselves. In *The Earth, the Temple and the Gods,* the American art historian Vincent Scully has suggested that ancient monuments of worship were located in places favorable to the contemplation of the sky because this was an essential component of religious experience.[9] In the monuments of ancient Greece, the physiognomy of the horizon and therefore the location of the building used to be integrated into the architectural design. The "henges" of Britain and similar Neolithic and Bronze Age monuments elsewhere seem to have been sites where the populace assembled to worship the encompassing sky. The alignments of Carnac suggest points of departure for priestly processions and for pilgrimages to the surrounding country. The force of tradition certainly accounts in large part for the persistence of place, but the emotional impact created by the physical setting must also contribute to the ability of certain sites to remain *hauts lieux* despite changes in religious beliefs and in social structures.[10]

Throughout history, the growth of civilization has been associated with the persistence of urban centers. The Bible derives its name from the city of Byblos, a word which means papyrus scroll, but also refers to an ancient seaport on the Lebanese coast, twenty-five miles north of Beirut. Philo of Byblos wrote in the second century A.D., on the basis of old Phoenician texts, that "Kronos put a wall about his habitation and founded Byblos of Phoenicia, the first city." And in fact, there is archaeological evidence that a small fishing community existed on this site as far back as seven thousand years ago. Although the early inhabitants of Byblos, the Giblites of the Bible, were at first fishermen and farmers, the location of their city soon put them in contact with Egypt and Mesopotamia. Progressively they became involved in international trade, since their harbor was the center for the shipment of the cedarwood that the Mesopotamians, and especially the Egyptians, obtained from Lebanon for their temples, tombs, boats, and furniture. Even though Byblos thus came to share in the civilization and wealth of Egypt and the rest of the Near East, it retained for a thousand years some aspects of the archaic culture it had developed during the time when fishing and farming made it self-sufficient. It still exists today under the name of Jubail, a living symbol of the role that cities have played from the beginning of historical times in the evolution of civilized life.[11]

Famous cities have exhibited a persistence that transcends their geographical location, the quality of their climate, or their natural resources. Like the hallowed sites, they have remained true to character despite changes in religious, economic, and political philosophies. In this regard, cities can be compared to living organisms which acquire certain distinctive characteristics early in their development and thereafter retain their personality structure while growing and aging. Paris and London, for example, can be recognized in descriptions written more than eight hundred years ago, at a time when both cities were still extremely small and primitive according to modern standards.

This is how the French cleric Guy de Bazoches saw Paris in the twelfth century:

> "The city lies in the lap of a delightful valley crowned on both sides by hills which Ceres and Bacchus make beautiful, striving with one another in their eagerness. The Seine, by no means a humble stream among a host of rivers, takes its rise in the east and in midcourse divides its proud current into two branches, thus making an island out of the center of the city. Two suburbs stretch forth on either side, and even the lesser of these arouses the envy of many an envious town which it surpasses. Connecting each suburb with the island is a bridge of stone, the name of which is derived from the amount of traffic that falls to its lot. The bridge facing the north, the sea, and England is styled the "great bridge" and the one which faces the Loire on the opposite side is called the "little bridge."

According to Guy de Bazoches, the so-called great bridge

> is densely crowded with a wealthy, bargaining throng, swarms with boats, groans under riches, overflows with merchandise: for lo! there is nowhere its equal.
>
> The little bridge, on the other hand, is given over to walkers, strollers, and disputers of logic. On the narrow strip of land that forms the island the royal palace towers up to lofty heights and audaciously overlooks with its shoulders the roofs of the whole city. Reverence for it is commanded not so much by the marvelous structure of the building as by the noble authority of its rule. "This is that house, the glory of the Franks, whose praises the eternal centuries will sing. This is that house which holds in its power Gaul mighty in war, Flanders magnificent in wealth. This is that house whose scepter the Burgundian, whose mandate the Norman, and whose arms the Briton fears."

The description of Paris closes with a tribute to the island, from ancient times the home of philosophy and of the seven sisters—the liberal arts.[12]

William Fitzstephen, an English contemporary of Guy de Bazoches, wrote that ". . . among the noble cities of the world celebrated by Fame, the city of London in the kingdom of the English is the one seat that pours out its fame more widely, sends to farther lands its wealth and trade, lifts its head higher than the rest." Fitzstephen goes on to praise London's mild climate, piety, fortifications, site, manners and customs, and the character of its citizens. London's piety is shown by the presence not only of an episcopal church but of no less than thirteen larger conventional churches besides one hundred and twenty-six lesser parish churches. "Above all other citizens, the citizens of London are regarded as conspicuous and noteworthy for handsomeness of manners and of dress, at table and in the way of speaking. The city matrons are true Sabine women." The city is very well organized so that the different businesses are distributed in different quarters. In the suburbs are "spacious and beautiful gardens . . . planted with trees."

The long account of the sports of the London youth with which Fitzstephen closes shows that even at this early period the English were devoted to outdoor athletics and games. Besides shows and cockfights, he tells in detail of ball games, gymnastics, wrestling, dancing, and more strenuous horseback exercises—sham battles, tourneys, and combats in the water with lances. In winter, when the "great fen or moor which waters the walls of the city on the north side" was frozen, boys and girls engaged in sports upon the ice. Nor were young people alone interested in athletics, for in the twelfth, as in the twentieth century, "the ancient and wealthy men of the town came forth to see the sport of the young men and to take part of the pleasure in beholding their agility."[13]

Among large American cities west of the Mississippi, San Francisco is the only one which was not settled by the westward spread of immigrants over land. Many of its earliest inhabitants were "gamblers, prostitutes, rascals, and fortune seekers, who came across the Isthmus and around the Horn. They had their faults but they were not influenced by Cotton Mather." As the old song used to put it, "The miners came in '49/The whores in '51/And when they got together/They produced the native son."[14] The new city thus developed without Puritan influence. However, it was soon given a special character by the large numbers of immigrants who came to it from northern Italy. Unlike poor Sicilians and Neapolitans, these North Italians had a great awareness of European cultures and created an atmosphere similar to that of cosmopolitan Mediterranean harbors but without the Mediterranean poverty.

Not having arisen as a WASP settlement, San Francisco acquired from the beginning the mood of a large European continental city, with sections where anybody could engage in behavior of his own choice, no matter how far out. Indifference toward conventional mores and openness to cultural innovation made it a mecca for persons in search of new life styles. And this is what the city has remained, making its citizens smilingly tolerate beatniks, hippies, and topless waitresses, as well as almost any form of social and cultural experimentation.

Each city responds to experiences and challenges in a characteristic manner which tends to accentuate its uniqueness; this organic process of development accounts for the permanence of characteristics despite the upheavals of history. London started as the capital of a small Belgic tribe, then became in succession a provincial capital in the Roman Empire, a Saxon capital, a Norman capital, and eventually the capital of a world empire. This diversified past gives confidence that London will retain its importance and glamor, though Great Britain has now become a relatively small nation. Much the same can be said of Paris. Through countless upheavals involving the religious faith, philosophical doctrines, political allegiance, and social tastes of her inhabitants, Paris has remained the Ville Lumière and continues to symbolize the art of reconciling sensual pleasure with intellectual sophistication, bourgeois common sense with revolutionary zeal. As to Rome, she has deserved for two thousand years the title of Eternal City, first as the creator of the greatest empire in the Western world, then as the seat of the universal Catholic Church, and now as the magnet of intellectual and political ferment in unified Italy.

Ecologists have demonstrated that highly diversified natural systems are the most stable, and this is equally true for urban systems. The cities which have remained great and glorious over long periods of time are those with a rich variety of population, economic enterprise, and social functions. Diversity endows them with the resilience required for surviving the upheavals of history and for maintaining identity in the midst of endless changes. The cities that once derived wealth from a single type of enterprise, whether exploitation of forest products, mining of gold, or extraction of oil, are likely to become ghost towns when bypassed by technology. Great centers of navigation, in contrast, have a much better chance to survive because they have a more diversified economy.

As D.H. Lawrence wrote in his *Studies in Classic American Literature:*

> Every continent has its own great spirit of place. Every people is polarized in some particular locality, which is home, the homeland. Different places on the face of the earth have different vital effluence, different vibration, different chemical exhalation, different polarity with different stars: call it what you like. But the spirit of place is a great reality.[15]

This spirit of place continues to manifest itself in regionalism —not to be confused with nationalism. One thousand years of French national unity under kings, emperors, dictators, and democratic governments have not weakened the differences in human mood between Perigord and Provence, Brittany and Burgundy. In the United States, the centralization of federal power in Washington does not decrease the differences between Vermont and Virginia, Colorado and California. Regional characteristics will not disappear, since topography, geology, and climate give to each country "its own flowers, nat shine especially there," and even more its own skies which etermine the moods of the people and the landscape. Under he moist New England skies, the green mountains of Vermont nd New Hampshire make men different from what they vould be if they lived in "the blue mountains of Arizona, blue s chalcedony, with the sagebrush desert sweeping grey-blue n between" under the scorching Southwest skies.[16] On Medi-erranean shores, all aspects of life, including literature and specially the plastic arts, are inevitably influenced by the tark quality of the landscape and the feeling that, wherever ne goes, the sea may be around the corner beating against ocks. The Mediterranean sky can be so luminous and the tmosphere so translucent that objects seem to give off light. Jnder the skies of the North Atlantic, in contrast, the light eems to be absorbed into the objects which acquire from it a nysterious quality. Rembrandt and Constable differ from El Greco and Cézanne, not only in styles or subjects of painting, out much more profoundly in the effects that different kinds of light had on their senses and on their minds.

Man is intensely affected by the spectral composition of he light to which he is exposed. The so-called daylight from luorescent bulbs does not deserve its name; it provides very ittle long-wave ultraviolet radiation and emits yellow and red adiations in a ratio quite different from that present in sun-ight, and its physiological and psychological effects on man are unlike those exerted by natural light.[17] There are profound differences also between the effects of light in temperate hu-mid regions and in the southwestern United States or Mediter-ranean types of countries. Old civilizations learned empirically to compensate for the qualitative and quantitative differences of sunlight in the various parts of the world. They controlled the degree of exposure by proper orientation and design of dwellings, windows, inner courts, and other artifacts of everyday life. Old Delhi, for example, is so structured that its narrow streets and its courts provide effective as well as charming shelters against the Indian sun, whereas the modern avenues and open parks of New Delhi are almost incompatible with human use during the summer months.[18] As one travels northward in Europe, it becomes obvious that the sunlit areas of buildings, porches, and courts progressively increase in size and that much of life is organized around these areas to take better advantage of sunlight.

The size and shape of rooms, as well as the distribution and character of fields, woodlands, and even of roads, also affect man through his sensory organs. Hardly anything is known of these important aspects of human life, but through the somnambulist wisdom innate in mankind, they have found expression in the marvelous diversity of dwellings and landscapes that have emerged in the various parts of the world. Emerson traced the regional diversity of architecture to historical and social influences:

> The Doric temple still presents the semblance of the wooden cabin in which the Dorian dwelt. The Chinese pagoda is plainly a Tartar tent. The Indian and Egyptian temples still betray the mounds and subterranean houses of their forefathers. . . . The Gothic church plainly originated in a rude adaptation of the forest trees with all their boughs to a festal or solemn arcade. . . .[19]

Regional styles, however, also may have practical origins. Everywhere, until modern times, the steepness of the roof has been largely determined by the amount of snowfall. The open verandas and balconies which were so functional in New Orleans before air conditioning would have had little use in a Cape Cod cottage.

Since regional styles emerged from local needs and resources in periods when transportation was limited and difficult, it would seem that their raison d'être has been destroyed by technological standardization and the increased mobility of populations. However, the revolt against the homogenization of human life is giving a new life to regionalism. The persistence of regional characteristics is of special interest in the United States, where a large percentage of the public moves on the slightest pretext from one part of the country to another and therefore seems to have become rootless. Even under these conditions, however, it takes only a few years for John Doe, his wife, and especially his children to acquire habits peculiar to the region in which they settle. Whatever their origin, they become New Englanders, Virginians, Californians, or Oregonians—outwardly at least—by adopting the suitable type of clothing, ways of life, turns of phrases, and even the manner of eating their salad—as a first course in California, with the main course in the Midwest, and before the dessert in the East.

Regionalism is also reviving in France, despite the continued centralization of power and wealth in Paris. The ancient French provinces were defined by natural boundaries and persisted through the Ancien Régime, but during the Napoleonic era they were submerged in the purely administrative departmental structure. Now, efforts are once more being made to cultivate the traditional customs and styles which used to give so much color and diversity to the French land, just as the Welsh and the Scots are affirming their identity in Great Britain.

Regional characteristics can persist even with a highly mobile population, because unconsciously, and indeed often eagerly, most people become identified with a place. As Lawrence Durrell states: "If you want to intuit the inner mystery of the [British] island, try watching the sun come up over Stonehenge. It may seem a dull and 'touristic" thing to do, but if you do it in the right spirit, you find yourself walking those woollen secretive hills arm in arm with the Druids."[20] Likewise, even if the Provence region of France did not have its history and monuments, the architectural quality of its landscapes and the brilliance of its skies would still make it a magnet for those who want to escape from the sodden skies of the North Atlantic.

The social and cultural history of a nation is reflected not only in the behavior and tastes of its people but also in the manner its landscape is shaped by human activities. In all settled parts of the world, national landscapes derive much of their distinctive character from the way people make a living, take their pleasure, and conduct social intercourse. Fields, fences, waterworks, parks, houses, barns are at least as important in determining the appearance of a landscape as are such natural features as hills, woods, streams, and lakes. Natural characteristics are not sufficient to account for the profound differences in landscapes between England and France, or the northeastern United States and the Province of Quebec; these differences reflect habits, tastes, and needs which in turn are expressions of national cultures. In brief, nations come into existence and persist as distinct physical entities not so much by reason of natural forces as because national cultures exist and govern the management of their landscapes.

Tastes are frequently more important than needs in determining the appearance of landscapes. People try to shape the natural world as they would like it to be, and the effects of their interventions usually outlast economic necessities and may almost mask geographic realities. Man, not nature, created the moors of Scotland, the straight avenues through the forests of France, the grassy slopes of Vermont. The pastoral character of England is to a large extent an expression of the early English fondness for the bucolic, an attitude which was strengthened by reaction against the massive industrial development of the nineteenth century. The pastoral ways of life became anachronistic half a century ago in most parts of England, yet attempts to maintain a bucolic atmosphere continue today in urban as well as in rural settings. Whether in London or in the countryside, the national tendency is to shun plans that are formal, geometrical, and too evidently contrived. This esthetic attitude contrasts sharply with the French taste for majestic boulevards and long vistas down straight avenues, formal parks and promenades with wide panoramas, which is as evident in the provinces as it is in Paris.

The very concept of the city park reflects social tastes and therefore national characteristics. From the beginning, the use of greenery in London was guided by one of those unwritten laws which carry so much weight in England—namely, that a person shall not be disturbed in his private life and shall have access to nature. According to the Swiss art historian Sigfried Giedion, "The rule runs as follows: the residential quarters of a city should, as far as possible, merge into greenery. They should be inconspicuous." In contrast, the parks and especially the "squares" created in Paris during the mid-nineteenth century by Baron Haussmann were intended for public life and set right in the midst of noise and dust of traffic. An English landscape architect visiting Paris in the early twentieth century expressed his admiration for one of these public "squares" by noting "the number of people who are seated in it, reading, working, or playing," but he failed to emphasize that little effort had been made to use greenery as a protection against traffic.[21] An exciting form of this urban use of space is the Italian piazza, that of Siena, for example, which looks like a grand stage on which the public is both actor and audience.

The irrelevance of most city parks in the United States to American life does not derive from poor design but from failure to relate them to regional and national taste. Wherever single dwellings greatly outnumber apartment houses, their backyards provide outdoor settings for social life, and public parks are left to derelicts. A personally planted willow tree substitutes for noble elms and oaks planted in the public domain generations ago. On the other hand, certain ethnic groups in the large American cities have a greater emotional need for settings in which to act out their aspirations than for trees, lawns, and peaceful benches on which to think and dream. Several of the modern parkways have emotional overtones as well as practical utility and esthetic beauty, because they serve the traditional American longing for the open road, or at least for movement. Stephen Vincent Benet's line, "We do not know where we are going but we are on our way," is the affirmation of a national characteristic that Americans derive from their immigrant and pioneering past.[22] The sense of life is to be discovered not so much through the inner search for identity as in a Rembrandt portrait or through well-designed social orders, but rather in unstructured happenings or by moving freely on the open road.

Certain imperatives of nature, of course, create constraints on man's attempts to shape his landscapes and dwellings. Especially among pre-industrial people, the shape of buildings and their roof lines are determined by temperature, insulation, rainfall, the character of the terrain, and also the kinds of materials available for construction. Igloos, tepees, the hogans of the Navajos, the well-insulated adobe houses of the Pueblos, the open and well-ventilated dwellings of the Yagua people in the Amazon valley constitute economical and practical solutions to special environmental problems in a specific place.

Despite technological standardization, environmental factors still profoundly affect the design of landscapes and dwellings. In modern farm practice, the danger of erosion is averted by contour plowing, much as it has been for centuries by the traditional methods of terracing in areas as different as Japan, Peru, and southern Europe. Even when using the same standardized or prefabricated construction materials, architects are trying once more to adapt the design of houses to local climatic conditions with results comparable to those attained in past centuries, as can be readily observed when one travels from north to south or east to west in the United States or from the North Sea to the Mediterranean in Europe.

On the American continent, the immense scale of many vistas and of the natural features they contain inevitably influences the design and size of human constructions. The width of the rivers and the length and height of the bridges create new dimensions for the human landscape. In the Old World, most bridges were built chiefly for communication between human beings, whereas the great modern bridges of America are primarily designed for through traffic. The buildings of old cities are clustered in compact groups and are served by short and often tortuous streets; in contrast, the gridiron pattern which early became established in the United States—Jefferson proposed it for Washington—encouraged the development of long streets which progressively evolved into highways. The moment you set foot on one of them, Jean Paul Sartre wrote, it has to go on to Boston or Chicago. And the ultimate consequence may be the linear city.

Historical accidents also play a role in giving an enduring shape to landscapes. The city of Washington was first planned by a Frenchman, Major Pierre Charles L'Enfant, who chose to build it on the flats along the two rivers, according to the principles of the French Renaissance. An Italian architect, more at home with the tradition of building on elevated areas, would have been more likely to locate the city on the southeast-facing slopes above the present location.[23] San Francisco developed on its present site because when the city was born the harbor was the most accessible approach. If California were settled today, San Francisco would probably become the suburb of a major city across the bay.

The size of the country may be one of the factors influencing attitudes toward land use. The British have felt increasingly during recent decades that their cities must not be allowed to spread across the surface of the nation, eating up land unchecked. This attitude, which is obviously motivated by the need to preserve open space in a small and crowded island, has made urban-rural planning a dominant preoccupation of modern England. In contrast, few Americans yet realize that open land will soon become scarce. They still tend to believe that if one place is no longer good enough, it can be abandoned for a better one, as was done in the past. This attitude considers the land as a resource that can be used, even squandered, with little thought to the future.

Considerations such as love for the rural atmosphere in England, the longing for open vistas in France, the compactness and stability of life in conservative societies, the openness and fluidity of the economic enterprise in the United States are thus reflected in the national landscapes and impose on them evolutionary patterns from which escape is almost impossible. Everywhere, the persistence of place results from a complex interplay between nature and culture. In certain special situations, the principal qualities are clearly contributed by nature, as in the Grand Canyon or Niagara Falls. In other situations, human activities are the dominant force, as in London and Paris, but even in the most urban environments, nature contributes to the spirit of the place. The rivers of London and Paris, the hills of Rome and San Francisco, the openings to inland America and to the Atlantic Ocean in New York, and the stimulating climates of all these cities have provided favorable conditions for a regional superstructure which retains its unmistakable identity even as it evolves. Persistence of place is the expression of a spirit which is so powerful that it can unify a heterogeneous resident population as well as indoctrinate and sometimes convert the visitors and immigrants that come to it in search of a unique experience or opportunity.

All urban areas in prosperous industrialized countries are of course becoming increasingly alike in their superficial aspects, but this is not a new phenomenon. The Greek and Roman temples of a given period exhibit much uniformity, as do Gothic cathedrals and their sculpture. There is uniformity also in the Renaissance houses with their formal gardens, the slums of the industrial revolution, the brownstone era in New York, the opulence of the bourgeois dwellings everywhere at the turn of the century during the Belle Epoque.

Furthermore, the trend toward greater uniformity which we are now experiencing may not be as deep or as persistent as is feared. When the traveler awakens in an American luxury motel neither his eyes nor his nose can recognize any local atmosphere in the room, but the manner of the waitress and the walk of the people in the street soon tell him where he is. Although the technologists and bankers of New York, London, and Stockholm deal with the same problems and can speak the same language, the fashionable sections of their respective cities continue to look different, as do suburbs, satellite towns, and green belts; the new communities of Sweden and the new towns of England do not have their counterparts in the United

States. The subways of New York, Montreal, Toronto, London, Paris, and Moscow all operate according to the same technological principles, but their employes and passengers follow the beat of different drums.

International styles in materials and methods obviously facilitate some of the operations common to the whole planet, but human beings search for distinctiveness in their surroundings. Regionalism has an enduring justification in the cosmic, terrestrial, and historical characteristics of each particular place. Because it is rooted both in human and in physical nature, environmental diversity will persist within the political ecumenism of One World. Natural and cultural forces will overcome technological and political imperatives and continue to nurture the *genius loci* which accounts for persistence of place.

CHAPTER 7

Humanized Nature

I grew up in small villages of the Île de France, north of Paris, near Picardy and Normandy. This is a land without any notable characteristics except those conferred upon it by several millennia of continuous human occupation. The hills have such low profiles that they would be of little interest without the venerable churches and clusters of houses which crown their summits. The rivers are sluggish and the ponds muddy, but their names have been celebrated so often in poetry and prose that they evoke the enchantment of peaceful rural scenes. The sky is rarely spectacular, but painters have created a rich spectrum of visual and emotional experiences from its soft luminosity.

Ever since the primeval forest was cleared by Neolithic settlers and medieval farmers, the province of the Île de France has retained a humanized charm that transcends its natural endowments. To this day, its land has remained very fertile, even though much of it has been in continuous use for more than two thousand years. Far from being exhausted by intensive agriculture over such long periods of time, the land still supports a large population and a great variety of human settlements. Its hamlets, villages, towns, and cities have uninterruptedly nurtured the glories and follies of civilization, despite the ebb and flow of men's fortunes.

These observations about my native country are not dictated by chauvinism; I know they apply just as well to many other parts of the world. Certain very ancient landscapes, particularly in Asia and Europe, have remained fertile and are still the sites of sophisticated cultures even though they have long been occupied by man. In North America also, some of the most attractive and prosperous agricultural lands are found in areas which were covered with forests three centuries ago but which have been intensely cultivated ever since. Amish farms in Pennsylvania illustrate the way wise ecological management can be as creative of soil fertility and as lastingly successful in the New World as it has been for millennia in the Old World. Repeatedly and under a variety of conditions, man has thus converted wilderness into humanized landscapes which have become biologically richer with time and have been propitious to the emergence and growth of civilization. The words of the French poet Charles Péguy (1873–1914), as he presented the Beauce country to Notre Dame de Chartres, can be adapted to humanized landscapes all over the world:

Deux mille ans de labeur ont fait de cette terre
Un réservoir sans fin pour les âges nouveaux.
(Two thousand years of human labor have made of this land
An inexhaustible source of wealth for the times to come.)

Even as a schoolboy whose direct knowledge of the world was limited to the Île de France country, I had learned that Europe possesses an immense variety of landscapes far grander, rougher, more diversified, more colorful, and more sublime than the cultivated fields, flowered meadows, manicured forests, gentle hills, and peaceful rivers of my own birthplace. The picture books devoted to the *Spectacles de la Nature* which long remained my only view of the outside world gave me the impression that much of the European continent was still wilderness. But now that I am familiar with most of the United States and have traveled over a good deal of the earth, I realize that there is little original wilderness left in Europe. What I had assumed to be primeval nature had in reality been altered by man for thousands of years, in most cases since the Stone Age.

Man's influence is difficult to recognize in certain European landscapes, because it has been exerted so slowly and progressively that it has created a second nature. All European forests, for example, have been used by the peasantry since time immemorial; many of them have been under state management for several centuries. Mountain slopes and valleys have been progressively adapted to human purposes by a multiplicity of interventions, rarely recorded because they were minor and empirical. Even the highest European mountains have become humanized. Except for their glaciers, the Alps and Pyrenees have acquired a gigantic parklike quality.

Eric Julber, a Los Angeles lawyer fond of mountain climbing, has described how a trip to Switzerland convinced him that one need not be a "nature purist" to enjoy the excitement of scenery at high altitudes.

> Switzerland is crisscrossed with roads, some in use since Roman times; its mountain valleys are heavily grazed and farmed; hotels and restaurants are everywhere, even on the tops of some mountain peaks. Where the automobile cannot go, railroads will take you; and when the going gets too steep for the cogwheel trains you catch an aerial tramway, suspended on a wire.
>
> Many of the most remarkable viewpoints are acces-

> sible by some type of comfortable transportation, so that all over Switzerland people sit on restaurant patios 10,000 feet high, eating pastry and admiring nature—and they got there without walking.
>
> (And when I say people, I mean lots of them, for tourism is Switzerland's primary industry.)
>
> Switzerland is everything the purist in America despises. It is roads, rails, restaurants, hotels, crowds and filling stations. It is beauty made easy. It is comfort. It is climbing without suffering.[1]

All over Europe, man has thus created a semiartificial landscape by converting primeval nature into an orderly arrangement of farmlands, pastures, and wooded areas, all of which are linked by roads and trails which may extend beyond the timberline and onto the glaciers. Much of Europe is so carefully groomed that it resembles a work of art. Man has recreated it in his own image. The same applies, of course, to other humanized regions of the Old World.

The wonderful harmony that now exists in many parts of Europe among the various components of nature cannot therefore be regarded as a spontaneous expression of wilderness; it is instead the outcome of a continuous and intimate collaboration between man and the site on which he lives—what Rabindranath Tagore referred to as the wooing of the earth. Jacquetta Hawkes's *A Land,* mentioned earlier, can be read as a prose poem celebrating the creation of the English landscape from wilderness by the tender coaxing of man in the course of ages. As Claude Lévi-Strauss wrote in *Tristes Tropiques,* even the wildest sceneries of Europe reveal order and proportions—a marvelous ordonnance of which Nicholas Poussin has been the incomparable interpreter. "Travel in America, and you will realize that this sublime harmony, far from being the spontaneous expression of Nature herself, is the result of agreements long sought for between mankind and the site in question."[2] At its best, the European landscape is a creation of peasants, painters, and poets.

In contrast to Europe, the other continents still possess large areas which have not been significantly affected by man. This is true of the Amazon valley, the Himalayas, the Arctic, and the Antarctic. There are also many different types of undisturbed nature in the United States. The Rockies, the Sierras, the Everglades, the Northwest, the Southwest, the various national parks, although they receive large numbers of tourists every year and are affected by close and distant technological activities, illustrate nevertheless the immense variety of landscapes on the North American continent which have not yet been completely transformed by man and still retain their primeval genius.

The American wilderness had no appeal for the early European settlers or the later immigrants. In *The Machine in the Garden*, the American literary critic Leo Marx has shown that what they looked for in the New World was not the dense forests, high peaks, immense streams and exciting sceneries, but rather a place in which to escape from corruption; it was the setting for a civilized pastoral way of life.[3] William Byrd, owner of the Virginia plantation Westover, set forth in quaint words what he regarded as a desirable human environment: "A Library, a Garden, a Grove, a Purling Stream are the innocent scenes that divert our leisure."[4] Jefferson's Monticello came close to this ideal, which was clearly far removed from life in the wilderness. The primeval forest was full of terror for the New England Puritan—the site of evil and witchcraft. The Plymouth Pilgrims found the region around Provincetown Harbor a "heidious and desolate wilderness full of wild beastes and wild men."[5] As the early settlers and immigrants began to move westward, one of their dominant urges was to cut down the forest, not necessarily for its timber but because they longed for the safety and comfort of cultivated fields and teeming cities.

Today we seem to have moved far away from the eighteenth-century pastoral attitude and to have overcome the fear of the forest. Our contemporaries in all age groups commonly talk and behave as if the civilized environment evoked by William Byrd in the eighteenth century had no appeal for them, and as if they valued only undisturbed wilderness. And yet! Despite the commonly professed ideal that wild and exotic environments are the only ones worth attention, the landscapes which provide the most lasting pleasure for the largest number of persons, young as well as old, are still those in which man has tamed wilderness. Even completely artificial environments created by profound alterations of nature are more sought after than wilderness. For one John Muir or Daniel Boone trying to remove himself as far as possible from human settlements, there are millions of nature lovers for whom the country means humanized nature. Even Thoreau, when he settled by Walden Pond, built his cabin within walking distance of Concord, where he went every week for dinner.

Increasingly, all over the world men move to urban areas. Some manage to enrich their lives with the intense excitement and challenges provided by mountain climbing, rapids running, or big-game hunting, but this kind of enjoyment rarely extends over prolonged periods of time. For most people, wilderness is an occasional, or merely a one-time experience. In practice, the only manner of direct contact with nature is through tame forms of camping and outdoor cooking. Even in the United States, where extensive wilderness is readily accessible, few are the persons who do more than enjoy it vicariously or at best visually from a comfortable distance. For most outdoor lovers, now as in the past, the word "nature" evokes chiefly landscapes which have been modified by human intervention, either for profit or for pleasure.

Man feels alien in wilderness and has run away from it for several hundred generations. He has increasingly sheltered himself from it by manipulating nature and in many places creating new environments. He developed the essential characteristics of human life precisely while shaping comfortable and pleasant niches for himself out of the wilderness. The prehistoric Sumerians and Egyptians probably never moved far from the agricultural settlements they had created along their rivers. The very land on which the great cities of Babylonia were to rise had literally to be created. "The prehistoric forerunner of the biblical Erech was built on a sort of platform of reeds, laid criss-cross upon the alluvial mud."[6] And Cicero affirms with quiet finality in *De Natura Deorum,* "By means of our hands we create a second world within the world of nature."[7]

Thus, civilization began in a man-made world and could not long survive in wilderness. But, paradoxically, it is almost certain that mankind needs wilderness in order to survive. The biological and philosophical reasons for the need of wilderness are so complex and subtle, however, that it seems best to reserve this discussion for Chapter 8.

Man's efforts to create his own environment from wilderness is strikingly illustrated by his age-old and constant warfare against the forest. The fact that most of our cultivated plants are sun-loving and cannot grow under trees indicates that clearing the forest was an essential step in the development of agriculture and therefore of civilization. This process has been traced back to the Stone and Bronze ages in several parts of Europe. In the southwest of England, for example, pollen analysis of Dartmoor peats has provided evidence that before man's arrival in Devon the upland was very similar to the surrounding lowlands with regard to soil and forest vegetation.[8] With human occupation, however, the forest began to shrink. The bare moorlands of the present landscape probably began to emerge like a tonsure during the Neolithic period, while the lowlands remained forested until medieval times. Once the destruction of the trees had begun, grazing animals and the leaching of impoverished soil by the heavy rainfall prevented the re-establishment of the forest. In Devon, much of this deforestation process had been completed by the Bronze Age, but in other areas of Europe it continued into the Middle Ages. When the European settlers first came into contact with the wilderness of the New World, their struggle against trees was thus not only a question of survival but the continued expression of an attitude which has roots deep in the past.

In *Mountain Gloom and Mountain Glory*, the American writer Marjorie Nicolson shows that, until the nineteenth century, mountains and forests have been almost universally regarded as "Nature's Shames and Ills" and "Warts, Wens, Blisters, Imposthumes" upon the otherwise fair face of nature.[9] The appreciation of wilderness for its own sake is largely an acquired taste influenced by peculiar social forces. In Europe, it began to gain momentum as a philosophical reaction against the artificial refinements of seventeenth- and eighteenth-century social life, and it was nurtured by the writers and painters of the Romantic period during the nineteenth century. The awareness that urban blight and squalor increased the load of disease also favored the pro-wilderness movement. "Foul air prompts to vice and oxygen to virtue," was a public-health truism of the 1890s, a view which led to the conclusion that health could best be maintained amidst unspoiled nature. The cure of tuberculosis and of mental disorders was sought in sanatoria, preferably located in wild places or at least as far as possible from the corruptions of civilized life. Eventually wilderness came to be admired not only for its health-giving qualities but also for its esthetic value as, for example, by the painters of the Hudson River School.

Very early, however, interest in nature degenerated into artificial and even ridiculous postures. At the Petit Trianon, Marie Antoinette and her court used gilded crooks to tend well-groomed sheep. Along the Hudson, nature lovers placed ruined arches in secluded spots to enhance the romantic quality of the landscape, and they admired dead trees as if these were architectural relics. It is not a long step from this false esthetic sense to the transfer of London Bridge in 1969 from London to Arizona for enhancing the market value of a real-estate development in the desert.

During the nineteenth century, many visitors to the Far West seemed to be moved as much by historical evocations as by the authentic splendor of the wilderness; the stratified sedimentary and volcanic rock formations reminded the tourists of castles, temples, and other monuments of ancient civilizations. These pseudo-architectural oddities still contribute today to the tremendous popularity of Yellowstone Park and of the Garden of the Gods in Colorado Springs. In fact, it was the entertainment value of the wilderness rather than its primeval quality which prompted Congress to designate the first national park (Yellowstone) a "pleasuring ground for the use and enjoyment of the people." The very word "park," instead of wilderness, indicates that the intent of Congress was less to preserve natural landscapes undefiled by human associations than to provide environments for interesting and pleasurable experiences away from the city.

Then as now, few were the hearty souls eager to dissociate themselves from the pleasure of human companionship and the comforts of civilization. Writing in 1870, N.P. Langford predicted that Yellowstone Lake would soon "be adorned with villas and the ornaments of civilized life. . . . The march of civil improvement will reclaim this delightful solitude, and garnish it with all the attractions of cultivated taste and refinement."[10] Unfortunately, this kind of "civil improvement" can readily degenerate into the slum-like facilities which now disgrace some of the national parks.

The great majority of persons, in any case, have no opportunity to experience and enjoy nature except in its humanized aspects—cultivated fields, parks, gardens, and other manifestations of human settlements. In consequence, it is not enough to save the Redwoods, the Everglades, the Grand Canyon, and as much wilderness as possible; it is equally important to protect the esthetic quality of urban settings and farmlands. Figuratively speaking, we must improve Coney Island.

In antiquity, historians made little effort to separate the description of a place from the narration of the events which had taken place in it. Physical geography and human history were thus always intermingled. This was justified since man is both the creator and the creature of his environment; wherever there is human life, it is impossible to dissociate nature from man.

The individuality of each particular area of the earth is determined by the system of dynamic relationships between the land and the life it harbors, especially the human beings. Except in the case of true wilderness, the land can be understood only when considered in relation to man. The human occupation of an oasis in the Sahara changes the character of the region, as does a settlement along a tropical river; Alaska will never be the same after the oil pipeline has been installed, nor will the African savanna after it has been invaded by hunters and tourists. In most parts of the world, a succession of different peoples have occupied each locality and used or developed its resources. They have spread themselves through the land as best suited their needs, transforming it by works that expressed their particular ways of life.

Even the decision to set apart certain areas of the earth as protected wilderness involves value judgments which are purely human in character. Ancient people protected the areas which they regarded as the abode of their deities. Assyrian kings maintained reserves for hunting lions. John Muir prized the High Sierras for their loneliness. Yellowstone became a national park because of its picturesque quality. The Adirondack Forest was preserved to maintain the watershed of the Hudson River.

Furthermore, as I have already emphasized, immense areas of what is generally called nature have in reality been profoundly altered by man. In many cases, the consequences have been undesirable, as when overgrazing destroyed the vegetation and created deserts or impoverished lands thousands of years ago. The erosion of certain areas of the Mediterranean basin dates from Greco-Roman times and even earlier. More interestingly, some of the most beautiful parts of the world have acquired their present characteristics from the systematic work of humble people over many generations. In many parts of the Old World, the individuality of the various geographical regions and of the villages which are organic parts of them reflects the local agricultural economy; for example, peasants have molded the land of Tuscany by rounding the hills and shaping the slopes into an architectural structure of terraces on which they grow their crops.

The unconscious shaping of nature to meet the necessities of life is eventually supplemented by conscious esthetic efforts. While much of the Italian farmland has been sculptured by the anonymous labor of the peasantry, the Italian Renaissance garden represents a sophisticated geometrical design consciously derived from the landscape. In France, the relatively flat and soft landscapes north of the Loire Valley have generated both large farms and classical parks; the opening of long perspectives *(la magie des perspectives infinies)* has been for several centuries an essential part of the French landscape. The English agricultural economy, which put great emphasis on cattle, horses, and sheep, inspired a different kind of landscape, characterized by large meadows in valleys where streams meander, lakes reflect the diffuse light, and woodlands occupy the hilltops.

The transformations of the earth by the works of man have frequently revealed and given life to potentialities that would have remained unexpressed in the state of wilderness. The Charles River valley around Boston, as well as the valleys of the Thames and the Seine around London and Paris, would be rather uninteresting landscape, if they had not acquired disciplined charm from becoming an integral part of human artifacts. The word nature thus is properly applied not only to wilderness but also to humanized landscapes which have been managed in such a manner as to bring out inherent characteristics that were concealed before human interventions.

Throughout the Old World, many landscapes incarnate age-old occupation by man. The American continent, in contrast, has been influenced by more recent social forces. Whereas the lands of the Old World first evolved organically under the influence of humble people governed largely by their senses and biological needs, much of the New World was rapidly transformed by immigrants who derived their motivation at times from utopian ideals but more frequently from dreams of wealth, and who were therefore guided by their brains rather than by their hearts or their senses. Property to be handed on to one's son is likely to be maintained in good condition. In contrast, the land tends to deteriorate when it is exploited to serve gross selfish interests or when economic efficiency and productivity are the sole criteria.

Over immense areas of the United States, man abandoned the land as soon as he had exhausted its readily available resources—timber, coal, minerals—leaving only ghost towns, deserted camps, and eroded slopes as witnesses of his passage. Elsewhere monocultures have transformed the land into gigantic open-air factories specialized in the production of a few cash crops. Monoculture can be highly productive, but as generally practiced it destroys the humus and impoverishes the soil. It has the overpowering grandeur of large-scale modern technology but limits the expression of the variety and sensual quality of nature. Although immense fields of cotton, corn, lettuce, cabbages, or artichokes have a beauty of their own, they do not provide the charm of a walk through diversified country.

Fortunately other forces of a more local and subtle character have been also at work in shaping the relation between man and nature in the United States.

The first settlers in America naturally planned their villages, dwellings, and farms according to the social patterns they had known in Europe. The court of Massachusetts Bay Co., for example, decreed that no house should be built more than half a mile from the meeting house. Soon, however, local conditions led to types of planning that differed from the European patterns; minor modifications were first dictated by the fear of Indian attacks and by the proximity of the forest. Progressively, local economic opportunities created regional patterns. In Virginia, plantations were established on the numerous estuaries where each could have its own docking facilities. Since ocean-going vessels could dock, unload, and take on cargo right at the farm, there was little need for the conventional type of commercial town. As a result, Virginians had little incentive to adopt city life even after they had acquired wealth. They favored instead the Jeffersonian ideal of a pastoral society.

In Pennsylvania, the cheapness of the land and the ease with which it could be obtained led the German immigrants to abandon the farm-village organization they had known in the Rhine valley; farms of several hundred contiguous acres made the traditional kind of village life all but impossible. Still larger tracts of land became available to the settlers who moved west and who could thus take advantage of modern agricultural machinery for the creation of huge farms.

It is easy to overstate the differences between the Old World and the New World; nevertheless some characters and uses of the land in the United States warrant generalizations that are not valid to the same extent for other continents. There exist in the United States immense areas of true wilderness, which inspire universal admiration, but which are directly experienced by only a very small number of devotees. There are also vast remnants of the different regional types of farming which call to mind the eighteenth-century dreams of a return to nature. Finally, there are huge fields of industrial agriculture, immensely productive but emotionally neutral because they represent nature tamed into a state of subjugation; the wheatfields and cornfields of North America have given to farming a monstrous magnificence which has little in common with the traditional peasant agriculture in the Old World.

Man has now transformed a large percentage of the globe by his agricultural and industrial enterprises. Eleven percent of the *total* land surface of the earth is used as cropland, 10 percent as range land, and 20 percent as managed forest. Of the remainder, the largest part is either almost constantly frozen or is too cold or too mountainous for normal human occupation or utilization. The rest consists of marginal areas, and especially of unmanaged forests, some of which may be utilized in the near future. If one adds to this inventory the increasing encroachments of industry, housing, communication networks, and other needs of modern life, it can be calculated that in most of the world expansion in the use of land will end by about 1985. Practically all the earth's land surface compatible with human life will then be humanized.

The date 1985 is taken from the proceedings of a 1970 symposium on "Man's Impact on the Global Environment," organized by the Massachusetts Institute of Technology.[11] Its closeness to Orwell's *1984* symbolizes the widespread belief that complete humanization of the earth will be as destructive to the quality of the natural world as the social takeover by Big Brother's technology to the quality of human life. This pessimistic mood pervades a recent anthology on *America the Vanishing: Rural Life and the Price of Progress*, which begins with accounts of the fresh delight experienced by early discoverers and interpreters of the American scenery and ends with the anguish and protests of modern ecologists and nature lovers, from Rachel Carson to Joseph Wood Krutch.[12] The two most common moods of present discussions about nature seem to be nostalgic tears for what was and disapproving frowns at what is. In fact, no one can reasonably doubt that we shall destroy the fitness of the planet for human life (perhaps earlier than 1985) if we do not immediately take steps to correct the disordered relationships between man and environment caused by the present-day ways of life and blind technological drives.

In the foreword of *Reason Awake!*, I wrote that: "When man truly enters the age of science he will abandon his crude and destructive efforts to conquer nature. He will instead learn to insert himself into the environment in such a manner that his ways of life and technologies make him once more in harmony with nature."[13] Although these words still reflect my convictions, they no longer satisfy me entirely because they seem to imply a rather static view of man's relationships to nature—as if it were not a historical fact that man has always manipulated nature. Since he now occupies a very large percentage of the total land mass of the globe, most places derive their distinctive individuality not only from their physical characteristics and from the animal, plant, and microbial life they naturally harbor, but also and increasingly from human activities.

Climate, geology, topography determine what forms of life can prosper in a given place, and these living forms in turn alter the surface and the atmosphere of the earth. Each particular place is the continuously evolving expression of a highly complex set of forces—inanimate and living—which become integrated into an organic whole. Man is one of these forces, and probably the most influential; his interventions can be creative and lastingly successful if the changes he introduces are compatible with the intrinsic attributes of the natural system he tries to shape. The reason we are now desecrating nature is not because we use it to our ends, but because we commonly manipulate it without respect for the spirit of place. The very word "desecration," now often used to lament the damage men are causing to the earth, implies belief in the sanctity of nature—as if its relation to human life had a sacred quality.

Certain geographers claim that for geography to become truly scientific it must study in detail the mechanisms through which the natural environment determines human activities. The natural environment, however, does not determine behavior; what it does is to offer options among which human beings select according to their culture, their capabilities, and their personal tastes. Men have created their environments by manipulating nature to suit their wishes. The Pennsylvania forest can be transformed into Amish farms or into golf courses. The American desert can be turned into a Mormon settlement or a Las Vegas. The Tuaregs continue to live as nomads in the Sahara, while the Israelis make the sand bloom in the Negeb desert.

Economic imperatives have of course profoundly influenced the domestication of nature, but esthetic values have also played a role. Tastes concerning landscape design have their origin in the Dutch and English painters of the seventeenth century and even more in their southern contemporaries Salvatore Rosa, Claude Lorrain, and Nicholas Poussin. Each in his own way, these three painters used Italian scenery to create idealized pictures of pastoral ways of life—an ideal which found its way into the design of parks and gardens all over Europe. In England, the landscape gardeners adapted the new pictorial vision of the Italian hill country to the design of large estates, and the influence of their work, in turn, spread rapidly through the country. The scenic charm of present-day England still expresses esthetic values that first emerged from seventeenth-century painting.

Most landscapes have thus been shaped by men who organized terrain, water, and vegetation according to patterns evolved from their culture and personal tastes. In addition, landscapes acquire a further quality from the myths created about them by painters, writers, and musicians, and from the great events with which they have been associated. The Australian aborigine or the Navajo Indian sees his land through the spectacles provided by the legends of his tribe, whereas the civilized Westerner looks at the various places of the world through the memory of paintings, novels, poems, melodies, and historical facts which crowd his mind. The Brooklyn Bridge is more exciting because Thomas Wolfe has described how he used to walk across it from Brooklyn Heights and because Hart Crane idealized it in his poem, "The Bridge." Genius of place symbolizes the living ecological relationship between a particular location and the persons who have derived from it and added to it the various aspects of their humanness. No landscape, however grandiose or fertile, can express its full potential richness until it has been given its myth by the love, works, and arts of man.

CHAPTER 8

Franciscan Conservation Versus Benedictine Stewardship

History is replete with ecological disasters; the most flourishing lands of antiquity seem to have been under a malediction. Mesopotamia, Persia, Egypt, West Pakistan were once the sites of civilizations which remained powerful and wealthy for great periods of time but are now among the poorest areas of the world. Their lands are barren deserts, many of their ancient cities abandoned, most of their people so poor, malnourished, and diseased that they have no memory or even awareness of their magnificent past. Since the same situation is true for much of India, China, Southeast Asia, and Latin America, it would seem that, contrary to the views presented in the preceding chapter, all civilizations are mortal.

Civil strife, warfare, famine, and disease certainly contributed to the demise of ancient Eastern civilizations, but the desolate appearance of their lands today would seem to indicate that the primary cause of the decline was the depletion of the soil caused by prolonged occupation by large numbers of people. Exhaustion or destruction of water resources probably followed and dealt the final blow. Babylonian civilization, for example, disappeared after its system of irrigation was destroyed by the Mongols, but its environment had begun to degenerate long before this final disaster.[1]

The English archaeologist Sir Mortimer Wheeler has examined in detail the fate of Mohenjo Daro, the archaeologically famous city-civilization that flourished from 2500 to 1500 B.C. on the plains of the Indus River in present-day Pakistan. This civilization, which prospered some four thousand years ago, at the same time as Mesopotamian and Egyptian civilizations, differed from them in its architecture, art, and technology. Like them, however, it disappeared because, in Wheeler's words, it was "steadily wearing out its landscape."[2] In modern ecological jargon this means that its environment was being destroyed by overuse or misuse. Pessimists have therefore much historical evidence for their thesis that civilizations inevitably ruin their environments.

There is, however, another side to the question. The American geographer C.O. Sauer is of the opinion that "the worn-out parts of the world are the recent settlements, not the lands of old civilizations."[3] For more than a thousand years, Japanese agriculture has remained highly productive without decreasing the fertility of the soil or spoiling the beauty of the landscape. In Western Europe also, as mentioned in Chapter 7, many areas opened to agriculture by the Neolithic settlers remain fertile today after several thousand years of almost continuous use. This immense duration of certain cultivated landscapes contributes a sense of tranquility to many parts of the Old World; it inspires confidence that mankind can survive its present ordeals and learn to manage the land for the sake of the future.

These contrasting views of the relationships between civilization and the land may not be as incompatible as they appear. All the great Eastern civilizations which wore out their soil were located in and around semiarid and arid zones. Under such climatic conditions, which prevail over approximately 35 percent of the world's land mass, productive agriculture depends upon irrigation, and damage to the soil can be rapid and almost irreversible. In contrast, Western Europe, Japan, and certain other parts of Asia are blessed with a greater and especially a more constant rainfall, which enables their soils to recover fairly rapidly after they have been damaged by ecological mismanagement. Climatic conditions, however, cannot account entirely for the fate of the world's civilizations. They do not explain the sudden disappearance of the Maya, Khmer, and other great civilizations which once flourished in humid countries. In Mexico, the end of the Teotihuacan culture occurred suddenly, around A.D. 800, during a moist period. The primary cause was probably the fact that the protective forests of the region had been cut to provide fuel for the extensive burning of lime. The erosion that ensued, coupled with the destructive effects of cultivation, was apparently sufficient to offset the blessings of returning moisture. Ecological mismanagement was also responsible for the deterioration of agriculture around the Mediterranean basin in the ancient world and is now creating similar problems in many temperate regions, including the United States. The land has remained fertile under intense cultivation only where farmers have used it according to sound ecological principles. Unwise management of nature or of technology can destroy civilization in any climate and land, under any political system.

Environmental degradation in the modern world is commonly traced to technological excesses, but the roots of the problem go far deeper. When George Perkins Marsh visited the Near East in the middle of the nineteenth century, he was shocked to find deserted cities, silted harbors, and wastelands instead of flourishing civilizations. Technology could not then be blamed for soil turned barren, forests destroyed, and ancient bodies of water replaced by salt and sand flats. Marsh properly concluded that ecological errors had led to the deterioration of agriculture in the Mediterranean countries, and he recognized also that good agricultural practices had preserved the quality of the land in other parts of the world. His book *Man and Nature*, first published in 1864 and revised in 1874 under the new title *The Earth as Modified by Human Action*, advocated conservation practices but chiefly from the agricultural point of view.[4]

While Marsh emphasized the quality of agricultural lands, another aspect of ecological concern was taking shape in the United States—the efforts to save the quality of nature. One of the most articulate spokesmen of the new movement was the American ecologist Aldo Leopold (1887–1948), whose primary commitment was to wildlife and to undisturbed wilderness. Leopold advocated an ecological conscience in all aspects of man's relation with nature and as one of the founders of the Wilderness Society was influential in securing government approval for the protection of America's first wilderness area at the head of the Gila River in New Mexico. He preached a "land ethic" in his book *A Sand County Almanac*, which has become the Holy Writ of American conservationists.[5]

Marsh's influence was not great, probably because he wrote at a time when the methods of modern agriculture were producing enormous increases of crop yields, and his teachings therefore seemed irrelevant. In contrast, Leopold rapidly gained a large following because the obvious damage done to nature by the new technologies had created a public mood receptive to his plea for a new ethic of man's relation to nature.

A curious expression of the present public concern for the environmental crisis has been the theory, which became academically fashionable during the 1960s, that the Judeo-Christian tradition is responsible for the desecration of nature in the Western world. This view seems to have been publicized for the first time around 1950 by the Zen Buddhist Daisetz Suzuki.[6] But it was given academic glamor by Lynn White, Jr., professor of history at the University of California at Los Angeles, in a much publicized lecture entitled, "The Historical Roots of Our Ecologic Crisis."[7] It is a measure of its popular success that this lecture has been reproduced *in extenso*, not only in learned and popular magazines but also in *The Oracle*, the multicolored, now defunct journal of the hippie culture in San Francisco. Whether valid or not, White's thesis demands attention because it has become an article of faith for many conservationists, ecologists, economists, and even theologians. The thesis runs approximately as follows.

The ancient Oriental and Greco-Roman religions took it for granted that animals, trees, rivers, mountains, and other natural objects can have spiritual significance just like men and therefore deserve respect. According to the Judeo-Christian religions, in contrast, man is apart from nature. The Jews adopted monotheism with a distinctly anthropomorphic concept of God. The Christians developed this trend still further by shifting religion toward an exclusive concern with human beings. It is explicitly stated in Chapter 1 of Genesis that man was shaped in the image of God and given dominion over creation; this has provided the excuse for a policy of exploitation of nature, regardless of consequences. Christianity developed, of course, along different lines in different parts of the world. In its Eastern forms its ideal was the saint dedicated to prayer and contemplation, whereas in its Western forms it was the saint dedicated to action. Because of this geographical difference in Christian attitudes, the most profound effects of man's impact on nature have been in the countries of Western civilization. To a large extent, furthermore, modern technology is the expression of the Judeo-Christian belief that man has a rightful dominion over nature. Biblical teachings thus account for the fact that Western man has had no scruples in using the earth's resources for his own selfish interests or in exploring the moon to satisfy his curiosity, even if this means the raping of nature and the contamination of the lunar surface.

Since the roots of the environmental crisis are so largely religious, the remedy must also be essentially religious: "I personally doubt," White writes, "that ecologic backlashes can be avoided simply by applying to our problems more science and more technology." For this reason, he suggests that the only solution may be a return to the humble attitude of the early Franciscans. Francis of Assisi worshiped all aspects of nature and believed in the virtue of humility, not only for the individual person but for man as a species; we should try to follow in his footsteps, so as to "depose man from his monarchy over creation, and abandon our aggressive attitude toward Nature." "I propose Francis as a patron saint of ecologists," is the conclusion of White's essay.[8]

In my opinion, the theory that Judeo-Christian attitudes are responsible for the development of technology and for the ecological crisis is at best a historical half-truth. Erosion of the land, destruction of animal and plant species, excessive exploitation of natural resources, and ecological disasters are not peculiar to the Judeo-Christian tradition and to scientific technology. At all times, and all over the world, man's thoughtless interventions into nature have had a variety of disastrous consequences or at least have changed profoundly the complexion of nature.

The process began some ten thousand years ago, long before the Bible was written.[9] A dramatic extinction of several species of large mammals and terrestrial birds occurred at the very beginning of the Neolithic period, coincident with the expansion of agricultural man. His eagerness to protect cultivated fields and flocks may account for the attitude "if it moves, kill it," which is rooted deep in folk traditions over much of the world. Nor was the destruction of large animals motivated only by utilitarian reasons. In Egypt the pharaohs and the nobility arranged for large numbers of beasts to be driven into compounds where they were trapped and then shot with arrows. The Assyrians, too, were as vicious destroyers of animals—lions and elephants, for example—as they were of men. Ancient hunting practices greatly reduced the populations of some large animal species and in some cases led to their eradication. This destructive process has continued throughout historical times, not only in the regions peripheral to the eastern Mediterranean, but also in other parts of the world. In Australia, the nomadic aborigines with their fire sticks had far-reaching effects on the environment. Early explorers commented upon the aborigines' widespread practice of setting fires, which under the semiarid conditions of Australia drastically altered the vegetation cover, caused erosion, and destroyed much of the native fauna. Huge tracts of forest land were thus converted into open grasslands and the populations of large marsupials were greatly reduced.

Plato's statement in *Critias* of his belief that Greece was eroded before his time as a result of deforestation and overgrazing has already been mentioned. Erosion resulting from human activities probably caused the end of the Teotihuacan civilization in ancient Mexico. Early men, aided especially by that most useful and most noxious of all animals, the Mediterranean goat, were probably responsible for more deforestation and erosion than all the bulldozers of the Judeo-Christian world.

Nor is there reason to believe that Oriental civilizations have been more respectful of nature than Judeo-Christian civilizations. As shown by the British scientist and historian Joseph Needham, China was far ahead of Europe in scientific and technological development until the seventeenth century A.D. and used technology on a massive and often destructive scale.[10] Many passages in T'ang and Sung poetry indicate that the barren hills of central and northern China were once heavily forested, and there is good reason to believe that, there as elsewhere, treelessness and soil erosion are results of fires and overgrazing. Even the Buddhists contributed largely to the deforestation of Asia in order to build their temples; it has been estimated that in some areas they have been responsible for much more than half of the timber consumption.[11]

The Chinese attitude of respect for nature probably arose, in fact, as a response to the damage done in antiquity. Furthermore, this respect does not go as far as artistic and poetical expressions would indicate. The classic nature poets of China write as if they had achieved identification with the cosmos, but in reality most of them were retired bureaucrats living on estates in which nature was carefully trimmed and managed by gardeners. In Japan also, the beautifully artificial gardens and oddly shaped pine trees could hardly be regarded as direct expressions of nature; they constitute rather a symbolic interpretation of an intellectual attitude toward scenery. Wildlife has been so severely reduced in modern Japan that sparrows and swallows are the only kinds of birds remaining of the dozens of species that used to pass through Tokyo a century ago.

One of the best-documented examples of ecological mismanagement in the ancient world is the progressive destruction of the groves of cedars and cypresses that in the past were the glory of Lebanon. The many references to these noble evergreen groves in ancient inscriptions and in the Old Testament reveal that the Egyptian pharaohs and the kings of Assyria or Babylon carried off enormous amounts of the precious timber for the temples and palaces of their capital cities.[12] In a taunt against Nebuchadnezzar, king of Babylon, the prophet Isaiah refers to the destructive effects of these logging expeditions. The Roman emperors, especially Hadrian, extended still further the process of deforestation. Today the few surviving majestic cedars are living testimony to what the coniferous forests of Lebanon were like before the ruthless exploitation which long preceded the Judeo-Christian and technological age.

All over the globe and at all times in the past, men have pillaged nature and disturbed the ecological equilibrium, usually out of ignorance, but also because they have always been more concerned with immediate advantages than with long-range goals. Moreover, they could not foresee that they were preparing for ecological disasters, nor did they have a real choice of alternatives. If men are more destructive now than they were in the past, it is because there are more of them and because they have at their command more powerful means of destruction, not because they have been influenced by the Bible. In fact, the Judeo-Christian peoples were probably the first to develop on a large scale a pervasive concern for land management and an ethic of nature.

Among the great Christian teachers, none is more identified with an ethic of nature than Francis of Assisi (1182?–1226), who treated all living things and inanimate objects as if they were his brothers and sisters. His tradition has continued to express itself in many forms among Judeo-Christian people, as for example in the philosophical concept that all living things can be arranged in a continuous series—the Great Chain of Being;[13] in Albert Schweitzer's reverence for life; in the semitranscendental utterances of writers such as Wordsworth, Thoreau, or Walt Whitman. The Darwinian theory of evolution provided a scientific basis for the intuitive belief in the universal brotherhood of all living things. Most modern men have come to accept or at least to tolerate the thought, so disturbing a century ago, that man belongs to a natural line of descent which includes all animals and plants. It is not unlikely that the Franciscan worship of nature, in its various philosophical, scientific, and religious forms, has played some part in the emergence of the doctrine of conservation in the countries of Western civilization and its rapid spread during the past century.

While it is easy to believe that wilderness should be preserved wherever possible, the reasons generally given to advocate the maintenance of undisturbed ecological systems and the preservation of endangered species are not entirely convincing. Despite what the conservationists say, nature will go on even if whooping cranes, condors, or redwoods are exterminated, just as it has gone on after the extinction of millions of other species that have vanished from the earth in the course of time. The fossil beds with their myriad of long-vanished forms testify to the fact that man is not the first agency to alter the biological composition of the earth.

Environments which are being upset by smogs, pesticides, or strip mining are not destroyed thereby; they will become different by evolving in directions determined by these challenges. We may not like the consequences of these changes for ethical, esthetic, or economic reasons, but it is nevertheless certain that the disturbed environments will eventually achieve some new kind of biologic status, as has been the case in the past after all great ecological disasters.

The advance of continental ice sheets during the Pleistocene destroyed much of the flora and fauna and in many places removed the soil down to the bedrock. But nature is so resilient that the rocks made barren by the glaciers eventually acquired a new flora and new fauna. Destruction always results in a different creation. The American chestnut *(Castanea dentata)*, which had been a dominant member of the forest in the eastern United States, was all but eradicated following the accidental introduction of a fungus from Asia in 1906; today, the dead chestnut trees are turning into humus, and their place in the forest canopy has been taken by several species of oak.

In 1883, the small island of Krakatoa, situated between Java and Sumatra, was the site of a tremendous volcanic eruption. The explosive force was so great that as much as two-thirds of the island was blown away. The accompanying tidal wave caused immense damage along all the nearby coasts, and volcanic dust spread over vast portions of the globe. A careful search through the island, one year after the eruption, revealed only one spider and a few blades of grass. But twenty-five years later, 202 species of animals were found in the course of a three-day search. Fifty years after the eruption, the biological recovery had gone so far that 880 animal species could be counted and a small forest covered much of the island. Most of the new forms of life had come from Java and Sumatra.[14] The Pacific atolls of Bikini and Eniwetok, which were pulverized by multiple nuclear blasts between 1946 and 1958, similarly had returned to an almost normal state in 1964, despite the destruction of their topsoil.

Changes occur even under natural conditions, because nature continuously evolves. As pointed out by C.O. Sauer, the classical concept of "ecologic climax" is a postulate which tends to replace reality. Climax assumes the end of change, but the ecological reality is a dynamic state; the biological equilibrium is never reached because natural and human influences continuously alter the interplay between the various components of the ecosystem.[15]

Final or stable communities are exceptional in nature and they are impossible wherever there is human activity. Every form of agriculture, even the most primitive, involves the creation of artificial ecosystems. Since most of the temperate world has now been transformed by man, the balance of nature is at best an artificial and static concept unrelated to the conditions that prevail in most of the world.

Although the need to maintain the balance of nature cannot provide a valid case for conservation, there are other strong reasons for protecting environmental quality and preserving as much wilderness as possible. Some of these reasons were cogently stated in the 1860s by George P. Marsh:

> It is desirable that some large and easily accessible region of American soil should remain as far as possible in its primitive condition, at once a museum for the instruction of students, a garden for the recreation of lovers of nature, and an asylum where indigenous trees . . . plants . . . beasts may dwell and perpetuate their kind.[16]

It has now become obvious that the pollution of rivers and lakes is creating grave economic problems because the United States is coming close to a shortage of water for home and industrial needs. Polluted air damages buildings and vegetation; automobile exhausts kill evergreens and dogwoods along the highways, as well as the celebrated pines of Rome. In all its forms, air pollution is deleterious to human health and increases medical problems.

A scientific justification for taking a conservative attitude toward changes in nature is that the long-range outcome of human interventions into natural ecosystems cannot be predicted with certainty. Past experience has shown that many of these interventions have resulted in unforeseen ecological disturbances, often disastrous for man himself.

Another justification is that the progressive loss of wilderness decreases biological diversity. This in turn renders ecological systems less stable and less likely to remain suitable for a variety of species, including man. Conservation of natural systems is the best guarantee against irrevocable loss of diversity and the simplest way to minimize ecological disasters. Consider what might happen if—as has been seriously suggested by some "experts" in lumbering companies—native forests were completely replaced by artificial forests. This could certainly be accomplished by planting seedlings of the few desired species and growing them under controlled conditions with generous use of fertilizers and protective sprays. The artificial forest would probably be economically profitable for years or decades, but if such tree farms became victims of infection or other ecological accidents, and if there were no sizable natural forest communities left in the climatic and soil regions where the artificial ones had been established, starting the reforestation process anew would be extremely difficult. Undisturbed native marshes, prairies, deserts, and forests are at present the best assurance against the potential hazards inherent in the truncated, oversimplified ecosystems that are being created by the monocultures of a few strains selected for specialized properties, especially in view of the fact that these strains require massive use of chemical fertilizers, plant hormones, pesticides, and other synthetic products. As the American ecologist David Ehrenfeld stated in *Biological Conservation*, the prospect of vast blighted zones choked with weeds and scarred by erosion is more than a Wellsian fantasy.[17]

Above and beyond the economic and ecological reasons for conservation, there are esthetic and moral ones which are even more compelling. The statement that the earth is our mother is more than a sentimental platitude, since, as I said early in this book, we are shaped by the earth. The characteristics of the environment in which we develop condition our biological and mental being and the quality of our life. Were it only for selfish reasons, therefore, we must maintain variety and harmony in nature. Fortunately, as ecologists have estimated, the amount of ecological reserves needed in North America approximates ten million acres, which is far less than 1 percent of the total land area of the continent. But even if the economic impact were greater than this statement suggests, the conservation of wilderness would be justified for a number of spiritual values on which a dollar sign cannot be put. The ever-increasing popularity of the national parks, the presence of aquariums and plants in city apartments, may indicate that pigeons, dogs, cats, and even people do not suffice to make a completely satisfying world. Our separation from the rest of the natural world leaves us with a subconscious feeling that we must retain some contact with wilderness and with as wide a range of living things as possible. The national parks contribute a value that transcends economic considerations and may play a role similar to that of Stonehenge, the pyramids, Greek temples, Roman ruins, Gothic cathedrals, the Williamsburg restoration, Gettysburg battlefield, or the holy sites of various religions.

Ian McMillan, a California naturalist, has written of the struggle to save the California condor: "The real importance of saving such things as condors is not so much that we need condors as that we need to save them. We need to exercise and develop the human attributes required in saving condors; for these are the attributes so necessary in working out our own survival."[18] Conservation is based on human value systems; its deepest significance is in the human situation and the human heart. Saving marshlands and redwoods does not need biological justification any more than does opposing callousness and vandalism.[19] The cult of wilderness is not a luxury; it is a necessity for the protection of humanized nature and for the preservation of mental health.

Francis of Assisi preached and practiced absolute identification with nature, but even his immediate followers soon abandoned his romantic and unworldly attitude. They probably realized that man has never been purely a worshiper of nature or a passive witness of his surroundings and natural events. Human life was naturally close to nature during the Stone Age, but Paleolithic hunters and Neolithic farmers altered their environment. By controlling and using fire, domesticating animals and plants, clearing forests and cultivating crops, they began the process which eventually humanized a large percentage of the earth. Every form of civilization, each in its own way, has since contributed to the shaping of the earth's surface and thus altered the composition of the atmosphere and the waters. Even persons who thought they were returning to the ways of nature usually transformed their environment more than they knew. "Sometimes as I drift idly along Walden Pond, I cease to live and I begin to be," Thoreau wrote in his *Journal.* But he used a canoe to drift on the pond and he cleared an area along its shore to grow beans and construct his cabin.

Thus, human life inevitably implies changes in nature.

Indeed, man shapes his humanness in the very process of interacting constructively with the world around him and molding nature to make it better suited to his needs, wishes, and aspirations. Stonehenge, Angkor Wat, the Parthenon, the Buddhist temples, and the countless other places of worship created by man before the Judeo-Christian era represent forms of human intervention which exacted as large a toll from nature as did the construction of the Judeo-Christian shrines or the immense American bridges and industrial plants.

Christianity acknowledged early that human beings differ in their spiritual needs and aspirations; each of its important saints symbolizes a different approach to the human problem. In the article quoted earlier, Lynn White, Jr., suggests that Saint Francis's example can help mankind to achieve an harmonious equality with the rest of creation, as if animals, plants, and even inanimate objects were really our brothers and sisters. This doctrine is not quite congenial to me, because I like gardening and landscaping and therefore tend to impose my own sense of order upon natural processes.

Benedict of Nursia, who was certainly as good a Christian as Francis of Assisi, can be regarded as a patron saint of those who believe that true conservation means not only protecting nature against human misbehavior but also developing human activities which favor a creative, harmonious relationship between man and nature.

When Saint Benedict established his monastery on Monte Cassino during the sixth century, his primary concern was that he and his followers should devote their lives to divine worship. However, though he was an aristocrat, he knew the dangers of physical idleness, and he made it a rule that all monks should work with their hands in the fields and in shops. As a result, the Benedictine monks achieved an intimate relationship with the world around them. One of the still dominant aspects of the Benedictine rule is that to labor is to pray. Saint Benedict had not intended his monks to become scholars. But in the course of time a great tradition of learning and of artistic skills progressively developed in the Benedictine abbeys, along with the continuation of some physical work.

Lynn White, Jr., the very historian who has advocated that ecologists take Saint Francis as their patron saint, has also emphasized the social importance of the fact that "the Benedictine monk was the first scholar to get dirt under his fingernails."[20] For the first time in the history of human institutions, the Benedictine abbey created a way of life in which practical and theoretical skills could be embodied in the same person. This new atmosphere proved of enormous importance for the development of European technology and science. The Benedictine abbeys did not immediately launch into scientific investigations, but by encouraging the combination of physical and intellectual work they destroyed the old artificial barrier between the empirical and the speculative, the manual and the liberal arts. This created an atmosphere favorable for the development of knowledge based on experimentation.

The first chapter of Genesis speaks of man's dominion over nature. The Benedictine rule in contrast seems inspired rather from the second chapter, in which the Good Lord placed man in the Garden of Eden not as a master but rather in a spirit of stewardship. Throughout the history of the Benedictine order, its monks have actively intervened in nature—as farmers, builders, and scholars. They have brought about profound transformations of soil, water, fauna, and flora, but in such a wise manner that their management of nature has proved compatible in most cases with the maintenance of environmental quality. To this extent, Saint Benedict is much more relevant than Saint Francis to human life in the modern world, and to the human condition in general.

The Benedictine rule was so successful during the early Middle Ages that its monasteries burgeoned over Europe, and their numbers reached many thousands. They differed somewhat in their interpretation of the rule, but all were organized along similar religious and social patterns. All the Benedictine monks and nuns accepted the cloistered life and regarded manual labor not as a regrettable necessity but as an essential part of spiritual discipline. They practiced a democratic administrative system of home rule and tried to achieve a living relationship with the physical world around them. The monastic rule was so broadly human that it permitted different attitudes toward nature and man. For example, while the original Benedictines generally settled on the hills, the monks of the Cistercian branch preferred the valleys. This topographical variation in the location of the monasteries proved to be of great economic and technological significance because it broadened the influence of the Benedictines in the development of Europe.

The Cistercians played a social role of particular importance precisely in this regard, because they established their monasteries in wooded river valleys and marshy lands which were infested with malaria and therefore ill suited to human occupation. With their lay helpers, they cleared the forests and drained the swamps, thus creating, out of the malarious wilderness, farmlands that became healthy and prosperous. They achieved such great fame in the control of malaria by eliminating the swamps that they were entrusted with the task of draining the Roman Campagna.

Cistercian life was of course not motivated by the desire to create agricultural lands. A mystic attitude toward nature certainly played a role in their selection of secluded places for the worship of God. Saint Bernard was sensitive to the poetic quality of the site when he chose to establish his Cistercian monastery in Clairvaux:

> That spot has much charm, it greatly soothes weary minds, relieves anxieties and cares, helps souls who seek the Lord greatly to devotion, and recalls to them the thought of the heavenly sweetness to which they aspire. The smiling countenance of the earth is painted with varying colours, the blooming verdure of spring satisfies the eyes, and its sweet odour salutes the nostrils. . . . While I am charmed without by the sweet influence of the beauty of the country, I have not less delight within in reflecting on the mysteries which are hidden beneath it.[21]

Saint Bernard believed that it was the duty of the monks to work as partners of God in improving his creation or at least in giving it a more human expression. Implicit in his writings is the thought that labor is like a prayer which helps in recreating paradise out of chaotic wilderness.[22]

While the primary commitment of the monks was to divine worship, they devoted much effort and inventiveness to practical problems:

> Cistercian monks were so devoted to the Virgin that everyone of their hundreds of monasteries was dedicated to her; yet these White Benedictines seem often to have led the way in the use of power. Some of their abbeys had four or five water wheels, each powering a different workshop.[23]

All types of Benedictine monasteries, in fact, were involved in technological activities. The monks developed windmills and especially watermills as sources of power on their holdings. This power was used for the conversion of their agricultural products into manufactured goods—leather, fabrics, paper, and even liqueurs such as Benedictine and Chartreuse, which achieved world-wide fame. Thus these medieval monasteries prepared the ground for the technological era in Europe.

When practiced in the true spirit of the Benedictine rule, monastic life helped the monks to establish close contact with the natural world through the daily and seasonal rituals and works which were coordinated with cosmic rhythms. The Benedictine rule also inspired a type of communal organization which was both democratic and hierarchic, because each monk or nun had rights in the monastic organization but also had to accept a certain place in the social order. This complex social structure found its expression in an architectural style beautifully adapted to the rituals of monastic life and to the local landscape. Benedictine architecture, in its several variant forms, thus achieved a functional beauty which made it a major artistic achievement of Western civilization.[24]

Many human interventions into natural systems have been destructive. Technological man in particular uses landscapes and water, mountains and estuaries, and all types of natural resources for selfish and short-range economic benefits. But his behavior in this regard is not much worse than that of the people whose activities caused erosion in West Pakistan, in the Mediterranean basin, in China, or in Mexico. The solution to the environmental crisis will not be found in a retreat from the Judeo-Christian tradition or from technological civilization. Rather it will require a new definition of progress, based on better knowledge of nature and on a willingness to change our ways of life accordingly. We must learn to recognize the limitations and potentialities of each particular area of the earth, so that we can manipulate it creatively, thereby enhancing present and future human life.

Conservation, according to Leopold, teaches what a land can be, what it should be, what it *ought* to be. Although this aphorism has much appeal, it is misleading because it implies a questionable philosophy of ecological determinism and of man's relation to nature. It assumes that some invisible hand is guiding biological processes to the one perfect state of ecological harmony among the different components of a particular environment, whereas experience shows that different satisfactory ecosystems can be created out of the same set of environmental conditions. The aphorism seems to suggest, moreover, that man should not interfere with the natural course of ecological events, a view which does not square with the existence all over the world of successful parks, gardens, agricultural fields, and managed forests.

Francis of Assisi's loving and contemplative reverence in the face of nature survives today in the awareness of man's kinship to all other living things and in the conservation movement. But reverence is not enough, because man has never been a passive witness of nature. He changes the environment by his very presence and his only options in his dealings with the earth are to be destructive or constructive. To be creative, man must relate to nature with his senses as much as with his common sense, with his heart as much as with knowledge. He must read the book of external nature and the book of his own nature, to discern the common patterns and harmonies.

Repeatedly in the past and under a great variety of religious traditions and social systems, man has created from wilderness new environments which have proven ecologically viable and culturally desirable. Because of my own cultural tradition, I have chosen to illustrate this creativeness by the

Benedictine way of life—its wisdom in managing the land, in fitting architecture to worship and landscape, in adapting rituals and work to the cosmic rhythms. An Australian aborigine, a Navajo Indian, a Buddhist, or a Moslem would have selected other examples, taken from their respective traditions, but the fundamental theme is universal because it deals with man's unique place in the cosmos. Human life implies choices as to the best way to govern natural systems and to create new environments out of wilderness. Reverence for nature is compatible with willingness to accept responsibility for a creative stewardship of the earth.

CHAPTER 9

Fitness, Change, and Design

Before the arrival of the white man, the life of the various American Indian tribes was organized around local resources. The culture of the Plains tribes was dependent on the huge herds of buffalo, that of the Pacific Northwest tribes on the abundance of fish and timber. Writing in the middle of the eighteenth century, the Swedish explorer and naturalist Peter Kalm gave in *Travels in North America* a lively picture of Indian life around Lake Champlain:

> We often saw Indians in bark boats close to the shore, which was, however, not inhabited, for the Indians came here only to catch sturgeons wherewith this lake abounds and which we often saw leaping up into the air. These Indians lead a very singular life. At one time of the year they live on the small store of corn, beans, and melons which they have planted; during another period, or about this time, their food is fish, without bread or any other meat; and another season they eat nothing but game such as stags, roes, beavers, etc., which they shoot in the woods and rivers. They, however, enjoy long life, perfect health,

> and are more able to undergo hardships than other people. They sing and dance, are joyful and always content, and would not for a great deal exchange their manner of life for that which is preferred in Europe.[1]

During the period when the Vermont Indians observed by Peter Kalm were still dependent on a gathering and hunting economy, there were Europeans who could devote their whole life to cultural occupations. The English clergyman Gilbert White, for example, spent fifty years observing and recording the animal and plant life in the parish of Selborne, Hampshire, where he had been born in 1720. His letters, grouped in *The Natural History of Selborne*, describe a seemingly unchanging natural and social scene and give the impression of perfect fitness of man to civilized nature in eighteenth-century England.[2] Samuel Johnson was a contemporary of Gilbert White but unlike him had no desire to settle away from London. His idea of perfect happiness was "driving briskly in a post-chaise with a pretty woman." The eighteenth-century lives of Peter Kalm's Lake Champlain Indians, of Gilbert White, and of Samuel Johnson thus symbolize widely different types of relationships between man and environment, each with its distinctive interpretation of fitness.

Fitness, however, is always ephemeral. The Indians no longer fish for sturgeon from bark canoes. The English countryside began to change during Gilbert White's own lifetime as a result of the agricultural revolution and the enclosure of land. A modern Samuel Johnson would be more likely to be immobilized in traffic than to be driving briskly.

The changes in appearance of human settlements from one period to another illustrate that fitness between ways of life and the external world is never perfect and at best transient.

The old parts of ancient villages and towns usually seem tightly woven into the countryside. In many cases, they fit snugly in a hollow or on top of the hills; the church appears deliberately framed by noble trees either at the summit or on a gentle rise; the houses are built of native stone in a suitable local style and are sensibly arranged as if to form an organic whole; the old community is contained in a natural way, perhaps by a stream on one side and by slopes on the other; the gardens lead into agricultural fields which progressively merge with open country or forest. Each one of us can think of such a village or town as the symbol of fitness between human habitations, sites of activity, and nature. Such fitness, however, was achieved at a time when the life of the village or town depended on subsistence farming and local commerce. It is related to past conditions and therefore cannot endure. Whatever the efforts made to preserve human settlements in their present forms, villages, towns, fields, and roads will inevitably be transformed because the ways of life change continuously. Buildings, agricultural and industrial equipment, channels of communication must keep in step with changes in styles of commerce, of industry, of farming, and even of leisure. What is often regarded as natural in human settlements constitutes in reality the expressions of particular ways of life at particular times.

Since most landscapes have been shaped by man, they too can change profoundly and rapidly under the influence of human interventions. An especially drastic alteration of the English landscape occurred in a short time at the beginning of the eighteenth century, as a result of the Enclosure Act.[3] In order to facilitate the introduction of certain types of agricultural improvements, the Enclosure Commissioners, operating under the authority of acts of Parliament, imposed a square grid of fields on the countryside almost without regard to the natural layout and characteristics of the land. The farming country was thus converted into a patchwork of semirectangular fields, each five to ten acres in area, divided by ditches and straight lines of hawthorn hedges, with trees growing through the fields in regular rows. This specialized landscape, which is now endowed with so much history, and celebrated by so much literature, is commonly regarded as typical of the English Midlands. But it is a very artificial human creation, carried out for the sake of agricultural efficiency against much popular objection.

When this ruthless reshaping of the English countryside began more than two hundred years ago, the results were at first unattractive, especially because hedges and trees had to be started from small seedlings. Violent opposition to the enclosure policy came not only from the poor people whose life it disorganized but also from nature lovers. "Disgusting" was the word commonly used by connoisseurs of scenery to qualify the new regimented landscape. Even considerably later, the famous landscape architect Humphrey Repton (1752–1818) condemned the hedges because, according to him, they destroyed "the union of hill and valley."[4] As time went on, however, the hedges and trees grew in size and grace. The mature landscape, now rich in songbirds and other wildlife, became *the* English landscape. Even those Englishmen who know that the cut-up landscape is the artificial consequence of the Enclosure Act are as anxious to preserve it in its present form as their ancestors were to keep the older countryside it replaced.

Public policies in England are now changing again. The hedges, ditches, and trees must go because they are incompatible with modern agricultural techniques. The traditional "fields," as they are called in the Enclosure terminology, are being rapidly regrouped to create much larger tracts of land suitable to high-powered agricultural equipment. The very word "field" is thus reacquiring its original Anglo-Saxon meaning, which is not hedged enclosure but open space.

The new trend is of course destroying the habitats of many wild plants and animals; as everywhere else in the world, modern agricultural practices cause the disappearance of song birds. Nature lovers and ecologists are trying to save as many hedges, ditches, and trees as possible; furthermore, they hasten to study the fields about to be destroyed and treat them as archaeological relics. But lamentation is not universal. Certain connoisseurs of scenery are beginning to realize that the new agricultural system is giving to the landscape of southern and eastern England a quality of openness which permits large sweeps of vision. Man is thus creating a new kind of scenery for the Midlands of England, and a similar situation is developing in the northwest of France.[5]

If Samuel Johnson were living today and wanted to drive briskly in the company of a pretty woman, it would be in a fast motor car rather than in a chaise, on a smooth parkway rather than on a country lane. The curves and slopes of roads, and the trees, bushes, signs, and even billboards that line them must be designed to fit the speed of the vehicle and the physiological responses of the traveler. Flowers, hedges, grassy surfaces, and winding lanes are pleasing at low speed, but at 60 miles an hour they blur and can become a nuisance or even a danger. Flowers can be appreciated by a stroller, the bubbling of a brook can be perceived from a horse-drawn carriage, but the best landscape for fast automobile travel is a spacious, uncluttered expanse. While speed makes new demands of accommodation on the body and especially on the eyes, it also enhances the perception of the large anatomical features of the terrain. There was fitness between slow-motion vehicles and the cozy, delicately etched countryside of pre-industrial days, but automobile and air travel is better adapted to the immense vistas of the open land which has been made necessary by modern agricultural equipment.

In its large sense, fitness denotes fine adjustments among the various components of a system. In practice, however, it is rarely possible to study a system as a whole. I shall consider separately the environment's fitness for man and man's fitness to his environment, even though this is an artificial distinction, since both aspects of the problem are expressions of the same system.

The fitness of the environment for man involves unpolluted air, food, and water; good sanitation, elbow room, and satisfactory human contacts—in brief, the environmental conditions essential for physical and mental health. Indirectly, fitness for man involves also the subjective factors mentioned earlier as perceptual and conceptual environments. Finally, environmental health implies that the environment remains in a desirable ecological state for a long period of time. The very use of the adjective desirable points to the anthropomorphic attitude inherent in the human approach to environmental problems. Ecologic purists notwithstanding, all ecology is anthropomorphic in the final analysis. When the professional ecologist laments the fact that modern life transforms urban areas into environments which are suitable only for rats, roaches, or ragweed, he obviously judges the situation from man's point of view, not from that of rats, roaches, or ragweed. Man cannot discuss environmental fitness without introducing judgments of values. Except in the case of absolute wilderness, the earth's surface has been transformed for the sake of human ends and the process will continue. The problem is not whether man will or will not alter natural systems, but rather how he will do it. Since man is now a component of practically all ecological systems on earth, sound ecological management implies the kind of long-range views that will make it possible to maintain nature in a humanized condition suitable for the generations to come.

For man, as for animals, plants, and microbes, biological fitness is achieved in part through the genetic changes that occur in the course of Darwinian evolution. In human life, however, these changes are effective only in the very long run and for this reason are now of limited importance. Under usual conditions a person's fitness depends chiefly upon the adaptive responses he makes during his own lifetime to the forces of his total environment, which includes the natural world, the man-made world, and his perceptual and conceptual world. Fitness, so understood, can be achieved despite poverty and physical hardship, as illustrated by the excellent biological, mental, and cultural health of certain primitive people. But their fitness persists only as long as they remain isolated and hold on to their traditional culture. For example, the populations of American Indians, Polynesians, and Eskimos were decimated shortly after being exposed to the white man's diseases, ways of life, and social patterns.

The adaptive failures of a few primitive populations have provided history with some of its most spectacular tragedies, but the more common situation has been the adaptive success of mankind. The emergence of modern man during the upheavals of the Ice Age symbolizes the prodigious adaptability of *Homo sapiens.* This adaptability, which is still evident today, has enabled mankind to spread over all the earth, and it now enables all kinds of people to function successfully under all possible climatic and social conditions. The white man prospers in northern Scandinavia and in tropical Africa; the black man is gaining his place in all climatic regions of the United States; the yellow man runs successful businesses in every large city of the world; a Buddhist Burmese can be a monk in a Bangkok temple or Secretary General of the United Nations in New York.

Even though food production and consumption are among the most stable elements of a culture, man's adaptability extends to his nutritional habits. It is true that when a family emigrates, its members readily change lodging, clothing, and even language, but the kinds of food they eat, the way they prepare the meals, and the psychological nourishment they derive from these are usually the last links with the pre-migration style of life. Yet even national foods and eating habits do change. An Italian menu offers spaghetti and tomato sauce but neither is of Italian origin. The use of spaghetti was introduced into Venice in the fourteenth century by Marco Polo, who had become familiar with it at the court of the Great Khan in China. Tomatoes were introduced into Europe from Central America in the seventeenth century; they were then known in England and France as "love apples" because of their alleged aphrodisiac virtues, an idea which delayed their acceptance at the family table. Today tomatoes are considered indispensable because of their vitamin content. The ubiquitous corn and potato also are of American origin, as are many of the vegetables most highly prized all over the world. Rice has a complicated history; it reached China from India only two thousand years ago and Japan eight hundred years later. The fundamental grain of the Sumerian, Babylonian, Assyrian, and Egyptian civilizations was barley which was the main ingredient for making both bread and beer during early times. Wheat spread through the world from the Ethiopian highlands. Wine from the European grapes became one of the most widely accepted products of Western civilization.

Food habits remain markedly different from one national or social group to another because they are conditioned by early life, climate, and culture. They illustrate the fact that fitness involves not only physicochemical forces and ordinary biological processes, but also, and especially, cultural influences.

The cultural adaptability of human beings regardless of origin or color is made obvious by the population mixture in all the great cities of the world. Despite the prejudices resulting from the accidents of birth and education, almost any man can achieve fitness to almost any country; home is determined by birth, not by the color of skin, eyes, or hair. The people of Caucasian origin who have become Greek or German, Spanish or English, Sicilian or French, Mexican or North American differ in language, behavior, and biological characteristics, not because of genetic constitution but only because they have responded adaptively to their respective national environments. Black people originating from the Senegal or Sierra Leone are different in Paris from what they are in New York. Within a few generations the inhabitants of Chinatowns anywhere in America are likely to become conventional citizens and to raise oversized and alienated children. Changes can indeed occur so rapidly that they are detectable within one generation. The Jews born in the kibbutzim of Israel differ from their parents who had lived in the ghettos of Eastern Europe, and so do the young Japanese of today from their counterparts before the Second World War.[6] Man, in other words, is so adaptable that he can live anywhere on earth, but this adaptability is responsible for many of his present problems.

Except for the early part of the Neolithic era, which seems to have been placid, the history of mankind is a continuous record of wars, revolutions, famines, epidemics, and perennial conflict between families, social groups, and generations. The variety and violence of the struggles which occurred during the Pax Romana and the Pax Britannica suggest that peace and quiet are not of this world even under the best conditions.

There is reassurance, however, in the fact that all periods seem unique in the rate and depth of change to those experiencing them. The French humanist Louis Le Roy in the sixteenth century,[7] the English naturalist Alfred Russel Wallace in the nineteenth century,[8] and countless historians, philosophers, and plain people before and after them were convinced that they were witnessing technological and social changes of such magnitude that mankind would have to change or to die. Each generation has its own brand of "future shock."[9] Events have so often appeared apocalyptic that the end of the world has been forecast on many dates—all now safely in the past. Learned and sophisticated as we imagine ourselves to be, we nevertheless find it difficult to realize that the worlds we have lost were never quite as bad or as good as historians describe them. We do not even dare hope that the future will be better than we fear.

Perfect fitness, like perfect health, is a mirage, or at best a utopian dream which serves the useful purpose of encouraging us to work for better ways of life and better environments. My moderate optimism comes perhaps from my belief that, as Marcel Proust recognized, *les seuls vrais paradis sont les paradis qu'on a perdus* (the only true paradises are the paradises that we have lost). Like the hero of Alain-Fournier's novel *The Wanderer*, we spend our lives trying to recapture and substantiate a vision much richer in our memories than it was in reality. Wonderful fantasies take form in our minds or in society's collective consciousness. In the end, however, most people prudently but sadly bank the fires of youth and then try, like Voltaire's Candide, to find satisfaction in tending a small garden.

Many ancient settlements derive their charm from their fitness to natural surroundings; adobe houses look comfortably cool in the dry heat of the Southwest; high-pitched roofs look reassuring under the snows of the Northeast. But fitness has more subtle and more compelling cultural determinants. All successful forms of housing, farming, and landscaping are the outward manifestations of an underlying social philosophy; they express the habits, tastes, and aspirations of the people who created them. The modern factory conveys precision and efficiency, but the traditional family farm also had its genius. Each of its parts contributed to an independent existence under certain climatic conditions on a certain kind of land. Whether planning is conscious or subconscious, on a large or a small scale, a human settlement will achieve fitness only if it symbolizes a way of life, an institution, or an ideal—in other words, if it gives a true structural expression to fundamental needs.

Fitness of man to his environment and of the environment for man implies that neither man nor environment will deviate far from a position of equilibrium. There has to be some stability in the interrelationships between the components of the system under consideration. But in reality all living systems are irreversibly changed by almost any kind of experience; this is the reason why you cannot go home again. While it is true that human settlements like human beings retain their identity, they are modified irreversibly by almost any kind of life experience. Some of the modifications, however, are so slow that they are overlooked even by experienced observers. The historian Arnold Toynbee referred to the Polynesian civilizations as "arrested civilizations" because he believed that their isolation had protected them from outside influences and made them unchangeable. But Hawaiians do not take kindly to this theory. Social evolution had been going on continuously in the isolated Pacific islands before Captain James Cook and Louis Antoine de Bougainville introduced European influences in the eighteenth century.

The ability to evolve is fundamental for the continued existence of all human settlements. In the past, fitness between man and his total environment developed spontaneously and progressively in the course of everyday life, through the continuous self-correcting agency of feedback processes. The achievement of fitness is now more difficult, because the acceleration of technological and social change has not been accompanied by corresponding developments in the mechanisms for ecological and social adaptation. When the rate of change is as rapid as it is in technological societies today, there is not enough time for the achievement of fitness through spontaneous adaptive processes.

William James remarked a century ago, "Tight fit is what shapes things definitively; with a loose fit you get no results, and America is redolent of loose fits everywhere."[10] In William James's time, lack of fitness in American life was due in part to massive and uninterrupted waves of immigration; many persons living in the United States had not had the opportunity, the time, or the desire to become identified with the distinctive characteristics of their new country. At the same time, American technology was developing so rapidly that the adaptive processes could not possibly keep pace with the rate of change. To a certain extent, this is still truer in the United States than in the rest of the world, but everywhere fitness is losing ground to technological and social change.

In ancient settlements the fitness of cultural forms to natural surroundings was slowly achieved over many centuries through mechanisms which have little chance of operating now. At the beginning the choices that were made and the courses of action that were taken were largely empirical and almost subconscious, because purposes were not clearly defined. The goal to be reached was vague; in most cases, indeed, there was no conscious goal. The desire inherited from the past for a certain form of worship, the biological urge for some form of collective life, and always the search for comfort and safety evoked responses which were at first unconscious rather than cerebral, but which initiated large cultural movements. The great monastic orders, for example, were started by a variety of obscure forces which led the black-robed Benedictines to build their monasteries on the hills, the white-robed Cistercians in the valleys, the Dominicans to feel more at home in the towns, the Jesuits to operate by preference in cities. Other kinds of forces made the English develop a deep appreciation of animals and plants for their own sake, whereas the French early displayed an urge to use animals and plants in formal designs. And Americans, who have cluttered their continent with huge urban agglomerations, continue to extol the virtues of wilderness and pastoral environments and to depreciate city life.

Most cultural patterns probably have their origins in the fact that a slight bias in attitudes, forms, and techniques started almost by accident a collective process moving in a certain direction. As time went on, this bias progressively became more conscious and more strongly expressed, evolving eventually into standards of belief, behavior, and taste which helped to define social philosophies and goals.

The high degree of fitness achieved by the early creators of tools, of social structures, or of architectural forms was thus probably due, not to their gifts for design or to their vision of goals, but rather to the very process of building in which they were practically engaged. Early form-builders had the additional advantage that the situations with which they first had to deal were fairly simple. This made it relatively easy for them to create forms that fitted well. The shaping of a spade or a hammer must have involved at first the feelings of the body for the tool as much as the clear vision of a practical need. For a while tradition and the directness of the responses to new needs maintained the fit as culture evolved.

The distinctive kinds of dwellings and roofs that were so characteristic of each climatic and topographical region before the development of standardized building practices thus emerged from direct responses to environmental demands. One of the charms of travel in old countries is that their buildings and roofs through their fitness to local conditions still vividly express the spirit of the place. In most parts of the world, farmers have thus created through unconscious processes a variety of environments with a high degree of fitness simply because their buildings and implements had to be related to environmental conditions.[11] This is the reason that, as mentioned in Chapter 6, the kind of landscape created long ago by a given society becomes its most enduring memorial, as are the medieval farmlands of Europe, the rice paddies of Asia, or the fields bounded by dry-stone walls in New England.

Since technological and social innovations are now so rapid and numerous that fitness can no longer be achieved through spontaneous adaptive processes, conscious design must preside over change.

In social design, attention must naturally be given to factors affecting physical and mental health. There is no difficulty in recognizing and evaluating environmental influences which have direct and immediate effects on health, such as poisons, obvious malnutrition, acute infectious diseases. But the problem is far more difficult and in many cases more important when the effects on health are indirect and delayed, such as those due to pollution, noise, or crowding. A further complication comes from the fact that most human beings remain unaware of conditions which are not sufficiently bad to be profoundly disturbing, yet are potentially dangerous in the long run. Some early observations by the illustrious French microbiologist Louis Pasteur (1822–1895) are worth mentioning here, because they illustrate that the health effects of the environment depend not only on its physical characteristics but also on the changes it elicits in our biological and mental nature.

During the academic years 1864 to 1867, Pasteur was invited by the Ecole des Beaux Arts in Paris to give a course on the application of physics and chemistry to the fine arts. He did not publish his course, but fragments of the notes he used for teaching were discovered in his files after his death.[12] These fragments deal chiefly with the scientific aspects of oil painting—its origin and evolution, the chemical nature and reactions of pigments, the effects of different oils and fixatives on the stability of colors and of painted surfaces. The sections of Pasteur's course which are relevant here, however, are those in which he discussed the design and construction of buildings. In his first lecture he stated that architects, rather than painters or sculptors, would probably be the ones to derive the greatest benefit from his scientific teachings.

Pasteur introduced his argument by pointing out that human beings crowded in a poorly ventilated room usually fail to notice that the quality of the air they breathe deteriorates progressively; they are unaware of this deterioration because the change takes place by imperceptible steps and does not significantly affect their activities.

In order to illustrate the dangers inherent in the progressive acquisition of tolerance to an objectionable environment, Pasteur placed a bird in a closed container and allowed it to remain in the confined atmosphere for several hours. The bird became rather inactive but survived. In contrast, when another bird of the same species was introduced into the cage where the first bird had survived, it immediately died—of asphyxiation, Pasteur believed. The precise interpretation of this experiment is probably more complex than Pasteur thought. But he was nevertheless right in concluding that men, like animals, tend to make progressive adjustments to objectionable and even dangerous conditions, when these develop slowly without giving clear signs of the dangers they entail for biological or mental health. We are inclined to assert that man is immensely adaptable, but all too often such adaptation has to be paid for later by organic and mental disease. Pasteur's experiment illustrates, moreover, that sudden changes from one environment to another are more likely to have dramatic consequences than are progressive changes.

Fitness of the organism to the environment is thus conditioned not only by the characteristics of both components of the system, but also by the rates at which these characteristics change. As Hippocrates wrote in his treatise on "Humours," twenty-five hundred years ago, "It is changes that are chiefly responsible for diseases, especially the greatest changes, the violent alterations both in the seasons and in other things. But seasons which come on gradually are the safest, as are the gradual changes of regimen and temperature, and gradual changes from one period of life to another."[13]

Environmental design should go beyond concern with the avoidance of disease, pain, and effort. It should aim at creating conditions favorable for the development of man's anatomical and physiological potentialities. It should also take into consideration the cosmic rhythms which are inextricably woven into man's biological fabric and that condition even his mental processes. For this reason, environmental control, including air conditioning, should incorporate the kind of daily and seasonal fluctuations necessary for optimum biological and mental performance.

Ideally, environmental and social design should also take into account the irrational or suprarational components of human behavior. The sanity of technological man still depends upon the satisfaction of the urges which he inherited from his Stone Age past. Primitive hunters moved among streams and rocks, trees and grass, and were always close to both tame and wild animals. They engaged in a variety of physical occupations which were dangerous but which sharpened their wits. They had to make decisions on their own rather than being programmed for a limited technical role, but on the other hand their choices and movements had to be subordinated to the activities of their social group. One can take it for granted that biological and mental health demands environments providing both the biological freedom and the social subordination that created the human qualities of life during the Stone Age.

The need for direct participation in the affairs of the group is another aspect of human life that is universal probably because it has roots deep in the biological past. To a very large percentage of people, perhaps to all, this need is more intense than the thirst for knowledge or respect for pure reason. Man is a social animal in a deep biological sense. His life depends upon a hierarchical order that has similarities to that of other higher animals, wolves and primates, for example. The popular appeal of movie stars, political leaders, and other idols of the public scene (what Francis Bacon called "the market place") may express the biological need for recognizing the special position of one particular member of the group in the social hierarchy. There is a continuous gradation from the pecking order among chickens to charisma among men.

The creative effects of environmental design on the development of the body and the mind have their biological basis in the fact that the determination of human characteristics is far from complete at birth. The various organs, including neural tissue, develop or atrophy depending upon the quantity and quality of the environmental stimuli they receive throughout life. Our perception and interpretation of reality is thus conditioned by the size, shape, and color of landscapes, buildings, and rooms.

It is a sad commentary on our civilization that when we speak of the environment it is usually in reference to its undesirable effects. The very word "environment" now evokes the nightmares of industrial and urban life: depletion of natural resources, accumulation of wastes, pollution in all its forms, noise, crowding, regimentation, the thousand devils of the ecologic crisis. Just as the Pilgrim fathers regarded nature around Provincetown Harbor as hideous and full of demons, we fear the world we have created. As a result we are chiefly concerned with the avoidance of dangers and the maintenance of a tolerable state, rather than with the creation of new, positive values through the development of environmental and human potentialities.

Thinking about the environment only in such negative terms is not likely to take us far toward the establishment of desirable living conditions. If we limit our efforts to the correction of environmental defects, we shall increasingly behave like hunted beasts taking shelter behind an endless succession of protective devices, each more complex and more costly, less dependable and less comfortable than its predecessors. Today we develop afterburners for automobiles to protect us from air pollution and complicated sewage treatments to purify grossly contaminated water; tomorrow we shall turn to gas masks and to filters on our water faucets. Although technological fixes have transient usefulness, they complicate life and eventually decrease its quality. The ecological crisis will continue to increase in severity if we do not develop positive values integrating human nature and external nature.

Positive values can sometimes be introduced from the outside. More generally, however, they are found in the intimate relationships between man and the world in which he lives. The Greco-Roman civilization emerged under the Mediterranean skies, and this is where it has remained most creative and true to itself. In contrast, as expressed by the English writer Herbert Read in *High Noon and Dark Night*, northern Europe has generated a different kind of culture which has emphasized inner preoccupations instead of the concrete and luminous realities of the Mediterranean world.[14]

Most persons find it difficult to think of man-nature relationships in abstract terms. This is probably the reason that ancient people personified each place with a deity representing the attributes which gave it uniqueness and thus determined its vocation. The Latin word *vocatio,* originally "a summons," later referred to the divine call to a certain kind of function. Similarly, each part of the earth has one or several vocations, determined by its nature. The dictionary definitions of "nature" are "the essential character or constitution of something," or "the intrinsic characteristics and qualities of a person or a thing." In this sense the word nature accounts for the genius or spirit of place; it denotes the forces hidden beneath the surface of reality as well as the geographic, social, and human appearances.

Certain places have a fairly simple nature and therefore a limited range of vocations; for example, there are probably marked limitations to the kind of places that can be created from deserts, arctic areas, and even tropical lands. In general, however, places, like persons, have several potential vocations, which man can help to make living realities.

Consider the transformations of the primeval forest in the temperate climates. In some parts of the world, it has been systematically cropped and managed, as is the case with the European forests which have been under state control for several centuries. In North America, much of the primeval forest was transformed into prairie as a result of the fires set by pre-agricultural Indians. The prairie vegetation generated one of the richest soils in the world; even now that it has been replaced by agricultural crops, it still remains imprinted on the American imagination. In Scotland and England, certain parts of the primeval forest were destroyed by lumbering and sheep grazing and progressively transformed into moors; these moors are not economically productive, but they have nevertheless enriched human life by their romantic quality. All over the world, immense areas of the temperate-zone forest have been converted into arable soils, each region developing its own individuality in agricultural production, social structure, and esthetic character. Farmlands created out of the forest thousands of years ago are now cultivated by scientific techniques and support a large variety of crops; they express as well as architectural monuments the genius of each particular region. The Amish farms in the United States demonstrate that the soil derived from the temperate forest can long be maintained in a healthy productive state even with a limited technology.

Man's transformations of the land from one ecological state to another have not all been successful. For the land as for man, any change is likely to be damaging if it occurs too rapidly. Changes have given desirable results chiefly in situations where they occurred slowly, over several generations, thus enabling adaptive processes of a biological and social nature to create a new, acceptable relationship between man and environment. The Gaels who have occupied the Scottish Highlands for thousands of years are still there; they have progressively developed new trades and ways of life as their land slowly changed from forests to moors.[15] In contrast, the immigrants who moved into the virgin forests of Wisconsin devastated the area in a short time through massive and hasty lumbering; then they moved on leaving only ghost towns and eroded land. Whereas an old culture tends to hang on to the place in which it evolved, even when the economy is decaying, most modern immigrants only want to exploit the resources of the land as rapidly as possible and as a consequence ruin its quality. As an immigrant, Andrew Carnegie devoted his genius and energy to achieving financial success in the United States, then he spent part of his fortune to protect and improve the Scottish village where he had spent his early years.

There are many types of desirable landscapes. Some derive their appeal from their majestic scale, their splendor, their mystery, or their uniqueness. The national parks in the United States provide varied examples of sceneries on which man could not improve. Likewise, the Polar regions, the ocean masses, the great tropical river valleys have distinctive characters that owe nothing to human intervention. In most parts of the world, on the other hand, man has created from wilderness new structures which have acquired a life of their own. The river settlements of the Ivory Coast, the Mediterranean hill towns, the pueblos of the Rio Grande, the village greens of New England, and the old cities organized along peaceful rivers throughout the world are as many different types of landscapes which derive their quality not so much from topographic or climatic peculiarities as from the intimate association between man and nature. Thus, the transformation of the land by man can be a creative act. Increasingly it will become the expression of conscious purpose based on value judgments but it will be successful and viable only if the conversion of potentialities into humanized realities takes into account the constraints resulting from the natural characteristics of the system. To "design with nature" is the most fundamental law of landscape design.[16]

The formal gardens of Italy and France did not just happen through the caprice of wealthy men or the genius of a few landscape architects. They were successful because they fitted in the physical, biological, and social atmosphere of Italy and France at the time of their creation. Formal gardens and parks also flourished in England, but the English school achieved its uniqueness by creating an entirely different kind of park, better suited to the local conditions. The great English parks of the seventeenth and eighteenth centuries are characterized by trees grouped in meadows and in vast expanses of lawn. This style was suited to the moist climate of the British Isles. In France, many attempts were made in the eighteenth century to create gardens and parks in the English style, but with little success. As the English writer Horace Walpole remarked in a letter giving an account of his visit to the continent: "They [the French] can never have as beautiful a landscape as ours, til they have as bad a climate."[17] Walpole's witticism expresses the biological truth that a landscape style can be lastingly successful only if it is compatible with the ecological imperatives of the country.

The personification of natural attributes as genius of place was a product of imagination during the archaic and classical periods. The eighteenth-century English poet Alexander Pope made this concept more concrete and specialized in his famous line "Consult the genius of the place in all."[18] By this he meant that local topography, climate, and resources determine the kind of landscape and architecture best suited to a particular region. "It is pointless to superimpose an abstract, man-made design on a region as though the canvas were blank. It isn't. Somebody has been there already. Thousands of years of rain and wind and tides have laid down a design. Here is our form and order. It is inherent in the land itself—in the pattern of the soil, the slopes, the woods,—above all, in the patterns of streams and rivers."[19] The eighteenth-century English landscape architect Lancelot "Capability" Brown earned his nickname by his skill in detecting the esthetic potentialities of each place. When surveying an estate, he was prone to exclaim, "This place has capabilities," but he knew also that each place has limitations. The landscape architect Ian McHarg's visionary book *Design with Nature* continues and extends this great tradition.

Just as the climate in most parts of France is not really compatible with the green magnificence of the English parks, so the atmosphere in many American cities is unsuited to certain types of plants. This does not mean that plant life is out of place in urban agglomerations, only that more effort should be made to identify and propagate for each particular city the kinds of trees, flowers, and groundcover that can best thrive under its set of climatic and other constraints. Ordinary grass looks so pathetic in most cities, and the rows of plane trees so monotonous, that botanists and foresters should be encouraged to discover or create other plants congenial to urban environments.

A new kind of ecological knowledge is needed, moreover, to predict the likely consequences of technological interventions and to develop rational guides as substitutes for the empirical adjustments that time used to make possible. But while such knowledge can provide a scientific basis for understanding and developing the genius of the place, it alone cannot create an environmental philosophy. All decisions concerning the environment involve matters of taste and therefore value judgments.

During the eighteenth century, as I mentioned earlier, tastes concerning landscape architecture were profoundly influenced by the artistic style of a few painters of the previous century. They used Italian scenery, each in his own way, to create an idealized picture of the pastoral ways of life, and this ideal rapidly found its way into the design of parks and gardens all over Europe, and especially in England. Nature and climate are far different in England from what they are in Italy. But the English landscape architects succeeded nevertheless in creating a new kind of scenery by introducing into the *genius loci* esthetic considerations derived from seventeenth-century painting. Their success demonstrates that man's interventions into nature generate new values by giving form to potentialities that had remained hidden or unexpressed.

In the final analysis, the role of design is to create from the potentialities of nature desirable patterns which express purposes based on value judgments. Purposes eventually become embodied in institutions. Originally, the word institution did not refer to buildings, administrative structures, and other mechanisms of the work-a-day world. Rather it expressed a commitment binding diverse activities focused on a mutual concern; it denoted a concerted effort to create a coherent whole out of the multiple efforts devoted to this concern. Institutions, so understood, have provided the intangible state of grace that has inspired all great social and architectural achievements.

To be successful, the design which gives form to an institution must express a well-defined social role or life style—whether it be respect for authority as symbolized in palaces or public buildings, religious worship as in churches or monasteries, need for communication as in railroad or air terminals, love of nature as in parks or gardens. Values must come first and must preside over design because they provide the architectonic principles which give esthetic quality and spiritual coherence to the physical structure embodying the social purpose of institutions.

CHAPTER 10

A Demon Within

At the time I was writing these pages, Sir Kenneth Clark's television program "Civilisation" was being shown in New York—an opportune reminder that human history is a record of ambitions, illusions, and frustrations, a sequence of rise and fall that we seem doomed to repeat. The human adventure since the Stone Age indicates that Civilization, with a capital C, has been a continuous and universal process, but it also leaves no doubt that all civilizations are mortal. The wistful mood of Sir Kenneth's program, and of his book on which it was based, seems to have been meant to convey his regrets for the worlds we have lost rather than any enthusiasm or even sympathy for the ongoing activities which are shaping our own civilization.

In the final section of the program, entitled "Heroic Materialism," Sir Kenneth dutifully showed the Manhattan skyline as a prodigious symbol of what modern technology can contribute to civilization, but he did it with little warmth. Even as he referred to New York with the felicitous expression "the celestial city," the tone of his voice made modern urban America appear more remote, less real, and far less human than the medieval towns, the Renaissance palaces, the baroque churches, or the Victorian households he had shown in the earlier sections of his program. The photographs of Manhattan, taken at the proper angle in the proper light, did indeed convey the exciting grandeur of a celestial city, but one without inhabitants, as if it were not meant for the living.[1]

The modern urban environment, it is true, hardly seems to be made for man. It is shaped and managed by experts who know a great deal about means but seem unconcerned with human aspirations. The Swiss architect Le Corbusier's *machines pour vivre*, as he called modern dwellings, encompass all the skills of technological civilization, but they are grossly deficient in the amenities that foster civilized life. The history of the word "civilization" helps to clarify this paradox.

The word seems to have appeared in print for the first time in an essay published by the Marquis de Mirabeau in 1757, under the title "L'Amy des Hommes ou Traité de la Population." Mirabeau used it also in another unpublished essay, "L'Amy des Femmes ou Traité de la Civilisation," in which he gave credit to women for most of the attitudes and achievements he regarded essential for civilized life. However, Mirabeau and the philosophers of the Enlightenment gave the word civilization a meaning far different from the one we give it now. For them, it referred to gentle ways of life, humane laws, limitations on war, a high level of purpose and conduct—in brief, all the qualities that in the eighteenth century were considered the highest expressions of mankind. As late as 1772, Samuel Johnson refused to enter the word in his dictionary, because he felt it did not express any concept that was not covered just as well by the older word "civility."[2]

Johnson would probably have felt even more justified in rejecting the word civilization if he had known that its meaning would be extended to include manifestations of human life as different as Greek rationalism and Venetian sensuality, German romanticism and the dark satanic mills of England, Jefferson's pastoralism and the automated life of the modern world.

A special view of civilized life emerged during the Industrial Revolution. Throughout the nineteenth century, new technological developments brought about an immense increase in economic wealth, first in Europe, then in the United States, and progressively in other parts of the world. But the success of industrial civilization soon came to be measured almost exclusively in quantities of food and manufactured articles produced, rather than in the quality of human relationships. For almost a century, this attitude appeared justified by the fact that even though technological advances did not contribute to civility, they made human life more comfortable, healthier, longer, and richer in experiences. The word civilization thus came to lose its eighteenth-century meaning and to signify what the American economist John Kenneth Galbraith designates in a telling and derisive expression, as "the affluent society."[3] In present parlance, a society is civilized when it is affluent enough to move its outhouses indoors, to do away with physical effort, to heat and cool its homes with electric power, and to own more automobiles, freezers, telephones, and gadgets for leisure time than it really needs or can enjoy. Gentle behavior, humane laws, limitations on war, a high level of purpose and conduct have disappeared from the concept.

Despite all the scorn one can legitimately level against the present form of technological civilization, the fact remains that its materialistic goals and uncoordinated efforts have produced works of esthetic magnificence. Each of the towers of the Manhattan skyline was erected, not as a contribution to a common purpose, but as an independent display of power and pride; yet together they constitute an exhilarating architectural symphony. The performance of the affluent society has thus demonstrated that the crudest human urges can accidentally result in great material achievements. Civilized life, however, requires more than the marvels of technological civilization. It flourishes best in environments suitable for the expression of civility and of human potentialities. In the modern world, such environments are not likely to emerge without conscious social planning.

Throughout history, social planning has been concerned much less with the welfare of human beings than with the maintenance and development of institutions—the word "institution" being used here in the sense outlined at the end of the preceding chapter. In the past, family, church, royalty, nobility, capitalism, the bourgeoisie, the proletariat have been among the institutions which have most influenced the course of civilization. Today it is chiefly nationalism and technology that influence man's fate and determine the distinctive characteristics of the twentieth century.

We live in an age of nationalism. The advocates of the United Nations have been much more successful in defining national identities than in fostering international cooperation. The names Biafra and Bangladesh are now widely known, not because of the geographical or cultural characteristics of these countries, but because of their struggles for national independence.

On the other hand, this age has also seen the triumph of international technology. The cosmopolitan architecture of the United Nations buildings and their location in the completely artificial setting of mid-Manhattan symbolize a kind of technological mastery—unrelated to natural local conditions—which every nation strives to achieve. International technology penetrates daily life all over the world, whether it be in the form of pick-up trucks, television sets, transistor radios or ball-point pens. The electric guitar and Buckminster Fuller's geodesic domes are just as popular in the hippie communes as in the square suburbs.

As many other institutions have done, nationalism and technology now evolve as if they had escaped from human control and acquired a life of their own. They seem to harbor capricious spirits, which give them a benevolent attitude at times but which behave more often as demonic forces. Most nationalities have emerged as a consequence of the efforts by a group of people to achieve cultural identity or social equality. All too often, however, this search for collective dignity has brought to the surface the kind of passion for power that is one of the most potent threats to freedom and to the unity of mankind.

The idealistic and the demonic forces in nationalism are as powerful today as they were in the past but their expressions are changing, because human history is moving from its hallowed parochial traditions to the era of global technology. While national cultures are still being shaped by conscious political design, their evolution is now influenced at least as much by international technological forces as by local cultural forces. The one credo of technology which has been accepted practically all over the world is that nature is to be regarded as a source of raw materials to be exploited for human ends rather than as an entity to be appreciated for its own value. Oriental civilizations give lip service to the holiness of nature, but in practice they cut down forests, erode the land, drill for coal, oil, and minerals, engage in monocultures, and pollute their environments at least as ruthlessly as do Western civilizations. Scientific technology does not recognize political or cultural frontiers; it constitutes at present the one force which, for good and for evil, has sufficient vitality to transcend nationalism.

The historical development of any particular technology

can usually be traced step by step, from the empirical, almost unconscious skills of artisans to the complex procedures based on esoteric scientific knowledge. It is easy to document the many intermediate steps that led from the digging stick of the Neolithic settler to the simple plow of the Egyptian peasant and the motorized equipment of the Midwestern farmer; from the crude oil lamps used in the Paleolithic caves to nineteenth-century gas illumination and modern fluorescent lights; from the individual hand loom to the spinning jenny of the Industrial Revolution and the completely automated weaving machines. It is also easy to recognize that, as each particular technology became more powerful, it exerted a greater and greater influence on human life and progressively altered the shape of civilizations. All technologies were created by man to act as his servants, but many of them are now beginning to act, if not as his master, at least as a molder of his destiny.

Technology as a social institution has a history which is almost unrelated to that of particular technologies. Its beginnings may have taken place in the bands of Stone Age men loosely organized for the collective hunt of large animals and in the large groups of workers regimented during the Late Stone Age and the Bronze Age for the execution of such colossal projects as clearing agricultural lands in the Fertile Crescent or building the Egyptian pyramids.[4] Technology took on some of its modern aspects in the precise regulations which governed worship, labor, and most other aspects of life in the monasteries during the early Middle Ages. Some of its worst aspects became apparent even before the Industrial Revolution in the European "manufactures"—meaning literally "making by hand"—in which hundreds of men, women, and children were subjected to a strict routine of work, without the help of machines. Eventually, technology emerged as a highly integrated social structure involving scientific, managerial, economic, and political forces interrelated in such a complex manner that men are no longer able to understand its intricacies or give it direction.

Technology could hardly have become so powerful, however, if man had not recognized a long time ago that certain types of organization would help him to reach his visionary goals. In *Reason Awake! Science for Man*, I discussed how ancient authors had imagined many achievements of our times —such as flying and space travel, synthetic drugs and the transmutation of elements, thought control and the ability to see and hear at great distances—long before these imaginings would be converted into reality, and indeed without any factual basis, either empirical or scientific.[5] Benjamin Franklin, matter-of-fact though he was, believed for example that human life would be "lengthened at pleasure even beyond the antediluvian standard," although there was nothing in the science of his day to justify this faith. On a famous occasion, he gave carte blanche to technology by replying to a lady of the French court who questioned the usefulness of the experiments with captive balloons which were then carried on in Paris. "But, Madam, what is the use of a newborn baby?"[6] The same kind of unsubstantiated faith in a future shaped by science led the Marquis de Condorcet in 1793 to write his *Sketch for a Historical Picture of the Progress of the Human Mind.* Despite the turmoil caused by the French Revolution and at a time when his own life was being threatened, Condorcet affirmed that science and technology would soon take care of all human problems.

Most of the scientific and technological dreams of mankind have come to pass. In fact the achievements of modern scientific technology greatly exceed the most visionary imaginings of Franklin, Condorcet, and the other philosophers of the Enlightenment. But the consequences of these achievements for society do not correspond to eighteenth-century hopes. Even under the most favorable conditions, the present ways of life do not necessarily result in better health and greater happiness—let alone provide the proper setting for civility. Something has gone wrong with technological civilization during the past hundred years.

A common explanation for the social failures of scientific technology is that, because of its very power and its sophistication, it is now beyond human understanding and control. In his short story, "The Machine Stops," the English writer E.M. Forster refers to technology as an independent force, "that moves on, but not on our lines; that proceeds, but not to our goals."[7] Comparing runaway technology with the tribulations of the sorcerer's apprentice is an obvious theme which has been much in favor among novelists, poets, and humanists; it has recently been developed also by such illustrious scientists as Max Born (1968), Norbert Wiener (1966) and Dennis Gabor (1971).[8]

Sociologists have particularly emphasized the difficulties arising from the countless ramifications of technology into all aspects of the social structure. In a paper entitled, "Counterintuitive Behavior of Social Systems" (1971), Jay W. Forrester, Professor of Computer Science at Massachusetts Institute of Technology, went as far as to claim that "the human mind is not adapted to interpreting how social systems behave. Our social systems belong to the class called multi-loop non-linear feedback systems. In the long history of evolution, it has not been necessary for man to understand these systems until very recent historical times. Evolutionary processes have not given us the mental skill needed to properly interpret the dynamic behavior of the systems of which we have now become a part."

The "multi-loop non-linear" systems become even more complex when they involve, as they almost always do, technological components. Since the human mind cannot cope with such complex situations, the only hope, according to Forrester, is to create "properly conceived computer models" of social situations.

> Computer models differ from mental models in important ways. The computer models are stated explicitly. The "mathematical" notation that is used for describing the model is unambiguous. It is a language that is clearer, simpler, and more precise than such spoken languages as English or French. Its advantage is in the clarity of meaning and the simplicity of the language syntax. The language of a computer model can be understood by almost anyone, regardless of educational background. Furthermore, any concept and relationship that can be clearly stated in ordinary language can be translated into computer model language.[9]

A new form of panic is being generated among the general public by the thought that the human mind cannot possibly apprehend the complexity of the interrelationships between the social structure and scientific technology. The widespread belief that technology is governed by a demon which is starting to model society to its own image is derived from the real fact that the technological mentality is now permeating all social institutions and modes of thought. Not only do we live in a technological civilization; biologically and mentally we are being shaped by technological forces.

The alarm over the possibility of a technological takeover of our own lives was made more vivid, plausible, and fashionable by the French philosopher Jacques Ellul in *La Technique ou L'Enjeu du Siècle*, first published in 1954 and translated into English as *The Technological Society.*[10] This book has made Ellul the spokesman of the antitechnological elite.

As used by Ellul the word *technique* does not refer to particular technologies. It implies rather a highly rational attitude in dealing with all human problems, social as well as technical. From the point of view of *technique*, efficiency is the ultimate criterion of success. For the sake of efficiency social institutions and customs must be continuously changed, and traditions must be rejected even though they are the expression of ancestral wisdom. *Technique* demands that life be regimented, mechanized, and automated to fit the efficiency of machines; it implies also a centralized, bureaucratic, soul-less way of dealing with people, because this contributes to the efficiency of social life. Ellul regards it as a *fait accompli* that modern societies have been taken over by anonymous technological forces which operate independently of human control and have truly become the most influential kinds of social institutions.

On the basis of social views somewhat different from Ellul's premises, John Kenneth Galbraith concludes, both in *The Affluent Society* and in *The New Industrial State*, that the modern technological society is an almost self-contained system. The system still depends on the public, but it secures acceptance of its products through an artificial demand created by advertising and government policies. In practice, it is accountable only to an essentially autonomous "technostructure" which determines its direction and is self-regenerating.[11] In Galbraith's technostructure as in Ellul's technique, the efficiency of the social system is more important than the individual life of the human person.

The pursuit of efficiency demands of technological societies that they make plans; the correct execution of these plans requires in turn that human affairs be conducted with time-clock punctuality. Technology, especially technique in Ellul's sense, implies the surrender of individual freedom to a gigantic multiheaded bureaucracy consisting of government, corporations, labor unions, and last but not least the school and university systems which are charged with preparing citizens for the regulated, predictable ways of life required for social efficiency.

In general, men become so well adapted to their technologic and bureaucratic environment that they acquire the attributes of technical and social machines. Their souls may still crave spontaneous creativity but this desire generates painful conflicts because increasing standardization is almost incompatible with the free expression of emotional and intellectual spontaneity.

The scientific and social complexities of the technological enterprise are certainly responsible in part for its runaway course and its unpredictable effects on mankind. But this may not be the most important aspect of the role played by technology in modern life. Even before social intricacies and scientific sophistication had made technology difficult to understand and control, man had elected to direct it on a course which is almost antihuman. Most of the dangerous aspects of technological civilization arise, not from its complexities, but from the fact that modern man has become more interested in the machines and industrial goods themselves than in their use to human ends. The destructive demon in scientific technology is man's own creation.

Social and technological developments which were at first unquestionably beneficial become dangerous only after they have been applied to wrong ends or allowed to expand beyond reasonable limits. Building roads at first increases the richness of human experience, but the highways of Southern California and Long Island destroy the countryside and impoverish human life. Mechanical equipment can eliminate the drudgery of existence, but snowmobiles spoil the purity and pristine quality of the snowscapes. We tend to use the word progress in its narrow etymological sense of "moving forward" even when it is obvious that the road on which we travel leads to boredom, physiological misery, and social disasters.

It is not easy to discover the precise period in which the formula of progress, which made technology one of the exciting aspects of civilization, began to be so distorted as to be destructive of human values. But there were clear warning signals as early as 1900. An indication can be found in the sense of despair which pervades the chapter entitled "The Dynamo and the Virgin," in *The Education of Henry Adams.*[12]

A visit to the Palais des Machines at the 1900 World's Fair in Paris convinced Adams that mechanical forces had begun to replace spiritual and emotional motivation in the governance of human affairs. As he visualized the future, steam and electric power would not only stimulate industry but also become the gods of a new religion. By increasing man's ability to manipulate nature, technology would change the quality of his relationships with life forces; the cult of the Dynamo would replace the cult of the Virgin. Perceptive as he was, Henry Adams had not grasped the extent to which technology had begun to dominate and alter human life even in his own times. The change becomes clear when one realizes the contrast between the World's Fair held by the city of Chicago in 1893 and that held in 1933.

The 1893 Chicago World's Fair was in the classical Beaux Arts tradition, without any reference to the new styles of industrial architecture and furniture then being created in the United States. Only the European visitors praised the functional beauty of the modern tools and household equipment on display, as the true expression of the American genius. Forty years later the organizers of the 1933 World's Fair had acquired the technology religion. Their primary purpose was to celebrate the "Century of Progress" which had elapsed since the founding of the city in 1833. They were so impressed by the role of scientific technology in the creation of wealth that they advocated a world in which machines would determine the shape of human life. As they stated in the guidebook of the Fair:

> Science discovers, genius invents, industry applies, and *man adapts himself to, or is molded by,* new things. . . . Individuals, groups, entire races of men *fall into step* with . . . science and industry.[13]

A large sculptural group in the Hall of Science at the Fair was even more explicit than the guidebook in conveying the theme that machines had become more powerful than mankind. The sculpture represented a man and a woman with hands outstretched as if in fear of ignorance; between them stood a huge angular robot nearly twice their size and bending low over them with a rigid metallic arm thrown protectively around each of them. Technology reassuring and guiding mankind was indeed the theme of the Fair.

Since the organizers of the Fair believed that everything developed by scientific technology was good for man, they found it natural to use as a heading in their guidebook:

Science Finds
Industry Applies
Man Conforms

The phrases "man conforms" and "men fall into step with . . . science and industry" had sinister implications even in

 1933. They implied that man must conform to the environment created by industry, instead of using science and technology to develop conditions suited to his fundamental needs. The etymology of the word "conform" suggests indeed that man would actually be molded by technological forces. These implications, however, did not become widely recognized until the mounting roster of environmental problems made it obvious that the technological way of life is not necessarily conducive to health and happiness.

As one looks back on the evolution of the relationship between man and the machine since the nineteenth century, it becomes apparent that the dangers of technology do not come primarily from the fact that its social complexities make it a Frankenstein monster independent of social control, as asserted by Ellul and Galbraith, but rather from man's willingness to fall into step with industry and conform to technological imperatives. The ultimate form of this intellectual surrender is the meek acceptance, expressed in the article by Forrester previously quoted, that "the human mind is not adapted to interpreting how social systems behave," and that we must therefore trust, almost blindly, the information and instructions received from the electronic machines to which we feed whatever facts we can assemble and program. Yet it seems legitimate to assume that, once we acknowledge as a matter of course our inability to understand the behavior of the social systems in which we function, we shall in time lose all incentive to change these systems and shall let our fate be decided by anonymous forces.

One of the worst demonic forces in technological civilization is the craving for growth, which is enhanced by countless institutional devices ranging from national prestige to real-estate promotion and other forms of commercial advertising. If modern man is encouraged to expand still further his appetite for the products of industry, if he continues to assume that every innovation is worth having and justifies the rejection of worthwhile practices simply because they are old, if populations continue to increase beyond the capacity of the earth to support them and to absorb their waste products, then disasters are inevitable, whatever improvements may be made in the technological processes. Neither wealth nor knowledge can provide effective ways to deal with human excesses.

The demons to be exorcised are therefore not in technology but in the minds of men. The future of technological civilization depends upon man's ability and willingness to formulate objectives that are attainable, safe, and desirable. It will unquestionably follow that these objectives are the ones most compatible with the fundamental and unchangeable nature of man and with the conditions most favorable for his health, happiness, and mental development.

At the beginning of the Renaissance, Pico della Mirandola expressed the faith of scientific humanism when he affirmed that man could choose his destiny and could make himself angel or beast:

> Neither a fixed abode nor a form that is thine alone nor any function peculiar to thyself have we given thee, Adam, to the end that according to thy longing and according to thy judgment thou mayest have and possess what abode, what form, and what functions thou thyself shalt desire. The nature of all other beings is limited and constrained within the bounds of laws prescribed by Us. Thou constrained by no limits, in accordance with thine own free will, in whose hand We have placed thee, shalt ordain for thyself the limits of thy nature. . . . With freedom of choice and with honor, as though the maker and

> molder of thyself, thou mayest fashion thyself in whatever shape thou shalt prefer. Thou shalt have the power to degenerate into the lower forms of life, which are brutish. Thou shalt have the power, out of thy soul's judgment, to be reborn into the higher forms, which are divine.[14]

There is a painful contrast between Pico della Mirandola's defiant affirmation of man's dignity and the fatalistic attitude of those present-day scientists and sociologists who would have us believe that we shall do certain things simply because we know how to do them, or that we must resign ourselves to not understanding the operations of the social systems even though we have created them. This peculiar kind of fatalism is the real demonic force in the modern world, because it blunts the incentive to select what is most worth doing among all the things which can be done. It discourages the attempts to reform social structures when they have become incompatible with the operations of the human brain.

There was human grandeur and panache in George Mallory's famous answer to the question of why he had wanted so intensely to climb Mount Everest: "Because it is there." But the Mount Everest philosophy is not applicable to the problems of human societies. It is rather an expression of compulsive animal behavior: the parrot is programmed to alight on a stick, the mouse to run into a hole, the bear and the raccoon to move to a garbage can. The animal cannot escape from this compulsive behavior and therefore is readily caught in a trap. But man has more power of discrimination and greater freedom in selecting his course of action. He need not be caught in technological traps.

To accept as a fact of life that a certain technology will be used for the simple reason that we know how to use it, or that we shall continue to live under a certain social system after it has become too complicated for human understanding, is tantamount to an abdication of intellectual and social responsibility. Fortunately, the likelihood that this kind of abdication will continue much longer is not warranted by historical precedents. Repeatedly in the past men have rejected the ways of their predecessors, either because conditions had changed, or to assert their independence, or more commonly because they had made up their minds to exorcise the occult demonic forces that were in the process of dehumanizing life.

The real prophets of doom are not the pessimists who see mankind on a course of self-destruction, but the misguided fatalists—falsely called optimists—who see the future merely as more growth and an extrapolation of the present. There *is* a demon in technology. It was put there by man and man will have to exorcise it before technological civilization can achieve the eighteenth-century ideal of humane civilized life.

CHAPTER 11

Industrial Society and Humane Civilization

Just before 1900, American magazine writers were busy trying to imagine what the world would be like in the twentieth century. Some of their imaginings, recently collected in a book entitled *Looking Forward*, constitute an entertaining lesson in humility for the would-be prophets who are now writing about the future.[1] The changes predicted in the essays republished in *Looking Forward* have not materialized but, more interestingly, these essays contain no hint of the social and technologic innovations that have made life in the twentieth century different from what it was in the nineteenth century.

During the late 1800s, the steam engine rapidly led to the development of luxurious ocean liners with two or three very tall smokestacks. The prophets therefore predicted immense multifunneled steamships capable of crossing the Atlantic in a few days, but they made no mention of jet aircraft. Plant breeders were then producing new strains of fruits and vegetables and there was talk of strawberries as big as apples—but not of TV dinners. Feminine fashion was escaping from the tyranny of the Victorian era and the prediction was that dresses would eventually be so short as to expose the ankles, but even the most avant garde couturiers did not dream of miniskirts, hot pants, or bikinis.

Imagining the future is a risky enterprise, not only because scientific discoveries and technological inventions are largely unpredictable, but even more because men are not robots. Many times in the past they have rejected the ways of life of their predecessors simply to assert their independence of the immediate past. New technologies and attitudes do not necessarily evolve as logical developments of existing conditions. In fact they rarely do so, because the logic of events must always yield to the arbitrariness of human choices. The willed future is always different from the logical future.

Granted that so much is unpredictable in human affairs, predictions nevertheless have to be made in order to keep society going. Some long-range view of the future is needed to plan for roads, airports, factories, new towns, systems of education, programs of international relationships, and all the complex structures and institutions of the modern world. But while a prospective view is useful, there is no ground for assuming that change and progress will continue along present lines and that the social and technological developments of the future will be extensions of what exists today.

During the 1960s, famous scholars and technologists published articles and books prophesying that the year 2000 would be the beginning of a sociotechnological utopia. Drugs would eliminate pain; robots would make physical work unnecessary; teaching machines would substitute for mental effort; life would be completely mechanized and air conditioned in domed cities located not only on earth, but also in space or on the ocean floor; scientists would be able to program dreams, to alter the genetic constitution of living things, including men, and to produce babies in the test tube. This technological euphoria is well documented in *The Year 2000: A Framework for Speculation on the Next 33 Years*, published in 1968.[2] In more recent articles, such as "Planetary Planning" and "Can Man Shape His Future?" eminent scientists still defend the faith that scientific technology can make our dreams come true.[3]

The scenarios for the future written by competent technologic utopians are within the range of scientific possibility; yet they probably bear no more resemblance to what will happen in the twenty-first century than did the prophecies made a hundred years ago for the twentieth century. The future is more likely to be shaped by the necessity of correcting the damage now being done to man and his environment than by more and more sophisticated technological innovations. In any case, what is technologically feasible is not necessarily what human beings really want to do or to have. The coming generations may be more interested in clean trout streams than in gigantic industrial plants, in quiet neighborhoods than in larger airports, in folk dances and handicrafts than in super-television programs, in hiking or bicycle trails than in automated freeways. Future technology will certainly be influenced by the fact that the clamor for environmental protection is becoming as loud in the halls of Congress as on college campuses.

In all industrialized countries, the prophets of doom are now taking the limelight and publicizing the thousand devils of the ecologic crisis. According to them, the year 2000 will not be the dawn of a technologic utopia but a gloomy sunset for many forms of life, especially for human life. While I share the concerns of the prophets of doom, I doubt that man is close to self-destruction, except of course in the event of nuclear warfare. Most forms of life are immensely adaptable; mosquitoes become resistant to pesticides, algae grow luxuriantly in contaminated waters, and human populations continue to increase even when they are short of food and live in heavily polluted environments. The immediate danger is not the destruction of life but its progressive degradation. Pollutants impoverish the rich complexity of ecological systems and thereby reduce their stability. Environments which are too traumatic or are deficient in the proper stimuli progressively cause a loss in humanness. If present trends were to continue for a few more decades, mankind would indeed be doomed—not to extinction but to a biologically and emotionally impoverished life.

Industrial civilization has always had enemies in all social classes; workmen fear that it will deprive them of their means of livelihood, while humanists believe that it will create a society unsuited to the fundamental needs and aspirations of man. In fact, the movements of protest against scientific technology which we are now witnessing have had their counterparts throughout the past two hundred years.

At the end of the eighteenth century, a half-witted Leicestershire workman, Ned Ludd, achieved notoriety by destroying stocking frames. He thus provided a name for the so-called Luddite workers, who, between 1811 and 1816, destroyed machines in an attempt to prevent the use of labor-saving equipment in English factories. Similar acts of industrial vandalism also occurred in France during the nineteenth century; the word "sabotage" derives from the damage done to machines by workmen with their sabots—wooden shoes. Luddism and sabotage are thus the forerunners of the labor conflicts generated by the fear that automation will cause widespread unemployment.

William Blake's vituperations against the dark satanic mills and the haunting descriptions of industrial cities by the Belgian poet Emile Verhaeren symbolize a long continuity of feelings among sensitive people lamenting the degradation of nature and of human life by industrialization. Throughout the nineteenth century, furthermore, many novelists and sociologists believed that mankind would become enslaved by technology, much as Jacques Ellul and Lewis Mumford fear this today, and there were a few who hoped that man would eventually revolt against industrialization. William Morris advocated a return to ancient crafts, and Samuel Butler described in his novel *Erewhon* a society in which men had destroyed machines to avoid being destroyed by them. Even H.G. Wells came to lose his faith in scientific technology and gloomily asserted in "Mind at the End of Its Tether": "Everything was driving anyhow to anywhere at a steadily increasing velocity. . . . The pattern of things to come faded away. . . . The end of everything we call life is close at hand and cannot be evaded."[4] When Henry Adams visited the Galerie des Machines at the Paris World's Fair in 1900, he began to "feel the dynamos as a moral force; just as the early Christians felt at the Cross,"[5] but he dreaded also the consequences of a situation in which scientific technology would become the ruler of human life.

The contemporary protests against industrial civilization thus do not differ greatly from those of the past, and one might assume therefore that they will not be more effective in changing social and technologic trends. But granting similarities, there are also profound differences. One of the new factors in the situation is that the reform movement is now led by men and women who are young and who are beneficiaries of the present economic system. They do not suffer from industrialization in the same way as did the victims of the dark satanic mills and the *villes tentaculaires.* But they fear that if present trends were to continue, the physical environment would become progressively impoverished in sensual qualities, and the social environment would have to be so highly organized and regimented as to resemble that of the social insects. The present revolt against industrial civilization is concerned not only with the here and now but even more with the quality of life in the future. It goes as far as questioning the cult of progress.

Another fact which makes the present situation different from the past and more threatening is the much greater magnitude of the technological enterprise. Industry did cause damage to nature and to man during the nineteenth and early twentieth centuries, but its impact was limited to a small percentage of the earth and of its population. Now that scientific technology is ubiquitous as well as more powerful, it causes major disturbances in practically all natural processes. Furthermore, until a few decades ago there were still unexploited lands and resources, whereas men everywhere are now faced with the limitations of the finite earth. A level of ecological damage which appeared tolerable in the past, because man could move on to other parts of the world, is no longer acceptable, because all the habitable parts of the earth are now occupied. A few simple examples will suffice to illustrate how natural forces will inescapably bring about a halt in the quantitative growth of population, industry, and agriculture early in the twenty-first century, and probably even before.

Every decade since the end of the Second World War, the production of electric power has doubled in the United States, as well as in other industrialized countries. The production of manufactured goods, and of solid wastes and other pollutants, has increased at approximately the same rate. If this rate of growth were to continue for three or four decades longer, the result would be ten times as many transmission lines over the land, ten times as much garbage in the cities, ten times as much junk in the air, streams, and lakes, with, of course, the increased regimentation of life required by a larger population and a more complex society. Young people have good reason to reject a state of affairs which would condemn them to live under such conditions during their adult and later years.

Although future scientific and technological developments will achieve more efficient use of resources and energy and decrease the production of solid wastes and other forms of pollution, there are limits to the increase in efficiency and decrease in environmental damage that can be attained by more science and better technology. Shortages of skills, of time, and of money will certainly act as limiting factors, since practically all industrial operations must be improved within a very few decades if disaster is to be avoided.

Less obvious but probably more important in the long run are the limitations which have their origin in the laws of nature and are therefore immutable. The generation of electric power inevitably produces enormous amounts of heat which must be discharged either into bodies of water or into the surrounding air. Such thermal pollution cannot be avoided and it causes physical and biological disturbances in the areas where the heat is discharged. At present these ecological problems can perhaps be dismissed as merely local nuisances, although they are real enough to generate vigorous protests from the localities affected. But they will become of global importance as larger and larger power plants are built. The utilization of electric energy also releases heat into the environment. Air conditioners, while cooling the rooms in which they are used, raise the outside temperature, thereby increasing still further the need for air conditioning, and the demand for electricity, in a hopeless, vicious circle. No advance in scientific knowledge or technologic skill can possibly eliminate these difficulties.

Since the earth is limited in area, in its store of unrenewable natural resources, and in its ability to cope with pollutants, the size of the human population and the amount of industrial production obviously cannot continue to grow forever. Scientific knowledge supplements this commonsense judgment by providing quantitative facts on which to base informed guesses as to how long growth can safely continue. In my opinion, the danger point will be reached around the turn of the century. This does not mean, however, that we must abandon the hope for improving the quality of life. Before discussing this, however, I wish to digress in order to point out that the rapid industrial growth of the past two centuries was a freak in the history of mankind, not likely to occur again.

The industrial revolution gained its momentum from the use of steam. This was a great advance, since steam power is much more economical and practical than human and animal power. As the supplies of wood were limited, large-scale industrialization would not have been possible without coal, a fuel which had been produced and stored by nature and was readily available in huge amounts. In essence the industrial revolution resulted not only from the invention of new techniques, but even more from the utilization of fossil fuels. Ever since, the development of industry has implied the use of natural resources, such as mineral ores, oil, and uranium, extracted from the earth.

Millions of years were required for the accumulation of these natural resources but the supply of several of them will be depleted in less than a century if they continue to be used and wasted at the present rate. Seen in the light of these facts, modern technology creates industrial wealth only by destroying existing natural wealth and converting it into other forms suitable for human use. Much the same can be said of modern agriculture. To produce high yields of crops from his land, the industrialized farmer must use complex equipment, unrenewable oil as fuel for his machinery, and large amounts of fertilizers and pesticides, the manufacture of which also requires the use of fossil fuel and other unrenewable resources. Indeed, in the United States, and probably in other industrialized countries as well, the farmer spends more calories in the form of industrial equipment and supplies than he recovers from his field in the form of corn.[6] To this must be added the fact that many types of farming progressively deplete the soil of its humus, thus reducing its natural fertility. Soil humus can be regarded as a natural resource, which cannot be readily renewed after it has been destroyed.

From the Stone Age until the end of the eighteenth century the human race created magnificent civilizations by practices which had little destructive effect on natural resources, but rather commonly renewed these resources or even created new ones.

In the past, wood constituted the largest source of fuel and its supply could be constantly renewed by maintaining large enough areas as woodlands. Deforestation occurred in many places, but fortunately several countries had strict laws for the preservation of valuable trees and for the sound management of forests. As early as 681, an ordinance in Spain made it a crime to cut down trees without government permission and similar conservation policies have existed in other parts of Europe since medieval times.[7]

In the temperate and subtropical world, as I pointed out earlier, arable soil has been created from wilderness by prolonged human effort and has been constantly enriched by the proper rotation of crops and other forms of wise agricultural management. Until a very few decades ago the areas thus transformed into pastures and farmlands have been increasing. All over the world, pre-industrial societies drained swamps, cleared river banks, dug canals, built roads, established cities, and in a thousand other ways created out of wilderness and then progressively shaped and maintained the world which we now regard as the natural environment for human life, and from which we derive much of our wealth.

In contrast, industrial civilization has been based so far on an extractive economy. It has mined the wealth of fuels and mineral ores accumulated in the earth through geologic ages; it has mined the agricultural wealth accumulated in the form of humus; and it is now beginning to mine the mineral and biological wealth of the oceans, even if this means the contamination of water with oil spills and the destruction of aquatic species.

Mining, however, lasts only as long as it is economically profitable. Once the supply of resources is depleted or the cost of extracting these becomes too high, the site is usually abandoned. Ghost towns and wastelands are the tragic witnesses of extractive civilization over much of the earth.

Thus, paradoxical as it may sound, the nineteenth and twentieth centuries have been more destructive than creative, because they have used and often wasted wealth stored in the form of natural resources. Modern men have benefited from this extractive economy and have had the illusion that the benefits were due entirely to scientific knowledge and technical know-how. The rapid technological growth of the past two centuries, however, was possible only because man has been ruthless in exploiting unrenewable natural resources and in creating conditions which degrade the environment. But this phase of human life will soon have to end, if we are sincere in our desire to replenish the supply of resources for future generations and to re-create for them a livable environment.

In nature, the products and wastes of biological communities are continuously re-utilized by being recycled into the system, instead of being left to accumulate as pollutants. To a large extent, this was also true in ancient human societies. Their wastes were of a kind that either could be consumed by animals, or could readily undergo microbial decomposition, or could serve as fertilizers—the composts and manures of the old-fashioned farms or the night soil of Oriental populations.

There is no reason to believe that animals and primitive people are more concerned with the neatness of their environment than we are. All anthropoids are careless eaters and destroy more than they eat. Among primitive men, the gluttony of tribal feasts is commonly associated with sloppiness and waste, as for instance in the potlatch ceremonies of some Indian tribes, where prestige is measured by the amount of possessions destroyed. The reason animals and primitive people do not pollute as much as our civilization does is simply that the solid wastes they produce and casually discard are in general rapidly eliminated by natural processes, whereas our kinds of wastes are largely indestructible. The bones, remnants of fruits, and articles of clothing left after the tribal feasts soon decompose, but the aluminum cans, plastic wrappers, and gadgets abandoned after our weekend outings persist along country roads.

Most natural systems approach a kind of steady state—namely, a state of affairs in which the biological community is more or less in equilibrium with its environment. Ideally, natural mechanisms regulate population size to a level compatible with the renewal of resources and with the maintenance of other conditions required for ecological health. When the natural regulatory mechanisms fail to function properly, profound ecological disturbances occur in the organisms and in the environment, commonly resulting in various forms of disease and in population crashes.

Throughout nature, the steady state thus seems to be a condition of health and often of survival, but there is a widespread feeling that this rule does not apply to modern human societies. The reason for this human conceit is that, for the past two hundred years, Western civilization has been concerned only with the first-order effects of technology, the goods and services it produces. In truth, there was apparent justification for ignoring the unfavorable side effects, in the fact that they did not reach an alarming magnitude until recent times. Furthermore, many years of scientific work were needed to define clearly the harmful effects of the countless products and influences which are part and parcel of life in the technologic world: ionizing radiations, chemical carcinogens, DDT and other pesticides, nitrogen oxides from motor cars, asbestos and volatile air pollutants, loud noise and excessive sensory stimuli. It has now become obvious, however, that the cumulative impact of these unfavorable side effects is causing ecological disturbances on a global scale. As a result, a shift is occurring in the assessment of values. Preserving the quality of life may soon be considered more important than promoting economic growth in assessing the social merits of technological developments.

Normal human beings, it would seem, should find it easy to shift their concern from quantity of production to quality of life. But in practice, the shift will be difficult, because we have been brainwashed into the belief that the betterment of life depends on quantitative growth achieved by an extractive economy. For most persons, indeed, the very phrase "steady state" implies stagnation eventually followed by decadence. Yet many historical examples demonstrate that great and beneficial qualitative changes can occur without significant quantitative growth. The Minoan civilization continued to evolve for more than twelve hundred years, arriving at a level of sophistication and refinement unmatched in the ancient world. Yet the island of Crete on which it developed is not much larger than Long Island and its contacts with Africa and the Near East were largely confined to trade. Throughout the modern world, social evolution has been most rapid and successful in some of the smallest countries, poorly endowed in the kind of natural resources required for industrialization—Denmark, for example. Indeed a strong case could be made for the view that it will be easier to focus our thoughts and efforts on the achievement of a higher quality of life once we have freed ourselves from the present obsession with quantitative growth.[8] In the final analysis, we must reconsider the meaning of progress.

Etymologically speaking, the word "progress" means simply moving forward in a certain direction on a certain road, even if it is a dangerous road. Progress is now identified with the kind of forward motion which makes it possible to produce on an ever-increasing scale, faster and faster, everything and anything that can be produced, irrespective of the damage done to human and environmental values.

Stephen Vincent Benét was dead serious when he expressed in his epic poem *Western Star*, published in 1943, the view that just moving forward was a true manifestation of the American genius.[9] He was then the voice of the blind American faith in the virtue of growth for growth's sake—as if more and more, bigger and bigger, farther and farther, faster and faster constituted a sure formula for the improvement of human life. This faith has dominated Western civilization since the beginning of the eighteenth century and is still widespread today. As late as 1971, a distinguished American business executive and sociologist found it worthwhile to uphold once more the value of the growth myth in an essay entitled "America Is a Growing Country." His very phrase "We cannot rule growth and progress out of our society" obviously implies that in his mind progress is dependent on growth.[10]

There are indications, however, that the Western world is beginning to outgrow the growth myth. A few years before his death, Jean Cocteau seriously suggested in his facetious way that progress might be nothing more than a logical development from false premises: *"Il est possible que le progrès ne soit que le développement d'une erreur."*[11] If there has been a fundamental flaw in the development of technological societies, it has been to identify the concept of progress with the belief that abundance of goods makes for human happiness; whereas it is obvious that, beyond a certain point, affluence becomes meaningless. Furthermore, great wealth is a social absurdity and an ethical monstrosity when it coexists with abject poverty.

Unlike the pioneers of Stephen Vincent Benét's time, we want to know where we are going and we care about our goals; just being on the way is no longer identified with real progress. The general public is demanding changes, even though in an erratic manner. All over the land, projects for highways, power plants, and factories have been abandoned because of local hostility; the SST, the Miami airport, the mid-Florida barge canal are but a few casualties of this new public attitude. If one can generalize from these examples, it would seem that soon either the rate of the technologic enterprise will have to be slowed down quantitatively or its program changed qualitatively.

The view that the era of quantitative growth must come to an end is not merely a daydream of unrealistic humanitarians and nature worshipers; it has been repeatedly expressed by hard-headed technologists and business men.

On April 22, 1970, which was celebrated as Earth Day in the United States, Charles Luce, chairman of the board of Consolidated Edison, was asked on a national television program how the electric power industry intended to deal with the ecologic problems for which it is responsible. He replied, "The answer to all of these environmental and resource problems is that we simply use less goods and services. In other words, *that we get off this growth kick our economy has been on throughout the history of our country.*"[12] This answer was truly one the most revolutionary statements that could be made in a country which has been built on the growth myth.

The English technologist Dennis Gabor, in *Innovations*, expresses the same view as Mr. Luce: "Unfortunately all our drive and optimism are bound up with continuous growth; 'growth addiction' is the unwritten and unconfessed religion of our times. . . . The insane quantitative growth must stop."[13]

Overcoming the addiction to quantitative growth, fortunately, is compatible with great qualitative changes. Societies can be viable and creative within the limitations imposed by a dynamic steady state if they turn their attention to the technological changes that will be needed for improving the quality of life. Luce stated as much in the television interview already mentioned: "We can redirect our growth into better channels." And Gabor expressed the same faith in his book: "Innovation must not stop—it must take an entirely new direction. Instead of working blindly towards things bigger and better, it must work towards improving the quality of life . . . towards a new harmony, a new equilibrium."

The redirection of scientific technology to new goals is essential, but much more difficult than keeping it on its present course. The scientific-technological complex that has functioned so effectively during the past hundred years will naturally tend to continue producing more and more of the same, almost automatically, by its own inertia. According to Newton's First Law, inertia refers to the fact that "a body remains in uniform motion unless acted upon by an external force." One can expect that the inertia of scientific technology will soon be overcome by extrascientific forces originating from social and political bodies. Increasing numbers of scientists are becoming professionally involved in the ecological crisis, not as a result of events internal to science itself, but because social and political pressures are creating a new climate of opinion.

Improving the quality of life is obviously more important than just increasing the quantity of things, but it is not easy to identify the qualitative changes which are most desirable for human beings. In fact, the very word desirable implies judgments of value and suggests that the quality of life is a purely personal matter. This subjectivity accounts for the vagueness of such phrases as "better channels," "new direction," "new equilibrium," "new harmony" used by Luce and Gabor in their suggestions that technology should be focused on human welfare. Life styles are much more difficult to define than increases in production. Creating a desirable social design would probably be impossible if life styles were entirely individual. But while each one of us lives in a private world and tries to do his own thing, it is also true that choices and value judgments have to be made within a narrow range defined by the unchangeable characteristics of the human species and by the mores of the social group.

When considered from this humanistic point of view, social problems cannot be the exclusive province of experts. Special knowledge is needed, of course, for the planning and execution of particular programs, and for the prediction of their probable consequences. But the public has a role in decision-making just as important as that of the experts, because in the formulation of social enterprises goals are as important as means. A society that accepts the tyranny of the expert is a sick society.

Civilizations commonly die from the excessive development of certain characteristics which had at first contributed to their success. Our form of industrial civilization suffers from having allowed experts to make growth and efficiency, rather than the quality of life, the main criterion of success. Among the hopeful signs of our times are the ground swell of dissatisfaction against this state of affairs and the awareness that, if things are in the saddle, it is because we have put them there. To repeat, the demonic force in our life is not technology per se, but our propensity to consider means as ends.

Largely in response to public pressure, legislative and governmental bodies are beginning to develop ways of evaluating the impact of technological and social innovations on human welfare. The present emphasis on assessing technology means that people today are considering goals to be as important as means in the development of industrial civilization—perhaps a significant step toward a return to the ancient concern for the good life. In this and other ways we seem to be somewhat more sophisticated than we were a decade ago. Most of us have dismissed the illusion that we are about to create a technological utopia, but we are also overcoming the fear that we shall soon witness the sunset of the human race. Industrial society cannot last long in its present form, but there are signs that it will emerge, phoenix-like, from its ashes in the form of a more humane civilization.

CHAPTER 12

On Being Human

Murals depicting the Crusades provided the background against which mathematicians, natural scientists, and philosophers discussed, once again, the possibility of discovering physicochemical explanations for the phenomena of life and for human behavior. During June 1971, an international congress organized by the Institut de la Vie around the theme "From Theoretical Physics to Life" met in the Palace of Versailles. The scientific sessions were held in the Salle des Croisades, so called because its walls are decorated with seventeenth century paintings illustrating the most notable events of the Crusades. Perhaps by intention, but more probably by accident, the speaker's platform was placed exactly under a painting of Pope Urban II extending his arms over the audience as he launched the first Crusade from Clermont Cathedral. The intent of the congress was to show that all the phenomena of life are the expressions of physicochemical forces. But while listening to the speakers, I could not help noticing, to my right and my left, scenes of Christians and Moslems slaughtering each other, and of ecstasy or despair as the Crusaders conquered or abandoned Jerusalem. The Crusades seemed far removed from the physicochemical explanations of behavior.

Some fifty illustrious scientists participated in the congress, with fields of specialization ranging from philosophy and mathematics through physics and chemistry to psychology and medicine. Among them were fifteen Nobel laureates. The scientific discussions were at first peaceful. There was general agreement that all the constituents and processes found in living things, including man, obey the laws of inanimate matter. There was a consensus also that life had originated some three billion years ago from organic matter produced out of simple chemicals by solar irradiation. No ill-feeling developed from the fact that there were almost as many hypotheses concerning the precise mechanism of life's beginnings as there were participants in the discussion. The atmosphere became tense, however, as soon as the discussions shifted from purely technical problems to the bearing of scientific knowledge on human behavior and on social action. When discussing the social aspects of science, the Nobel laureates and other illustrious scientists differed as much among themselves, in their attitudes and in their arguments, as would have a group of concierges or taxi drivers of Versailles.

The congress held in the Salle des Croisades showed that the technical problems posed by the relation of physics and chemistry to life are now within the possibility of scientific understanding. But the last phase of the program confirmed once more that it is much more difficult—if not impossible—to link the physicochemical aspects of life to the really important aspects of human behavior. As the medieval crowds shouted, "*Dieu li volt* [God wills it]" in response to the Pope's plea that they liberate the Holy Land, the sound of their voices and their emotional outbursts were the expression of physical and hormonal forces which are now well understood. But the processes occurring in their bodies did not account for their motivation.

Living things behave in many ways like complex machines, and so do their societies. An individual insect—ant, bee, or termite—moves about its day's business in a mechanical way, much like a mindless automaton governed by external stimuli. In the words of Professor Lewis Thomas of Yale University Medical School, "A solitary ant, afield, cannot be considered to have much of anything on his mind; indeed, with only a few neurons strung together by fibers, he can't be imagined to have a mind at all, much less a thought; he is more like a ganglion on legs."[1] Another aspect of the ant's nature becomes apparent, however, when one observes the functioning community, the ant hill. Thousands of ants crowded and working around their hill behave as a thinking, planning, calculating organism. So integrated is their behavior that the ant colony as a whole is more like a highly developed beast than a collection of individual insects. The same is true for other social insects. Termites, in particular, seem to generate a collective intelligence when the numbers in a colony reach a certain critical level.

There are countless other examples of separate creatures organizing to form complex social organisms. This occurs throughout the living world, among animals, plants, and even microbes, as well as among social insects. The integrated behavior of schools of fish, flocks of birds, or bands of mammals obviously has a biological basis, and there is reason to believe that a similar kind of force is at work in the type of group behavior in human populations obscurely referred to as mob psychology.

Man is *par excellence* a social animal, since he makes use of other human beings at every stage of his life. This dependence applies not only to his bodily, psychological, and emotional needs but also to the cultural attributes that determine the characteristics of a society. The members of a given human group are linked in complex systems for the collection, storage, processing, and retrieval of the immense variety of information that constitutes the collective property of the group. The linkage of persons into systems is probably as old as mankind and it is certainly more important than biological properties in determining the characteristics which differentiate man from animals. The explosive development of European science since the seventeenth century may have resulted in part from the use of a new system of communication among scientists—the prompt publication of fragments of research findings in specialized scientific journals. The English mathematician J.M. Ziman stated in 1969:

> A typical scientific paper has never pretended to be more than another little piece in a larger jig saw—not significant in itself but as an element in a grander scheme. This technique, of soliciting many modest contributions to the store of human knowledge, has been the secret of Western science since the seventeenth century, for it achieves a corporate, collective power that is far greater than any one individual can exert.[2]

The individual scientist may have only a dim view of the grand scheme to which his work relates; indeed he may have no view of it at all, but his professional activities—limited in scope as they may be—contribute nevertheless to the collective building of the scientific enterprise. His individual paper, even in an obscure journal, is part of a highly effective mechanism of information building.

Any social structure is thus largely built out of immense numbers of contributions by the anonymous members of the community. In this regard, much human work resembles that of social insects building an ant hill or a termite nest. Human communities, however, differ from animal communities in the fact that their history is marked by countless upheavals of internal origin, which profoundly alter the course of their development. To the slow, involuntary sleepwalk of biological evolution, man has consciously added discontinuities through revolutionary changes brought about by the sudden introduction or rejection of technologies and ways of life.

The domestication of plants and animals, the control of irrigation water in the river valleys of the Near and Far East, the development of weaving and pottery, the use of metals, the invention of writing, and all the other marvelous developments of Neolithic and Bronze Age cultures certainly involved numerous progressive changes over many generations. Taken together, these achievements deserve to be called a revolution when one considers how, despite the sparsity of populations and the difficulty of communication, they transformed the hunter-gatherer way of life into the complexities and splendor of prehistoric civilizations.

Throughout the historical period, new technical procedures and art forms have spread rapidly, as did, for example, Gothic architecture and sculpture; thus the famous smile of the Rheims angel was reproduced in many cathedrals of northern Europe within a very few decades. The use of steam and industrial processes spread like wildfire over the Western world, transforming industry, transportation, and ways of life. England had 97 miles of railway track in 1830, 1497 miles in 1840, and 4800 additional miles were laid in the year 1845. In a single decade, the stagecoaches disappeared from England and along with them a whole variety of trades.

The sudden transformations of life in our times are picturesquely epitomized by Lord Ritchie-Calder's experiences during his trips for the United Nations all over the world:

> In the Arctic, I "mushed" with the Eskimos who had Geiger counters on their dogsleds to seek uranium, and battery radio receivers to pick up the quotations of the Montreal metal market to see whether it was worth looking for uranium. In Nepal, on the slopes of the Himalayas, I listened with the Sherpas to radio accounts of *Nautilus*, the atomic submarine, going under the ice of the North Pole. In the High Andes of South America the disinherited heirs of the Incas were listening to the astronauts gossiping on the doorstep of space. During the worst days in the Congo, in the heart of darkness as Conrad called it, I watched the news bulletins from Cairo radio being picked up on radio receivers and the messages were being tapped out on the talking drums to be relayed through the swamp forest.[3]

Man's ability to transform his life by social evolution and especially by social revolutions thus stands in sharp contrast to the conservatism of the social insects, which can change their ways only through the extremely slow processes of biological evolution. In regard to other animal communities, however, the difference is not as clearcut. Recently the crows in Boston discovered the ease of riding on top of trolley buses. In London, birds developed the knack of removing the cover from milk bottles left on door steps so as to get at the cream. Colonies of primates have been known rapidly to acquire new social habits, such as washing potatoes in sea water before eating them, simply by imitating one of their members. And there are many well-documented examples of animals in the wild learning to function better in their environment by improving their skill in using local resources or otherwise changing their ways of life. The most that can be said, therefore, is that man can learn much more and much faster than any other living thing and can communicate his newly acquired skills so effectively that they rapidly spread to the rest of mankind. Even though his superiority over animals in this regard is relative rather than absolute, it is obviously considerable and it accounts in part for the rapidity of his social evolution.

Man's ability to bring about social changes, however, does not depend only on the rapidity with which he can learn new skills and transmit them to his communities. Unlike animals, he can and often does consciously reject techniques or habits that he had acquired and social attitudes to which he had been conditioned. In fact, his proneness to alter or even abandon certain ways of life makes possible or greatly accelerates revolutionary changes and thereby sets him completely apart from the rest of the animal kingdom.

Taoism, Buddhism, and Christianity are known today as specific doctrines defining the place of man in the order of things and his relation to other men. But the influence of Lao-tzu, Buddha, and Jesus began with their rejection of certain social and religious orthodoxies of their times rather than with the presentation of a systematic body of thought. Rejection of an objectionable state of affairs, as much as allegiance to a new faith, has commonly been the trumpet call of social revolutions, whether initiated by religious reformers such as Martin Luther, social reformers such as Karl Marx, or nameless soapbox orators.

The origin of some of the most spectacular and far-reaching movements of human history can be traced to a particular person, or more precisely to a view of the world seen by that person. The uniqueness of the initial visionary concept may partly explain why the natural sciences have contributed so little of importance to the prediction or explanation of great historical events; the scientific method is most successful when dealing with phenomena that can be repeated and manipulated by experimentation.

Islam, for example, was born unpredictably in the mind of Mohammed, who was a middle-aged merchant of Mecca in Arabia Deserta early in the seventh century. The group of Arabs to which he belonged was then a small tribe, extremely poor, largely illiterate, and almost entirely isolated from the rest of the world. Yet Mohammed and his immediate followers converted these destitute Arabs into a powerful fighting force which in little more than a century created an immense empire, prosperous, artistically refined, and intellectually sophisticated. The Arab empire eventually disintegrated but the spiritual legacy it derived originally from Mohammed remains one of the great forces of the modern world.

In just as mysterious a manner, the idea of the first crusade was apparently born in the mind of Peter the Hermit, a monk whose concern for the fate of the Holy Land was so obsessive that he might in other times have been sent to an insane asylum. Yet, by conveying his passion to anyone who would listen to him, Peter the Hermit was influential in starting the long series of crusades during which the uncouth European barons learned from the Arabs the refinements of civilization and furthermore built all over the Near East the extraordinary structures that are still admired today.

The wills of Mohammed and Peter the Hermit thus set in motion immense social forces, the impact of which extended for centuries over the whole world. Most of the great movements of human history likewise originated from individual decisions. In his monograph, *Three Lincoln Masterpieces*, the American lawyer Benjamin Barondess pointed out that America would have become a very different kind of country if Abraham Lincoln had not decided to run against William H. Seward for the Republican party nomination and thus been elected President just before the Civil War. In Barondess's words, "There is no such thing as History. There is only His Story. An act is without significance unless we know the actor."[4] But the real question is what it is that first motivates the actor to act.

We know a great deal about the physicochemical phenomena which make life possible and we can formulate reasonable hypotheses about their origin and evolution. We can imagine, even though we do not completely understand, how each particular living thing is shaped by genetic constitution, experiences, and environment. But this kind of knowledge does not explain the particular events in the minds of Mohammed, Peter the Hermit, and Lincoln which made each of them take a stand at a critical time and thus trigger social movements that changed the course of human history. Free will—at least as it is understood today—may not be compatible with scientific determinism, but it is certainly the strongest and most interesting force in human life. It constitutes what William James called the "zone of insecurity" in which lies all the dramatic interest; the physicochemical forces provide only the props and stage machinery.[5]

Great leaders accelerate historical changes and may even impose on them a pattern of their own choice. But many of the social and cultural revolutions of the past seem to have occurred spontaneously, as if circumstances had made the people concerned develop a collective will capable of overcoming existing conditions.

Social structures, even though defective and weak, commonly remain stable for long periods of time because people develop a superficial tolerance to even the most objectionable prejudices and environments. Thus, for a thousand years, the humble people of Europe accepted the view that the nobility was entitled to rule because they had been endowed by God with bluer blood and that the bourgeois owed their wealth to superior talents. For three centuries, the black people in America appeared to tolerate the idea that their white masters really belonged to a superior race. Today, most people in industrial societies seem to be convinced that environmental pollution, social regimentation, and other forms of social degradation cannot be avoided because they are the price of progress. But tolerance of an undesirable state of affairs rarely implies true adaptation. It corresponds rather to a passive acceptance, a form of resignation, which almost inevitably leads to withdrawal from the system and then to its outright rejection. This negative phase, in turn, is commonly followed by a search for new experiences and for other ways of life.

At the end of the Middle Ages, the dreariness of scholastic hairsplitting and disputatious verbosity generated a reaction which expressed itself through such writers as Boccaccio, Chaucer, Villon, and Rabelais, thus leading to the exuberant creativeness of the High Renaissance. During the mid-nineteenth century, a group of bold and gifted young men and women became bored with the stodgy comfort and rigid conventions of bourgeois life and sought for new experiences in the *vie de Bohème.*[6] Only a very small percentage of the population adopted the Bohemian life style, but this was enough to re-establish in the Western world saner human relationships and a more direct way of seeing nature. By cleansing their world of its dusty social and visual accretions, the Bohemians launched the phenomenal creativity of European cultures during the past century. The arts owe a great deal to the new modes of expression in music, poetry, painting, and other forms that emerged from the Bohemian episode.

A movement similar in spirit, but on a much larger scale, is now being directed against the banalities of mass-produced artifacts and the values resulting from economic affluence. Until the 1940s, the damage done to life by the industrial state and its megamachines was accepted passively. Social protest first took the form of the dejected escapism which gave such a drab complexion to beatnik life. But this was soon followed by a frantic search for new, positive experiences and modes of expression in the various forms of counterculture. The practice of ancient handicrafts and of unconventional human relationships, bold experiments in the organization of intentional communities, shared experiences in tribal life, new designs and bright colors in clothing, gay sounds as from the tinkling of bells, interesting odors from incense and flowers, rites organized around the real or imagined forces and cycles of the cosmos—all these manifestations of the countercultures, trivial and clumsy as they often are, are attempts to recapture ancient and lasting values which industrial civilization is in the process of destroying.

There are indeed values which have been woven into the biological and social fabric of human life for several millennia and which are still as essential as ever to well being and happiness. Their preservation does not require a return to cave life, but it demands the kind of social and technological reforms that will give man the opportunity to search for the fundamental satisfactions found only in nature, in human relationships, and in self-discovery. Henry Adams mourned the replacement of the cult of the Virgin by the cult of the Dynamo. In a more earthy and probably healthier way, the countercultures take up the plea for a world in which the flesh and the spirit are untrampled by the machine.

The present youth revolt against industrial civilization is amateurish and for this reason seems bound to fail. But, many times in the past, movements based almost exclusively on emotion and apparently devoid of power have proved capable of upsetting the most entrenched political and social systems. During the reign of Augustus, the Roman Empire was the largest, wealthiest, and most powerful political structure in the world. At that time also, the Synagogue ruled supreme in religious and social matters over the Jewish people in Palestine. The values enshrined in the Empire and in the Synagogue must have then appeared so stable as to be capable of lasting an eternity. Yet Jesus was born during this period of apparent stability, more than ten years before Augustus's death, and his teachings soon began to disturb the established order of things. Who could have imagined at the height of the Pax Romana that the Empire would collapse under the blows of the barbarians and that the barbarians themselves would so rapidly submit to the Cross? At first, the lowly Christians were less numerous and less well organized than the members of the countercultures are today. Nevertheless, they proved more influential than the Roman Empire, the Synagogue orthodoxy, or the vigorous tribes from the European forests and the Asiatic steppes, in determining the future of Western civilization.

In our own time, passive resistance, guerilla warfare, and sabotage—the weapons of the poor and the weak—have toppled the mighty colonial empires of the Western nations. Colonial wars and social revolutions have demonstrated time and time again that technological and political power can be overcome by the will of men. In fact, human will can intervene even in the purely biological phenomena of adaptation which in other living things blindly shape life by determining its fitness to the environment.

The modern theory of physiological adaptation began more than a century ago when the French scientist Claude Bernard (1813–1878) emphasized the importance of the fact that the fluids and cells in the body of higher animals and of man remain in an essentially constant state despite great and endless changes in their external environment. In one of the most famous phrases of the biological sciences, Bernard affirmed that this constancy of the internal environment is a condition essential to the independent life of higher organisms. His phrase, *"La fixité du milieu intérieur est la condition essentielle de la vie libre"* (The constancy of the internal environment is the condition of free and independent life), expresses the success of animal and human life in achieving independence from the vagaries of nature.[7]

Bernard guessed, furthermore, that the maintenance of stable conditions within the body is in some way dependent on neural and hormonal control[8]—a truth which was demonstrated half a century later by the American physiologist Walter B. Cannon (1871–1945). Cannon's famous book, *The Wisdom of the Body*, popularized the word "homeostasis," which he had introduced to denote the fact that under normal conditions, the animal body is capable of maintaining its internal processes in a state of equilibrium by constantly compensating for the disturbing effects of external forces.[9] A further elaboration of this concept was formulated by the American physicist Norbert Wiener (1894–1964), inventor of the word "cybernetics." Wiener pointed out that homeostasis constitutes a biological example of cybernetics, since each deviation from the norm in the body brings on a reaction in the opposite direction—in other words, a negative feedback.[10]

The recognition that all biological systems are controlled by feedback processes has greatly affected the course of many other sciences, sociology among them. The American sociologist Talcott Parsons, who was a colleague of Cannon at Harvard University and was certainly influenced by him, applied the concept of homeostasis to social systems and derived from it the doctrine called functionalism.[11] According to the functionalist view, every established society constitutes a system in equilibrium. When disturbances occur in it, they elicit adaptive responses from the various subsystems; the equilibrium is thereby restored and the society maintained in its original or slightly modified form. Each particular society is characterized by a "central value system"—a set of fundamental values which is accepted by most of its members and thereby contributes to its stability by bringing about adaptation and integration among the various components of the system.

Historically, Great Britain and the countries of continental Europe have differed greatly in their attitudes with regard to the use of feedback processes in technical devices and social systems. From the sixteenth to the eighteenth century, the continental mind was primarily interested in the control of technical and social operations by rigidly determined programs. This interest expressed itself, among other ways, by the construction of a great variety of complex and ingenious automatons and clock-driven planetariums. In sociology, it took the form of mercantilism and absolute government. The British, in contrast, turned to control processes in which the system was rendered essentially autonomous by inherent mechanisms which automatically maintained it in dynamic equilibrium. This type of control is illustrated by the feedback devices used in water clocks, windmills, and especially in Watt's steam engine.[12] In economics, the theory of autonomous control inspired Adam Smith's free market system, and in political science it led to the division of power in constitutional governments.

The cybernetic processes of responses operating through self-correcting feedbacks provide powerful and practical mechanisms of automatic control, but they are effective only as long as conditions remain fairly stable. This limitation, however, has often been ignored by biologists, ecologists, and sociologists, with the result that belief in the efficacy of homeostatic processes has tended to create the impression that all is for the best in the best of all possible worlds. The very word homeostasis seems indeed to imply that nature in its wisdom elicits responses that always bring the system back to original condition. For example, there is no mention of disease in Cannon's *Wisdom of the Body*, as if homeostatic negative feedbacks in physiological processes were always successful in preventing the harmful effects of environmental influences and in assuring healthy development. But this is far from the truth. In fact, homeostatic processes that appear to be successful because they exert a protective or reparative function at the time they occur commonly elicit malfunction at a later date. The production of scar tissue is a homeostatic response because it heals wounds and helps in checking the spread of infection. But in the liver or the kidney, scar tissue means cirrhosis or glomerular nephritis; in rheumatoid arthritis it may freeze the joints; and in the lung it may choke the breathing process. When the end results of homeostasis are evaluated over a long period of time, it becomes obvious that the wisdom of the body is often a short-sighted wisdom.[13] And much the same can be said for ecological and social systems. Lands that appeared highly fertile may rapidly deteriorate and social systems that appeared powerful suddenly collapse when these systems are subjected to influences which call forth an inadequate homeostatic response. Inflation leads to higher prices and wages which in turn generate more inflation.

Furthermore, the responses of a given system to disturbing influences commonly leave a permanent imprint on it; even when they appear to regenerate the equilibrium state, they change the system irreversibly and impose a new direction on its further development.[14] Living systems are characterized not by homeostasis, but by homeokinesis.

In sociology, the homeostatic attitude tends to make the adherents of functionalism insensitive to the potentialities for social change and to encourage in them a propensity to regard the fleeting present as an eternal order. Yet there are countless examples of creative changes in social development. From a feudal and agricultural country, Sweden was transformed within a century into a welfare urban society as a result of adaptive responses to industrialization. Over most of the world, the homeostatic feedbacks of the supply-and-demand economy are giving way to new systems manipulated by government intervention. And more importantly perhaps, as discussed earlier, changes of mood can completely alter the social and economic structure of a community, even without the use of force. The concept of homeostasis in sociology and economics, like the concept of climax in ecology, is a postulate which hardly ever fits reality.

To the extent that man is an animal, certain of his biological processes and behavioral responses operate through unconscious homeostatic mechanisms. But the most interesting aspects of his life have little in common with animal life. His uniqueness cannot be explained by his anatomical, physiological, or developmental characteristics, since these are only specialized expressions of tendencies found in apes. Man differs from the rest of the animal kingdom not by his biological endowments but by the use he has made of them, usually in a conscious manner. Being reflective and interpretative, he can embody his experiences in the form of cultural systems which facilitate the transfer of acquired knowledge from generation to generation. He can thus produce works of art, scientific concepts, moral codes, legal systems, and other organizations of experience which constitute the building stones of his psychosocial evolution—a process which is for mankind much more important than biological evolution. To a large extent, mankind is defined by its collective achievements—in other words, by its cultures.

Man is as much influenced by natural forces as are other living things; but he constantly tries to escape from his biological bondage. For this reason, his future is shaped not only by the immutable and inexorable forces of nature, the effects of which are predictable, but even more by individual and collective decisions, which are largely unpredictable. The great moments of history are the new departures that result from these decisions. These are determined not by the *reactions* of the body machine, which are essentially passive, but by purposeful *responses,* which always imply choices. These responses are guided by man's ability to visualize the future, and indeed by his propensity to plan for a future which transcends his own biological life.

Purposeful behavior is *terra incognita* because we do not understand the operations of free will and because the very concept of "state of consciousness" is extremely nebulous. There seems to be more hope, however, about the possibility of studying modes of responses. John Dewey went so far as to claim that: "The brain is primarily an organ of a certain kind of behavior, not of knowing the world."[15] William James also was more concerned with the willful aspects of behavior than with its determinism. He was less interested in the ultimate nature of things or their origin than in the consequences of action. According to him, the future is built from what he called the reserve energies in each individual. As everyone knows from experience, it is easier to react passively than to respond creatively by drawing on one's reserve energies; but to be human means to be creative. This involves choices which are often painful; hence the worried features in human faces at the moment of decision.

In man as in animals, admittedly, much of behavior is governed by instincts which operate without reference to consciousness and free will. Instincts come ready-made and enable the organism to deal decisively and often successfully with situations similar to analogous situations experienced by the species during its evolutionary past. As the French philosopher Henri Bergson (1859–1941) emphasized in *Creative Evolution*, however, it is precisely because instincts are so pointed and mechanical in their operation that they are of little if any use for adaptation to change; they are of no help in meeting flexibly and creatively the unforeseeable and fluid complexities of life.[16] Instincts provide biological security, but it takes awareness, free will, and purpose to achieve a life of adventure and creativity. The god within mankind is the spirit of purposeful and creative adventure.

The myths of ancient peoples are still meaningful to us because they express preoccupations and moods which are universal and eternal. Like rolling stones which gather moss when they come to rest for a while in a particular place, myths change their external appearance when they are adopted by a new culture, but their core of fundamental truth is not thereby altered. The story of Ulysses's travels and tribulations has taken many forms in different countries and different times, but its central theme has remained the trials of human life and man's search for his destiny.

Homer's Ulysses was a complicated person with many conflicting traits—as are most of us. He loved adventure, could withstand extraordinary hardships, but also was susceptible to the charm of Calypso and Circe and enjoyed idle life in the land of the Lotus Eaters. Above and beyond satisfying his sensual urges, however, he wanted to return home to Ithaca, either to rejoin aging Penelope or to resume his somewhat boring duties as a small landowner. For Homer, the fulfillment of human life seems to have been man's return to his origins.

The spirit of adventure took a more ambitious form in Europe during the Renaissance. For the Ulysses depicted by Dante in *The Divine Comedy*, neither the thought of home nor the love of comfort could still the desire that nothing remain concealed. When Dante's Ulysses reached the Pillars of Hercules, which were then the boundary set by God to man's ambitions, he exhorted his companions to go on: "You have your lives, not that you may live like beasts, but rather that you may strive for fame and knowledge." For five months the mariners sailed on, but eventually they encountered a storm of such violence that the sea swallowed up ship and men. By this tragic end of Ulysses's adventure Dante wanted to convey the moral that man is likely to founder when he transgresses the limits set by God to his ambitions. Christianity was willing to let man dream dreams but did not want him to ignore that certain areas of knowledge were forbidden to him.

By the nineteenth century, man no longer admitted any limitations to the enlargement of his existence. Progress, considered as an open-ended process, had then become the dominant social motto. When Alfred Tennyson restated Homer's theme in his poem "Ulysses," he made adventure, knowledge, and achievement the essence of the human condition. His hero urged the mariners

> To follow knowledge like a sinking star
> Beyond the utmost bound of human thought. . . .

For Tennyson's Ulysses, the ideal was to move ever onward, simply because some work of noble note might yet be done. In the United States during the nineteenth century, adventure and progress became almost completely identified with geographical, technological, and economic expansion. The historian Frederick Jackson Turner (1861–1932) claimed in *The Frontier in American History*, first published in 1920, that the ambition to reach the geographical frontier of the continent had been a dominant factor in shaping American attitudes and institutions.[17] Four decades later, the technologist Vannevar Bush wrote of "science the endless frontier" as a form of activity opening ever-new vistas for theoretical knowledge and practical applications.[18]

Modern man still craves both adventure and the comfort of the familiar; in fact he probably needs both for his mental health. Like Homer's Ulysses, he wants to re-establish contact with nature and with the past because he realizes that he cannot safely dissociate himself from his origins. Like Dante's Ulysses, he is willing to undertake hazardous tasks for the sake of knowledge and fame. Like Tennyson's Ulysses, he is still prone to move on and on, not only for profit but also for the simple reason that "some work of noble note may yet be done."

Now, however, man wishes to add deeper significance to his endeavors. Realizing that true fulfillment escapes him, he has begun once more to search within himself for a kind of satisfaction he has not found so far in his conquest of the external world. He knows that he can find biological happiness by achieving adaptation to his physical and social environment, but he realizes that this form of happiness is as limited in scope as the contentment of the cow. The best-adapted populations certainly experienced physical contentment, but their lives were probably deficient in other ways since they have produced chiefly what Toynbee called "arrested civilizations."

Modern man is not yet resigned enough to be completely satisfied with purely creature contentment. He still hopes that he can discover a philosophy of life that will be as creative and emotionally rewarding as that of classical Greece or of Western Europe in the thirteenth century.

Our greatest blessing, says Socrates in Plato's dialogue *Phaedrus*, comes to us by way of madness—mania. In this arresting statement, Plato does not mean mania as a disease, but rather as a state during which man experiences a kind of self-revelation occurring through the emergence of a powerful spirit from the depth of his being. Poetical words, tones, and gestures, and even prophecy are the expressions of enthusiasm—the god within. Apparently certain drugs can help in generating this inspired state. But Plato traced inspiration to the primeval forces that Greek mythology symbolized in the form of deities, especially Dionysos.

All ancient peoples have devised social practices to help overcome the limitations on life imposed by social mores. During the Dionysian ceremonies at certain times of the year, wine and dance were used to create a collective atmosphere of release from conventions—the kind of liberating experience which modern countercultures are trying to generate.[19] In ancient Greece, Dionysos was not only the god of wine; he was also Eleutherios, the Liberator, who loosened the lips and the hearts of men, thus helping them to achieve *ekstasis,* ecstasy. In its etymological sense, the word "ecstasy" means standing out of oneself, an attitude which may result in a profound change of personality. It denotes man's ability to escape from his past and also from biological and social conventions. This is a type of freedom which, as mentioned earlier, constitutes a striking difference between animal and human life. Throughout history, groups of men have placed themselves outside their societies and thus created new attitudes which became expressed in forms as different as countercultures, religion, or science.

Countercultures and the many types of intentional communities they commonly create are not social aberrations. For thousands of years, there have been attempts to provide alternatives for the existing social order in response to the perennial grounds for dissent: hierarchy and privilege, distrust of bureaucracy, disgust with hedonism and consumerism.[20] These are more than the dreamy schemes of dropouts, because they represent man's search for ways of life really suited to fundamental human needs.

Religion and science also constitute deep-rooted and ancient efforts to find richer experience and deeper meaning than are found in the ordinary biological and social satisfactions. As pointed out by Whitehead, religion and science have similar origins and are evolving toward similar goals. Both started from crude observations and fanciful concepts, meaningful only within a narrow range of conditions for the people who formulated them out of their limited tribal experience. But progressively, continuously, and almost simultaneously, religious and scientific concepts are ridding themselves of their coarse and local components, reaching higher and higher levels of abstraction and purity. Both the myths of religion and the laws of science, it is now becoming apparent, are not so much descriptions of facts as symbolic expressions of cosmic truths. These truths may always remain beyond human understanding, but at every stage of human development glimpses of them have enriched man in experience and comprehension. Together, religion and science make human life more than a flash of occasional enjoyments lighting up a mass of pain and misery; they save it from being a "bagatelle of transient experiences" and convert it into an adventure of the spirit.[21]

CHAPTER 13

Arcadian Life Versus Faustian Civilization

The legend of a Golden Age is so universal and so ancient that it must have a base of truth, as do most prehistoric legends.[1] At the very beginning of recorded history, more than five thousand years ago, the Sumerians evoked on clay tablets the idyllic land of Dilmun where their ancestors had led an Orphic life, free of sickness and old age, in a primitive paradise. For the early Jews, Palestine was a land flowing with milk and honey, as testified in many passages of the Pentateuch. And the Greek poet Hesiod described in *Works and Days*, written around 750 B.C., happier times when "men lived like gods . . . passed their days in tranquillity and joy . . . and the earth was more beautiful than now."[2] Every age has thus stated in stories or pictures a longing for the worlds we have lost, the melancholy mood so beautifully conveyed by Nicholas Poussin in his painting *"Et in Arcadia ego"* (And I too once lived in Arcadia).[3]

Poussin's painting shows three handsome young men reading the inscription *"Et in Arcadia ego"* on a tomb in a pastoral, semitropical landscape. It calls to mind the East African plateaus where probably the human species emerged several million years ago. But the mythical land of Arcadia might also be in other parts of the earth, indeed anywhere an abundance of game, fruits, and nuts made life relatively secure for pre-agricultural man.

As long as population density remained very low, the hunter-gatherer way of life could provide adequate nourishment without much physical effort. As a result, the cave man's life during the Early Stone Age may not have been as short, nasty, and brutish as is commonly believed. The study of bones, approximately fifty thousand years old, from various Neanderthal groups in fact indicates that the expectancy of life in the Early Stone Age was probably longer than used to be thought; a large percentage of bones from these groups were of people between thirty and sixty years of age. Even the view that life was then nasty and brutish may have to be changed in the light of recent discoveries by Ralph S. Solecki, professor of anthropology at Columbia University. In the Shanidar cave in Iraq, Solecki found evidence that Neanderthal people buried their dead on beds of woody branches and flowers—grape hyacinth, yellow groundsel, hollyhock, and yarrow. Furthermore, one of the Neanderthal skeletons found in the Shanidar cave was that of an adult man who had been blind and whose right arm had been amputated above the elbow early in life. This man had lived to the age of forty before a rock fall killed him, and since he could hardly have foraged for himself, he must have been supported by his people for most of his lifetime. These discoveries suggest that *Homo neanderthalis* was truly human as far back as fifty-thousand years ago.[4]

The Cro-Magnon people occupied sites where game was readily available and abundant. In consequence, they probably had much leisure time for social intercourse and for the creation of their weapons, tools, sculptures, and paintings. The beauty of these artifacts is further evidence that the qualification brutish is unsuited to the life of early man.

There still exist today a few pre-agricultural tribes that derive their sustenance almost exclusively from the hunter-gatherer way of life. The Australian aborigines, the Bushmen of the Kalahari Desert, the Xavante Indians of Mato Grosso in Brazil are examples of such pre-agricultural peoples who develop great physical vigor, speak a complex language, and have rich and subtle traditions, even though they live in environments much poorer than were those of the Paleolithic hunters. In view of the fact that irreparable damage is being done to these contemporary primitive people, it is fortunate that their ways of life have been recorded in their native habitats. Photographs and moving pictures reveal in particular qualities of tenderness and happiness rarely seen on civilized faces. The love of parents for their children, the excitement of children for the pleasurable things they find in nature, the expressiveness of smiling faces have not been improved by modern civilization.

As was recognized by the European explorers who first came into contact with Africans, Polynesians, Eskimos, and American Indians, many forms of primitive life are compatible with longevity, health, and *joie de vivre.* Disease and a very short life span, as well as miserable social habits, are expressions not of primitive life per se but of disturbances in the traditional ways of tribal existence during the first phases of contact with Western civilization.

The legend of the Golden Age may thus be the remembrance, poetized by time and by imaginative embellishments, of a very distant past when certain groups of people had achieved biological fitness to their environment. To a large extent, the fitness of primitive people was a product of Darwinian evolution, very similar to the fitness achieved by animals that live in the wild and are well adapted to the environments in which they have evolved. Biological memories long persist as a component of culture when they are transmitted orally in the form of myths or legends.

When more food became available through the practice of agriculture, the human population rapidly increased. But the agricultural ways of life probably brought about a decrease of man's fitness to his environment. Even though for many generations most people never moved far from small villages, and therefore were close to nature, their living conditions became increasingly unnatural, especially after social power structures began to organize large groups of human beings for collective enterprises such as irrigation projects or the building of temples. According to the French anthropologist Henri Vallois, who made comparative studies of skeletons from various periods of prehistory, the life span of the farming Neolithic people was shorter than that of the Paleolithic hunters.[5] Agriculture started man on his way to modern civilization, but the price was the end of the Arcadian way of life.

For thousands of years, men have dreamed of natural pleasures in some mythical Arcadia, but they have spent a very large percentage of their waking hours toiling to modify nature. Even stronger than man's biological urge for natural ways of life is his conviction that he can and should transform the world to make it a better and happier place. This was symbolized by the ancient Greeks in the myth of Prometheus, the demi-god who stole fire from Zeus and brought it down to man. According to the Prometheus myth the control of fire made man superior to animals by enabling him to make tools, warm his dwellings, engage in trade, develop medicine, and create the arts.

There is no indication in the myth—or in reality for that

matter—that Promethean man is happier than Arcadian man or than wild animals. But he differs from them in deriving a uniquely human satisfaction from manipulating nature to create new patterns and new values according to his desires. In Aeschylus's play *Prometheus Bound*, the demi-god takes immense pride in having enabled men to use nature for their own ends and thereby to become really human.

Promethean man believes that, through his techniques and his labor, he can re-create paradise by imposing order on the chaotic wilderness. During the Middle Ages, the Benedictine monks even felt it was their duty to improve nature, as if they were acting as partners of God in completing the Divine Creation.[6] They used fire, windmills, and watermills to convert wilderness into a modified form of nature more suitable to human use, more pleasing to human eyes, and, as they believed, more appropriate to the worship of God.

Arcadian life symbolizes biological adaptedness to the natural world, but Promethean man changed this world by bringing out its unexpressed potentialities through his work and vision. Cities and towns are obviously of human origin, but, as I have said, so is most of what we call nature, because the environments in which we now live have been created out of wilderness. Practically all aspects of life are artificial in the sense that they depend on profound modifications of the natural order of things. The life of the peasant is as artificial as that of the city dweller when he prolongs his activities after sundown with candles or electric light, when he shaves either with an old-fashioned blade or an electric razor, when he eats bread or canned goods instead of raw meat, fruit, and nuts. None of these activities is part of the primitive way of life.

Even people who are generally regarded as primitive have developed not only precise knowledge of their physical and biological environment but also rich and subtle languages, complex social structures, wonderful love songs and art forms, imaginative accounts of creation. Obviously, then, tools are not essential for the development of humanness or of cultures, but certainly Promethean life has immensely enlarged the range of man's experiences and has enabled him to populate the earth. Whereas the hunter-gatherer way of life could support a world population of only ten million to twenty million persons at most, the kinds of agriculture and of technology that existed even before the industrial revolution made it possible for a billion people to live on earth with a reasonable degree of comfort and safety. Many forms of knowledge and creativeness did not become possible until the various human groups had reached a critical minimum size and until Promethean life had widened the range of living conditions.

The achievements of Cro-Magnon man show that his intellectual potentialities were not significantly different from ours. There is no doubt, furthermore, that only people endowed with marvelous intellectual gifts could have created out of wilderness the immensely varied technologies and art forms of the Neolithic and Bronze ages. The world population was still very small ten thousand years ago, yet most of the artifacts on which daily life depends today had been invented by the time of the Sumerian civilization. Furniture, writing, social structures, religious worship, scientific knowledge, and art forms all reached very early a high level of perfection wherever men gathered in sufficiently large numbers.

The humanization of nature also reached a high level of quality long before the development of sophisticated techniques. In southern China, village sites have been selected from time immemorial according to the doctrine known as *feng-shui*—wind and water. This doctrine is concerned with the protection of persons against ghosts and evil influences.

But it teaches also that buildings be located in such a way as to be protected against storms and floods, exposed to warmth and attractive views, and readily accessible to farmlands, streams, and groves of trees—truly a simple formula for a contented life. Ancient Japan also provides wonderful illustrations of man fitted to his environment. The very word Nippon evokes a wonderfully integrated composition of natural scenery and climate, humanized landscape and architecture, formal ways of life and functionally elegant furniture. Such fitness could hardly have been achieved through conscious design; it must have developed more or less spontaneously in the course of the slow interplay between man and his total environment. As Bernard Rudofsky points out in *Architecture without Architects*, the architecture of primitive people is often fundamentally better than that of the present.[7]

The explorers of the Pacific during the eighteenth century soon became aware of the fact that, even though the Polynesians had been isolated from the rest of the world, many of them could readily adopt the European way of life and even enjoy its frivolities. Captain Cook and Bougainville each brought back from Tahiti a Polynesian—a noble savage—whom they introduced to the royal court in their respective capitals. Omai in London and Aoutourou in Paris made a sensation and soon participated in the activities of the fashionable world. Aoutourou in particular took an active part in the Paris social life which titillated him and which he could not resist though he found it absurd; one took one's pleasures more naturally in the South Sea islands but not so amusingly.[8]

The ready acceptance of the European way of life by the Polynesians in the eighteenth century has been duplicated whenever and wherever primitive people have come into contact with Western civilization. In our time, the peoples of the few tribes which are still in a Stone Age culture can acquire sophisticated technical skills and develop civilized ways if exposed to them early in life. Ancient man, or primitive man today, could function as an IBM employee, or even become president of the company, provided he had been raised under the proper conditions. But this proviso defines the limitations of primitive life.

Many of the potential attributes of man become expressed only if the individual receives appropriate stimuli at the proper time and under the proper conditions. One of the largest contributions of Promethean life has been to increase the variety of environmental stimuli, thus improving the individual's chance to achieve a more complete expression of his biological and psychological potentialites. For lack of knowledge, and also of will, modern societies have not yet learned to take advantage of this marvelous plasticity of man's nature. But the possibility exists and justifies the ancient belief, passionately expressed in Aeschylus's play *Prometheus Bound*, that Promethean life has not only enabled man to transform the earth but also helped him enrich his primitive animal nature with the qualities of civilized humanness.

The Prometheus myth symbolizes man's escape from animal bondage and the enlargement of his life. From the very beginning of civilization, however, man has used his skills not only creatively but often for destructive or at least selfish pursuits. He has engaged in countless military ventures, satisfied his ego with useless displays of wealth, and increasingly manifested cosmic arrogance and a tendency to believe that his powers are limitless. Technologic utopians that we have become, we regard ourselves, not as tenants or lodgers on the earth, but as its landlords. We identify progress with the conquest of the external world. Even George P. Marsh, the first

American prophet of ecology, asserted man's dominion over nature in uncompromising terms:

> The life of man is a perpetual struggle with external Nature. It is by rebellion against her commands and the final subjugation of her forces alone that man can achieve the nobler ends of his creation. . . . Wherever he fails to make himself her master, he can but be her slave.[9]

Perhaps not surprisingly, ecologists hardly ever quote this extraordinary, anti-ecological statement of their prophet.

It is a distressing fact that the Faustus legend is the only important one created by Western civilization. The activities of the learned and dynamic Dr. Faustus symbolize our own restlessness and our eagerness to achieve mastery over men and the external world, irrespective of long-range consequences. Faustus was willing to sell his soul to the devil for the sake of worldly pleasures and his own selfish ambitions, just as modern Faustian man does not hesitate to jeopardize the future of mankind in the pursuit of his goals.

In the United States, the Four Corners regional development for electric power is a current example of the problems man is creating for the near future. The Four Corners region, where Utah, New Mexico, Arizona, and Colorado meet, has abundant reserves of low-sulfur coal, a plentiful supply of cooling water from the Colorado River, and a low population density. This region therefore constitutes an ideal location for coal-fired plants which could supply electricity to Los Angeles, Las Vegas, Phoenix, Albuquerque, and other southwestern communities. However, the operation of these plants implies strip mining of coal, acid drainage, soil erosion, an enormous outpouring of stack effluents, the disposal of waste heat into the Colorado River—in other words, a variety of undesirable effects which will certainly upset the ecosystem over large areas for long periods of time. The present generation of energy users will no longer be around when succeeding generations are faced with the immense and costly task of repairing the environmental degradation caused by our undisciplined gluttony for electric power.[10]

A problem of even greater magnitude and potential danger is being created all over the world by the development of huge breeder nuclear reactors which will produce large amounts of plutonium—an incredibly dangerous substance. The prospect is made even more frightening by the plans to use the power produced by these plants for a variety of activities such as desalination of water, industrialized agriculture, urban developments. Even if we had all the technological and ecological know-how for the planning and management of these complexes (and what a big if!), it is likely that they would create social environments in which life would have to be highly regimented and would soon create the feeling of alienation. Modern man does not ask the help of the devil in the pursuit of his ambitions; instead he uses and misuses science and technology with little concern for the future.

The more complete the rule of Faustian man, and the longer he adheres to the philosophy that nature must be conquered, the faster will the environment be spoiled and the quality of human life degraded. If the future were to be strictly determined by the logical development of present trends, all aspects of creation over which man has control would be threatened with spoilage or destruction. Fortunately, as has been mentioned, the Faustian philosophy is under attack in many parts of the Western world and particularly in the United States. Ten years ago, no social movement existed to question the wisdom of building in a particular place a superhighway, a gigantic airport, a pollution-creating factory, a fossil-fuel or nuclear power plant. Now, in contrast, many such projects are being opposed by the public, often successfully. The increase in awareness of long-range consequences and in concern for the welfare of future generations has compelled profound changes in technological planning, as for example in the case of the Four Corners power development and of all other fossil-fuel and nuclear power plants. Western civilization, which invented the Faustian legend, is now becoming aware of its disastrous implications for the future. It is beginning to realize that the Faustian way of individual life is the way to racial death.

Most civilizations have been finally destroyed by military conquest, but in practically all cases they had been weakened by internal disturbances long before external enemies gave them the *coup de grâce*. The usual pattern is that a particular civilization develops to the point of absurdity certain characteristics which had contributed to its initial success and then to its power—just as certain animal species overdevelop organs in their evolution. Civilizations commonly behave as if they became intoxicated with their technological and social proficiency and lost critical sense in dealing with their own creations. This tendency is exemplified by the fate of Gothic architecture.

The architects of the twelfth and thirteenth centuries had such confidence in their technical skills that they built higher and higher cathedrals with more and more flamboyant ogives. In 1163, the vault of the nave in Notre Dame of Paris achieved the world's record with a height of 110 feet. This record was broken by Chartres in 1194 with 114 feet, then by Rheims in 1212 with 125 feet, then by Amiens in 1221 with 140 feet. Competition between cities became eventually as strong a motivating force in architectural design as was the glorification of God. Even though the nave of Amiens cathedral was so high that it gave a sense of insecurity, its splendor and boldness stirred the people of Beauvais to jealousy. When they began to build their own cathedral in 1227 they vowed to raise its vault 13 feet higher than that of Amiens. The Beauvais choir was brought to the promised height, but it had hardly been roofed when it fell. The Beauvais people rebuilt the choir, and once more it fell. A third time they built it, this time to 154 feet from the ground, but then they ran out of funds and the church was left without transept or nave for two centuries. Eventually, in 1500, the gigantic transepts were begun, and in 1552 a lantern tower was raised over the transept cross to a height of 500 feet. In 1573 the tower collapsed, bringing down with it large sections of the transept and choir. This was the end of the great period of Gothic architecture, and in any case the Gothic style had become less and less meaningful because it was no longer the spiritual expression of the age of faith. The Gothic experience provides a symbol for what has happened to many civilizations in the past, and for what is now happening to our own.

Like architectural styles, successful social structures have often been developed to a point of absurdity. The administrative genius of the Roman Empire in using the populations and the natural resources of the countries it conquered eventually caused its failure by making it completely dependent on these countries and even more by allowing it to grow beyond manageable size. The centralization of political power in the French monarchy helped to make France the greatest nation in Europe, but it reached the point of absurdity in Louis XIV's formula *"L'Etat c'est Moi"* (I am the State), which prepared the ground for the Revolution.

Our own civilization is also threatened by the absurd development of characteristics which were highly desirable when they first emerged. Thus the escape from physical drudgery has degenerated into contempt for physical work; the struggle for equality of rights has led to the belief that there is equality of talents; the use of the automobile for greater freedom of movement has turned into a compulsion; efficiency has become an end unto itself, destructive of diversity and of the quality of life; economic growth which originally produced more goods for more people is now largely pursued for its own sake, even when it means ecological degradation.

The ultimate form of the growth myth, which would be comical if it were not suicidal, is the affirmation, endlessly repeated from a myriad of official platforms, that our survival and the quality of our lives depend upon the production of more and more electric power. It is claimed that continuation of progress demands that the production of electricity continue to increase at a rate of some 6 percent a year, whereas in fact the population increases at a rate of only 1 percent a year.

For many years, there was not a truer slogan than "Better life through electricity." But the use of electricity now constitutes one of the best illustrations of a good thing overdeveloped to an absurd point. In urban areas, a very large percentage of electricity is used for obnoxious and absurd advertising, for raising high-speed elevators to absurd heights, and for absurd practices of air conditioning. In most parts of the country windows that could be opened to provide cross ventilation would greatly decrease the need for air conditioning. This, in turn, would decrease the amount of heat generated at the site of the power plant where electricity is produced, and in the city where heat is released by air conditioners. What is needed is not more electricity for air conditioning, but saner architectural design. The problem of air conditioning is important in itself because it accounts for a large percentage of the demand for electricity in urban areas; it also provides an outstanding example of the fact that social needs can be satisfied by techniques other than more and more electric power provided we escape from the obsession that everything in life depends on such power.

In 1971 Manson Benedict, professor of nuclear engineering at Massachusetts Institute of Technology, advocated the rapid development of fast breeder reactors, because, in his words, "An abundant supply of electricity . . . is essential to civilized society."[11] But countless highly civilized societies developed before electricity was used or even recognized. Furthermore, though the consumption of electric power per capita in the United States was very much smaller in 1940 than it is now, there is no evidence that the present U.S. society is more civilized or happier than it was then. Nor are European people less civilized than American people because they consume only half as much electricity per capita. What Benedict really meant is that an ever-increasing supply of electricity is essential for a society which measures civilization by power and therefore by the amount of electricity it consumes—a circuitous argument. Whether this is the most desirable kind of society is far from obvious and in fact is doubted by increasing numbers of people—including many professors of engineering.

Industrial efficiency has generated immense economic wealth, but is making Western civilization dependent on technological and social structures so complex that they are almost out of control—witness the power blackouts all over the land. Through specialization in knowledge, in management, and in technical skills, our society has succeeded in achieving fitness between the social forms of life and the kinds of environment it creates. But fitness and efficiency impose limitations on freedom. For example, there is such an intricate reciprocal relationship in the United States between working habits, automobile transportation, the packaging industry, and other aspects of life that modifying any component of the system is likely to cause serious social disturbances. The result is a fundamental conservatism which substitutes endless manipulation of details for significant changes.

Biology shows that the most specialized and the most efficient forms of life commonly find it difficult to undergo rapidly enough the necessary adaptive modifications when the environment changes. In human societies as well, adaptability decreases with increasing specialization. Overspecialized cultures, like that of the United States, might find it difficult to move on to the next phase of social evolution. The efficiency achieved through extreme specialization is not an effective attribute to carry us across the divide which separates present-day technological society from a more humane and culturally more sophisticated way of life.

The American public has been brainwashed during recent decades into the belief that progress means introducing into our lives everything we know how to produce—an endless variety of food additives, ever more powerful automobiles, higher and higher buildings serviced by high-speed elevators, a senseless consumption of electricity to create a more artificial life. This kind of progress demands little imagination and its likely outcome is at best a return to the dark ages. Fortunately, the future will not be a magnified form of the present, for the simple reason that the absurdities of current trends are generating forces which will soon change the course of technological societies.

Beyond certain limits of complexity, which may have already been reached, societies become increasingly vulnerable to accidents as well as to sabotage. Had the 1965 blackout in the Northeast occurred during a very cold spell in midwinter, it would have played havoc with plumbing in most cities. The nuclear-agricultural-urban complexes now being contemplated would offer frightening opportunities for accidents, especially through sabotage during periods of social unrest.

Other self-limiting factors inherent in the technological enterprise are shortages of natural resources. As pointed out during a 1971 meeting of the International Chamber of Commerce,[12] for example, the industrial demands for copper are increasing so fast and the world supplies are so limited, that copper may come to be regarded as a precious metal, an eventuality which would compel profound changes in many industries. The various forms of environmental pollution, of which the public is becoming increasingly aware and intolerant, will soon act as other limiting factors in industrial growth. New technological developments will of course make possible the recovery of metals from low-grade ores and will facilitate pollution control. But these developments would require additional electric power, which itself may soon become a limiting factor. The consumption of electricity in the United States has doubled every ten years since the 1940s. This rate of increase, however, will not last very long, were it only because both the production and the consumption of electric power inescapably generate heat. Thermal pollution will soon become intolerable, at first locally, then on the global scale.

Technological civilization has raised standards of living for large numbers of people, but paradoxically it has also lowered the quality of life in many places. Standards of living refer to economic affluence, a fairly objective value, whereas the quality of life is much more subtle and subjective. But its lowering is clearly perceived by most people; there is increasing awareness furthermore that present institutions are no longer contributing to the good life. Steam and electricity, growth and efficiency are words which are associated with the excitement of the modern era. This kind of excitement, however, dates only from the industrial revolution and has not yet deeply imprinted the general public. The scientific and technological institutions which have created it might be rejected if the public comes to question their relevance to human fulfillment. Despite the triumphs of scientific technology, the modern world still derives its color from art, music, and poetry and its catchwords from history and fiction. People could reject science more readily than singing, dancing, and story telling; they could find sufficient emotional and intellectual rewards seated with a brush in front of an easel or in a corner with a book.

A decline in the quality of life coinciding with an increase in economic affluence symbolizes the trend toward the absurd in technological societies. Present-day countercultures probably are the expressions of a deep-seated, almost subconscious social wisdom capable of generating protective responses against this trend.

Throughout history, countercultures have appeared irrational, at least in their outward manifestation. The prosperous young men and women who adopted a strictly cloistered monastic life during the Middle Ages, the nineteenth-century Bohemians who engaged in antics to protest against the pomposity of bourgeois life and art, certainly must have looked irrational to the majority of reasonable people of their times. But in fact, countercultures have commonly been motivated by a higher kind of rationality than that of the Establishment. What they express is not ordinary political dissent but rather the first stirrings of a true revolution in thought. They represent a soul-searching in quest of values which once gave zest to living and which are being lost—such as direct experience of nature, intimacy, uniquesness, and even eccentricity. The violence of the protests against present social trends is a warning that electronic gadgets, plastic knickknacks, and processed foodstuffs do not compensate for the degradation of nature into wastelands, of bright atmospheres into murky skies, of free behavior into regimented life.

The most obvious manifestation of a counterculture is withdrawal from orthodox society, as exemplified by the Franciscan and Benedictine monks in the Middle Ages, the Bohemians in the nineteenth century, and many young people today. Very different in manifestation but identical in origin is the questioning of formerly accepted social premises by members of the Establishment itself. The French Revolution was greatly facilitated by the fact that many members of the privileged classes—in the nobility, the higher ranks of the clergy, and the prosperous bourgeoisie—had lost faith in the institutions of the Ancien Régime. The need for a new social order had been recognized not only among philosophers and working people, but also in the fashionable salons. In her diary, Madame Vigée-Lebrun, who was Marie Antoinette's portrait painter, reports conversations that took place at the Château de Malmaison in the summer of 1788. To her dismay, she heard such respectable persons as the Abbé Sieyès and M. du Moley, the very owner of the chateau, defend the necessity for violent social changes. Ironically enough, one of the early victims of the upheavals brought about by the Revolution was du Moley himself, who had to sell Malmaison to Joséphine, then the wife of General Napoleon Bonaparte.[13]

A good-sized anthology could be compiled from statements made during the past decade by leaders of finance and technology who have expressed the view that industrial technology cannot continue much longer in its present form.[14] Don K. Price, dean of the J.F. Kennedy School of Government at Harvard University, went as far as to say, in his address as retiring president of the American Association for the Advancement of Science in 1969: "To me, it seems possible that the new amount of technological power let loose in an overcrowded world may overload any system we may devise for its control; the possibility of a complete and apocalyptic end of civilization cannot be dismissed as a morbid fancy."[15]

The most effective manifestation of the counterculture may not be the self-withdrawal of young people from society, but the widespread feeling in the Establishment that the time has come to challenge the rationality of endless economic growth and to formulate new social and technological policies. These new policies include not only a more equitable distribution of wealth but also the conservation of nonrenewable resources and the protection of the environment. It is widely realized that hope for the future lies not in technological fixes but in more intelligent social design and in a reformulation of the intangible values and sanctions of our culture.

The statements by Charles Luce and Dennis Gabor quoted earlier may come to have the character of self-fulfilling prophecies. If Americans do manage to overcome the growth addiction and to redirect the technological enterprise to new goals, it will be largely because many leaders of finance and technology are losing faith in the viability of present industrial and social institutions, just as the French nobility and clergy had lost faith in the institutions of the Ancien Régime. This change of attitude is reflected all over the world in the mode of thinking about the future. Traditional forecasting used to be influenced by social convictions and by personal eagerness for innovations. In contrast, modern futurologists try to consider multiple possibilities and even questionable probabilities; they are neither utopian nor apocalyptic but are sensitive to the fact that changing aspirations and life styles inevitably affect social and technologic planning.[16]

Because of its privileged geographical situation and its lateness in development the United States was probably one of the last industrialized countries to realize that the finiteness of the world imposes constraints on views of the future. American civilization, however, has been so wasteful and destructive of the earth's resources that it may now take the lead in emphasizing stability instead of growth, recycling instead of waste, socially oriented planning instead of development for profit. Nowhere in the world is there more painful awareness that ecological disasters and social chaos can be avoided only by profound changes in values and in life styles. Fortunately, there are many examples of social and environmental situations which appeared damaged beyond repair yet were rapidly corrected by pointed human effort.

A century ago, the great industrial cities of the Western world were in a worse state than ours are today. Poverty, alcoholism, drug addiction, prostitution, crime, pollution of air, water, and food, and every possible form of physiological misery and urban decadence could be found in London, Paris, New York, and other large industrial cities. For several decades, most prosperous people seemed to be unaware of the degradation of life and the environment within short distances of their opulent mansions. But social conscience was finally awakened—in part by the voices of public-minded citizens and even more perhaps by writers such as Charles Dickens, Émile Zola, Feodor Dostoevski, Maxim Gorki, Upton Sinclair. The movement toward political, social, and environmental reforms soon became so vigorous that many of the problems resulting from the first phase of the industrial revolution had been partially solved by the end of the nineteenth century. Our problems today differ from those of the nineteenth century, but there is no evidence that their solution will be more difficult once public concern and political power have been effectively mobilized to attack them. Progress would be much more rapid if, in addition to technical experts, there existed among us the kind of warm and eloquent voices which then activated political forces by making the public emotionally concerned with the gravity of the crisis.

Many historical examples can be adduced to show that Western societies have repeatedly experienced and overcome social and environmental difficulties at least as serious as those of our times. Alcoholism and drug addiction have had their ups and downs throughout European and American history. The painting "L'absinthe" by Edgar Degas evokes in a haunting manner the stuporous mood created in many men and women of the Western world, especially in France, by absinthe addiction; yet absinthe was effectively banned from the United States in 1912 and disappeared almost completely from the French scene after 1915. Even the problem of overpopulation may not be as intractable as it appears today. Throughout history, many populations have remained stable in size for long periods of time, or even decreased, in response to a variety of social conditions. This was true in the past for the Polynesian islands and for other areas where means of subsistence were limited either by lack of space or by shortage of certain natural resources. In modern times, birth limitation occurred in Ireland following the potato famine of 1850, and in France between 1840 and 1940 for complex social reasons and despite economic prosperity. There are indications that several European countries are once more approaching a phase of stable population, as did Japan in the 1950s.

The immense resilience of nature is demonstrated by the rapidity with which flora and fauna recovered, as mentioned earlier, on the islands which had been completely devastated by the Krakatoa volcanic eruption or by the nuclear explosions in the South Pacific. Further evidence of this recuperating power of nature is provided by the fact that landscapes spoiled by the pollutants of industrial civilization can often be improved simply by removing the conditions which had caused them to deteriorate. Lake Washington near Seattle was almost as polluted as Lake Erie; yet it recovered its pristine quality without treatment, less than ten years after steps were taken to prevent its further pollution. In Sweden, programs are on the way for the restoration of several types of lakes which had been damaged by pollution or partial drainage. Shallow lakes overgrown with reeds or with algal bloom and deep lakes suffering from oxygen depletion are beginning to revive.[17]

London had been grossly polluted for several centuries; yet dramatic changes for the better followed shortly after implementation of the amendments to the Rivers Act in 1951 and the Clean Air Act of 1955. The city has been free of its notorious pea-soup fogs for almost a decade; the amount of sunshine reaching it is now much greater than it was in 1950; the songbirds of Shakespeare's time are once more heard in the parks; herons have been seen recently, and fish can again be caught in the Thames.

History shows, moreover, that man can create new ecological situations which are desirable and stable. The so-called cane land of Kentucky might have been invaded, under certain social conditions, by worthless weeds, sedge, and scrub, but instead it became the wonderful bluegrass country after being subjected to ax, fire, plow, and cow by the nineteenth-century pioneers.[18] The countryside now served by the Tennessee Valley Authority was once ruined by the gullies and scourings of soil erosion. Today the renewed fertility of the land, as well as the beauty of the dogwood and judas trees blossoming on the hillsides above the winding lakes formed by the dams, illustrate the possibility of restoring the quality of nature and even of creating from it new environmental values.

Half a century ago, canals and locks were constructed to join Union Bay on the east side of Seattle with Lake Union, and this lake with salt-water Puget Sound. As the water level fell in the bay, vast marshes emerged along its gently sloping shores; in time, these marshes evolved into a rich wildlife habitat harboring more than a hundred different species of birds, as well as weasel, mink, muskrat, and otter. The marshes are unfortunately now used as landfill—a practice which threatens their wildlife and their beauty.[19] A similar situation is presently developing on the Mississippi River where a harbor-dredging project of the Corps of Engineers threatens a pool on the river near Keokuk, Iowa. Although this pool is not a natural body of water, it has served as a major stop-off for diving ducks on the Mississippi Flyway ever since it was created sixty years ago.[20]

In the heart of Poland's industrial region in Upper Silesia, a 1,500-acre refuge with a highly diversified fauna and flora has been developed on an area which had been used for 150 years as a dumping ground for wastes from nearby coal mines and for slag from blast furnaces. Similarly, much of the Brooklyn Botanic Garden is located on land which had been used as an ash dump by New York City; it is of interest that this land was transformed at the turn of the century by the work of a very few people and a team of horses.

Jamaica Bay on the south shore of Long Island was originally part of a rich natural salt-marsh ecosystem which included the land areas that now surround the Kennedy International Airport. For years, New York City used the bay as a garbage dump. The artificial islands thus created would have remained dreary masses of debris if it had not been for the devoted labor of a farsighted staff member of the New York Department of Parks, Herbert Johnson. Almost single-handed and with very limited funds, Johnson established on the landfills a vegetation of trees, shrubs, and grasses suited to the locality. Then nature took over. The plants grew rapidly as a typical wetland vegetation which attracted a variety of animal species, including such rare birds as the snowy owl, the glossy ibis, and the snowy egret.

The bird sanctuary and the man-made spoil islands of Jamaica Bay constitute great ecological success stories. But they are being threatened by the proposal to extend the Kennedy International Airport over part of the bay. One need not be a wildlife expert to know that the bird sanctuary would probably be destroyed by the runways. Furthermore, one need not be a transportation expert to know that, even though the operations of the airport would be somewhat facilitated by the extension of its runways, the improvement would be temporary and would be bought at the cost of further crowding of the airways. The Jamaica Bay–Kennedy Airport controversy is typical of many other environmental problems faced by the modern world, in that it transcends evaluation by the orthodox methods of science. There is no need of scientific studies to decide whether sacrificing the bird sanctuary or accommodating more airplanes should get preference. The decision involves only value judgments as to the relative importance of economic growth and urban quality. I am in favor of the birds.

Man-made ecosystems, on the other hand, present biological problems which are independent of social considerations. Jamaica Bay in particular cries out for long-range ecological studies, because these may provide indicators for what will happen to nature in industrialized areas. The Jamaica wetlands will remain under human influence even though they are protected; the bay is so close to the airport that jet aircraft will constantly fly over its wildlife sanctuary, and so close to New York City that the composition of its water, flora, and fauna will inevitably reflect urban pollution; in addition, since the bay is readily accessible to the public, the behavior and even the diet of the birds and other wildlife in the refuge will certainly be affected by human visitors. Jamaica Bay will thus constitute a microcosm for the study of the responses that natural forces make to the impact of technological forces. By allowing immense flocks of birds to share the skies with the huge jet aircraft, it provides at present a symbol for the hope that man can unite nature and technology in a viable organic whole.

Correcting the damage done to nature by industrialization is probably well within our powers, but to formulate new positive values for modern life will be much more difficult. We want, of course, better political and economic systems for a more adequate distribution of wealth and greater social justice; better planning of urban and rural environments, not only for reasons of efficiency, health, and esthetics, but also to enlarge and enrich human encounters; better engineering for less obsolescence and for more effective use of natural resources and of available energy; better chemical and biological methods for developing a new technology of recycling that will approach the productive economy of nature. Reaching these goals will enable us to escape from the present trends which would otherwise result in technological barbarism and a new version of the dark ages. Beyond this, however, there must be a renaissance, with the fresh and creative view of civilization that this word implies.

Man's conviction that he can shape his destiny through the exercise of will and knowledge is strikingly conveyed by the phrase "inventing the future"—the title of a justifiably famous book by Dennis Gabor.[21] We have indeed an enormous ability to imagine lands of Cockaigne in which life is effortless and behavior is governed by ideal systems of values. But, in practice, the futures we invent are viable only if they are compatible with the constraints imposed by the evolutionary past. This does not mean that the most desirable future is one which would take us back to the pretechnological womb. But it does mean that the unchangeable laws governing human nature and external nature must be kept in mind whenever plans are made to change the conditions of life. To discover these fundamental laws, we need to recapture the direct experience of reality out of which early man created concepts which remain basic to our own life today. We must also search for more fundamental patterns of reality through the abstractions of science, in the hope of understanding more precisely how we relate to the natural order of things from which man emerged. This search for the self and for our organic relation to nature may be what T.S. Eliot had in mind when he wrote in the *Four Quartets:*

> We shall not cease from exploration,
> And the end of all our exploring
> Will be to arrive where we started
> And know the place for the first time.[22]

We have not done enough to discover where we started from or to understand where we belong. Our efforts have been focused not on the search for reality but on the damage done to nature. During recent years, overpopulation, ecological disturbances, the dangers created by technology, and other instances of transgressing the laws of nature have been forcefully discussed.[23] I shall not consider these problems of the external environment but shall instead emphasize once more the practical importance of some internal attributes which the human species acquired during the Stone Age and which still operate in our lives today. This emphasis is justified by the fact that the deterioration of the psychological environment is as dangerous as environmental pollution but less well understood.

Loneliness is increasingly one of the curses of life in the urban agglomerations of the industrial world. The complexity of social and industrial structures is making human beings increasingly dependent on larger and larger population groups; the means of communication between and within groups are becoming more numerous, varied, and efficient. Yet, paradoxically, the outcomes of this interdependence and ready communication are the lonely crowd and also a pathological cult of personality. On the one hand each person tends to consider himself as unlike the rest of the group; on the other hand there is a frantic search for figureheads separate from the group but symbolizing its longings and illusions.

Modern cities are unfavorable to human relationships probably because they are almost incompatible in their present form with needs created during social evolution. Early man probably lived in bands of a fairly uniform size. The hunt for big game was a collective enterprise which demanded that the group be fairly large, and this generated complex social relationships. But the ecological limitations imposed by the hunter-gatherer way of life kept the group within a size determined by the availability of natural resources. Ten male hunters associated with forty women, old people, and children probably constituted a camp of reasonable size. Such a population unit was small enough that all of its members could interrelate and become a communal unity. In most cases, however, the hunting band and the camp were part of a larger breeding unit of several hundred persons living within a distance that permitted ready communication. By and large these determinants of population size apply to the few tribes which still live today under conditions approximating the primitive state. As mentioned earlier, social anthropologists use the magic numbers fifty and five hundred to define the range of group size most common in the hunter-gatherer way of life.

The practice of agriculture naturally resulted in much larger human settlements. But even though cities have existed for thousands of years, most human beings during prehistory and the greater part of history have lived in groups of relatively small size—whether as nomadic tribes or as village dwellers. In *The World We Have Lost*, the English writer Peter Laslett has shown that villages of some five hundred inhabitants constituted the fundamental demographic unit of England until the industrial revolution.[24] Recent studies of marriage records reveal, furthermore, that the average population group within which marriages are frequent—the so-called breeding community—rarely exceeds a thousand persons, even in large cities. It has even been claimed that the optimum size of the administrative structure in the modern corporation is of the same order as that of the primitive camp and the breeding community.[25] Whether he is part of a hunting tribe, an industrial city, or a late-twentieth-century corporation, man thus seems to function best in groups of less than a thousand persons and to find it difficult to deal personally with much more than a dozen. From time immemorial, armies have been organized on a similar numerical basis.

In the course of evolution, man naturally developed patterns of social relationships suitable for the size and structure of the groups in which he functioned. These patterns are apparent in many aspects of modern life. When the town of Longmond, Colorado, was established in the 1860s, its founders stated in the charter that "No man is integral within himself. We are all parts of one grand community and it behooves every man to know what his neighbor is about."[26] Experience has shown that this "grand community" must not be too large if it is to remain a true community.

Tastes change in social relationships as in other aspects of life, but irrespective of sophisticated communication techniques, patterns established thousands of years ago still influence the size and structure of social groups. Modern man is still psychologically conditioned by the range of human contacts that were possible during the Stone Age. He commonly finds village life stultifying and boring, yet he needs it emotionally. He spends much of his leisure time traveling in search of the village atmosphere and he endlessly illustrates it in novels and paintings. He even tries to re-create some aspects of it within the urban agglomerations—witness the appeal of block parties and the demand for neighborhood self-management in New York City. Much of the human charm of London and Paris comes from the fact that these cities still operate as if they were made up of a multiplicity of villages. American cities would benefit from the creation within their grotesque and obese structures of neighborhoods small enough to be capable of achieving identity and developing local pride.

The patterns of response established during evolutionary development may play a role even in artistic expression. Art is the product of a suggestive magic integrating subject and object and it always results from an intimate relationship between the artist and the external world. But the role of the public in the artistic experience has greatly changed in the course of time.

As commonly understood at present, the word art denotes a solo performance by the artist. Whether painting, sculpture, ornament, musical composition or interpretation, this performance is meant to convey the artist's message to a public who may provide understanding and feeling but is otherwise essentially passive. During most of human history, however, this type of creator-spectator relationship was uncommon. The ancient artifacts to which we now attribute artistic merit acted as triggers generating an interaction—a true trans-action—in which the public played a very active role. In fact, primitive art always involved tribal participation, as occurred obviously in the dance, and also in other important social activities. Early in the Middle Ages, the cathedral was a collective experience rather than a monument to be admired. Its construction and the religious celebrations it harbored provided stages for communal activity. The present tendency for a return to active participation by the whole social group in some forms of art suggests that we may be rediscovering the emotional value of this tribal experience.

There are many life styles and social designs compatible with the evolutionary past. But while man can do and can become many things, he cannot adapt to everything, and furthermore the expression of his potentialities is limited by social forces.

Each one of us lives in a particular society of which he accepts most of the mores even when he considers himself a nonconformist. To belong to a social group implies sharing with its members a vision of human fulfillment and accepting the concept of the ideal person it enshrines. This acceptance is illustrated by the widespread use of expressions epitomizing national characteristics. While there is no evidence whatever that nations differ significantly in the genetic endowment of their people, it is true nevertheless that such phrases as the sheer drive of the American, the ingenuity of the Japanese, the patience of the Chinese, the courage of the Yugoslav, the sangfroid of the Englishman derive validity from the fact that they denote attitudes regarded as highly desirable by these various national groups. We are all eager to retain freedom of judgment but we feel safe only within an accepted frame of conventions; absolute freedom would be unbearable because it would require an unremitting vigilance and involve at every moment an examination of all desires and activities.

Because he evolved as a social animal, man has a biological need to be part of a group and even perhaps to be identified with a place. He is likely to suffer from loneliness not only when he does not belong but also when the society or the place in which he functions is too large for his comprehension. Transient therapeutic experiences in encounter groups cannot satisfy the biological need to be a functioning part of a normal human community, a true supraorganism. Encounter groups, like technological fixes, at best alleviate or mask for a time the effects of a pathological state; they do not really correct it and they commonly generate new problems of their own.

Modern societies will have to find some way to reverse the trend toward larger and larger agglomerations and to recreate units compatible with the limits of man's comprehension—in other words, small enough that they can develop a social identity and a spirit of place. By cultivating regionalism, the United States could derive from its rich geographical diversity cultural values and also forms of economic wealth far more valuable because more humanly meaningful than those measured by the artificial criteria of a money economy.

Most human beings, probably all of them, crave the opportunity to express themselves in a unique manner. Even if industrial civilization manages to provide health, comfort, and peaceful relationships for all, it will fail in the long run if it does not create an atmosphere more favorable than the present one for the development of personality—in the strong sense defined earlier, the self-creation of the persona. There is something fundamentally irrational in a society which makes the ways of life of its members conform to the efficiency of technological operations, rather than to their individual needs and aspirations. Efficiency may be an essential criterion of modern technology, but man is not a machine. Diversity, not efficiency, is the sine qua non of a rich and creative human life.

Since persons differ in their endowments and aspirations, they need different kinds of opportunities and surroundings for self-expression and creation. Diversity is thus part of functionalism in the design of human settlements. Diversity may cause the world to become somewhat inefficient and even inconvenient, but in the long run it is more important than efficiency and convenience because it provides the variety of materials from which persons and civilizations emerge and continue to evolve. The inanimate world is a system running down and progressively losing its activities and varieties. In contrast, the living world evolves by widening the range of its activities and varieties. Without diversity, moreover, freedom is but an empty word. Men are not completely free if they do not have options from which to select in order to create out of their potentialities the kinds of lives they desire and the achievements by which they would like to be remembered.

Ideally each person—especially each child—should find in his physical and social environments stages on which to act out his life, in his own way. A meadow, an ocean shore, the banks of a river, a peaceful village green, the crowded plaza of a great city, a secluded room, or a busy street displaying the multifarious activities of daily life constitute so many different settings in which different kinds of human performance can be acted. Thinking of my own life as a child and a young man, I realize how I had the opportunity to select among a hundred different persons I could have become by selecting as the main stage for my life one or another of the hundred different atmospheres in streets, parks, and public squares of Paris—the plain folk jolliness of the Place de la Nation, the romantic mood of the benches along the Seine, the fashionable pretentiousness of the Parc Monceau, or the intellectual intoxication in the Luxembourg Gardens. Like Paris, certain other great cities of the world, such as Rome, London, New York, are uncomfortable and even traumatic, but they continue nevertheless to breed a wide range of talents because they offer a great diversity of stages on which very different kinds of people can act out lives of their own choices.

Moods concerning the future have changed drastically during the past few decades. Until the 1960s there was almost universal hope for a kind of utopia in which all human problems would be solved by science and technology. More recently, the prophets of doom have taken the limelight and have shown that the earth is becoming a poisoned wasteland soon to be unsuitable for human life. The really modern students of the future are more sophisticated. Like Professor Forrester at Massachusetts Institute of Technology, they program various combinations of known facts about the present world and read out from computers' analyses the social and ecological consequences of various courses of action.[27] But, in fact, the real future is likely to be very different from any of the predictable futures. Men are never passive witnesses of events, because they are endowed with free will. Once motivated, they take a strong position against trends and change the course of events. François Rabelais was expressing the attitude of a period which believed in free will and in its power to shape the future when he wrote at the beginning of the Renaissance: *"N'estez vous asceuré de vostre vouloir? Le poinct principal y gist: tout le reste est fortuit et dependent des fatales dispositions du Ciel."* (Are you not assured within yourself of what you have a mind to? The chief and main point of the whole matter lieth there: all the rest is merely casual, and totally dependeth upon the fatal disposition of the heavens.)[28]

The skeptics point out that the will to act is almost meaningless at the present time because we have no well-defined goals. We do not know what ought to be done, or even what we want to be done, among all the things that can be done. The truth, however, is that there has never been a precise answer to these questions. The future is always emergent and cannot be entirely planned. Now as in the past, seminal decisions will be made not on the basis of computerized abstract planning but through the vision and faith of men who have a holistic sense of what is feasible and enough courage to impose their will on events.

What is certain in any case is that a creative approach to the future is incompatible with the passive acceptance of technologic and economic growth—an attitude which is a form of social escapism and which would lead to collective suicide. Thoreau symbolized the need for an ecological point of view in social problems with the parable: "Can we do no more than cut and trim the forest? Can we not assist in its interior economy, in the circulation of the sap?"[29] By this he meant that we must regulate the uses we make of our environment instead of merely exploiting its resources and paying lip service to ecological considerations by making trivial embellishments. Unfortunately, ecological regulation is far more difficult than increasing industrial production. It takes only competent engineering and business experience to produce bigger and faster motor cars in ever greater numbers, but a much higher degree of technological imagination and social awareness is needed for adapting the automobile industry to the real needs of modern life. Industrial civilization will have to be reformulated on the basis of human ecological principles.

Thoreau's attitude, as described by Joseph Wood Krutch, comes close to my own view of contemporary problems:

> Thoreau was not a pessimist. He had faith in man's potentialities though little respect for the small extent to which man had realized them. He did not believe, as some do today, that man was a failure beyond redemption—he believed only that his contemporaries were failures because the true way had been lost a long time ago. . . . Thoreau's return to nature was a return to the fatal fork, to a road not taken, along which he hoped that he and others after him might proceed to a better future.[30]

Thoreau's attitude and Robert Frost's poem "The Road Not Taken" symbolize one of the most hopeful preoccupations of the modern world—the feeling that technological societies are engaged on a suicidal road but have a second chance to discover the good life if they are willing to retrace their steps. The general awareness of the defects in our present ways of life is creating throughout the Western world a social climate favorable to change.

Change does not imply that the past should be forgotten or rejected. In fact, the new road to progress will certainly take advantage of the most advanced technological culture. But this culture cannot possibly determine the way in which we perceive the world. We may understand the theory of electromagnetic waves intellectually and acknowledge the fact that they extend from 10^{-16} to 10^{8} meters, but our appreciation of color still extends only from red through purple to blue. As far as we are concerned, the real environment is that which we can perceive by our senses or which affects our bodies. The only world that is real for us is the primary phenomenal world in which the sun moves from east to west, the stars are hung in the skies, the reference of measurement is the human body. We remain Ptolemaic because this is the way we perceive the world during our early years, with the result that our reasoning, shaped by our senses, proceeds according to this initial way of thinking. Whatever road to progress he takes man will reach a desirable destination only if he is guided by the direct perception of his senses, and by the yearning for elemental modes of life.

Thoreau introduced *Walden* with an optimistic clarion call: "I do not propose to write an Ode to Dejection, but to brag as lustily as Chanticleer in the morning, standing on his roost, if only to wake my neighbors up." More prosaically, but in the same spirit, I conclude these pages with my own optimistic version of the humanistic faith: Trend is not destiny.

Envoi

I have lived through many springs, and the verdant memories I have of them can never dull the wonder of witnessing once more the renewal of nature. I can still smell the rich farm soil of the Île de France, fermenting in the first warm days of the year. I am still dazzled by the brilliant flowers emerging suddenly from the desert in the Mediterranean *guarrigue* or the American Southwest. During early April in the Hudson Valley, I am still exhilarated by the bright red buds of the swamp maples, the vibrant plumage of the bluebirds, the eerie calls of the peepers, the mourning doves, and the red-winged blackbirds.

The exuberance of nature in the spring appears almost indifferent to dangers. Undaunted by lawn mowers, dandelions return cheerfully every year, even on the most carefully tended lawns. Unconcerned with automobile traffic, woodchucks and rabbits graze along superhighways. Years ago, peregrine falcons used to forsake the cliffs of the New Jersey Palisades for the ledges of New York skyscrapers. And over Jamaica Bay immense flocks of birds take off not far from the flight patterns of jet aircraft over Kennedy Airport.

Despite the suffering, despair, and ugliness created by racial conflicts, national rivalries, food shortages, and pollution, the bells of Easter always lift me on waves of hope. To experience a spring day is enough to assure me that, eventually, life will triumph over death. On bomb craters in the midst of cities after the Second World War, delectable wild mushrooms appeared, as if to symbolize that life will continue to generate order and beauty from physical decay. Men have known for thousands of years that the phoenix can be reborn from its ashes. Our form of civilization may be sick and dying, but through the desolate, wintry climate of our times, there is beginning to emerge an effervescence of expectancy. Spring is calling, and men of good will are ready to proclaim once more, "The king is dead. Long live the king."

To assert that there is hope when everything looks so dark may appear a naive and pretentious illusion, but it is the kind of illusion that generates the creative faith of which Carl Sandburg wrote:

> I am credulous about the destiny of man,
> And I believe more than I can ever prove
> Of the future of the human race
> And the importance of illusions,
> The value of great expectations.[1]

It is often difficult to retain faith in the destiny of man, but it is certainly a coward's attitude to despair of events.

REFERENCE NOTES

SELECTED BIBLIOGRAPHY

INDEX

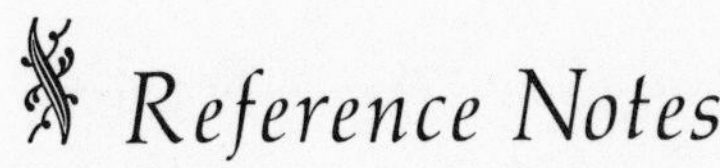

Reference Notes

INTRODUCTION: THE HIDDEN ASPECTS OF REALITY

1. Louis Pasteur, "Discours de Réception à l'Académie Française," *Oeuvres Complètes*, collected by Pasteur Vallery-Radot (Paris: Masson, 1933–1939), VII, 326–339. See also René Dubos, *Louis Pasteur—Free Lance of Science* (Boston: Little, Brown, 1950), 392.

2. Plato, *Phaedrus*, translated by H.N. Fowler (Cambridge: Loeb Classical Library, 1953), 465, 467.

3. Quoted in José Ortega y Gasset, *The Origin of Philosophy* (New York: Norton, 1967), 82.

4. Lawrence Durrell, *Spirit of Place* (New York: Dutton, 1969).

5. Leo Marx, *The Machine in the Garden* (New York: Oxford University Press, 1964).

6. "Toyota Chief Builds Shrine for the Souls of Accident Victims," *Wall Street Journal*, August 3, 1970.

7. Quoted in I.M. Lerner, *Heredity, Evolution and Society* (San Francisco: Freeman, 1968), 47.

8. E. Carpenter, F. Varley, and R. Flaherty, *Eskimo* (Toronto: University of Toronto, 1959); see also E. Carpenter, "Image-making in Arctic Art," in G. Kepes (ed.), *Sign, Image, Symbol* (New York:

Braziller, 1966), 206–225; Ladislas Segy, *African Sculpture Speaks* (New York: Hill and Wang, 1952).

9. Gerard Manley Hopkins, *A Hopkins Reader* (New York: Oxford, 1953).

10. Gary Snyder, *Earth House Hold* (New York: New Directions, 1969), 110.

11. Stephen A. Forbes, *The Lake as a Microcosm* (1887).

1. WORLDS WITHIN A WORLD

1. René Dubos, *Louis Pasteur. Freelance of Science* (Boston: Little, Brown, 1950), 183.

2. William James, *The Will to Believe* (New York: Longmans Green, 1907), ix.

3. Quoted in Russell Brain, *Some Reflections on Genius* (Philadelphia: Lippincott, 1960), 165.

4. John L. Stegmaier, "Cultural Endurance," *PHP*, August 1971, 96–97.

5. See John M. Brinnin, *The Sway of the Grand Saloon: A Social History of the North Atlantic* (New York: Delacorte, 1971).

6. Lewis Thomas, "Sensuous Symbionts of the Sea," *Natural History*, 80 (1971), 78.

2. A THEOLOGY OF THE EARTH

1. Walter Sullivan, *We Are Not Alone: The Search for Intelligent Life on Other Worlds* (New York: McGraw-Hill, 1964).

2. William Pollard, "God and His Creation," in Michael Hamilton (ed.), *This Little Planet* (New York: Charles Scribner's Sons, 1970), 59.

3. L.J. Henderson, *The Fitness of the Environment* (New York: Macmillan, 1913).

4. Joseph Wood Krutch, *The Desert Year* (New York: William Sloane Associates, 1952).

5. Quoted in C.G. Jung, *The Practice of Psychotherapy*, trans. R. F. C. Hull (London: Routledge & Kegan Paul, 1954), 196.

6. Quoted in David Mandel, *Changing Art, Changing Man* (New York: Horizon, 1967), 32.

7. Bronislaw Malinowski, *A Scientific Theory of Culture* (Chapel Hill: University of North Carolina Press, 1944), 200.

8. Henry Beston, *The Outermost House* (New York: Viking Compass, 1962), ix.

9. Paul Shepard, "Introduction: Ecology and Man—a Viewpoint," in Paul Shepard and Daniel McKinley (eds.), *The Subversive Science* (Boston: Houghton Mifflin, 1969), 1–10.

10. Scott I. Paradise, "Vandal Ideology," *Nation*, 209 (1969), 729–732.

3. DEEP ARE THE ROOTS

1. See Walter Menaker and Abraham Menaker, "Lunar Periodicity in Human Reproduction: A Likely Unit of Biological Time," *American Journal of Obstetrics and Gynecology*, 77 (1959), 905–914; U.M. Cowgill, A. Bishop, R.J. Andrew, and G.E. Hutchinson, "An Apparent Lunar Periodicity in the Sexual Cycle of Certain Prosimians," *Proceedings of the National Academy of Sciences*, 48 (1962), 238–241.

2. Vilhjalmur Stefansson, *The Friendly Arctic* (New York: Macmillan, 1953).

3. Richard B. Lee and Irven DeVore (eds.), *Man the Hunter* (Chicago: Aldine, 1968).

4. Gary Snyder, *Earth House Hold* (New York: New Directions, 1969), 92.

5. René Millon, "Teotihuacan: Completion of Map of Giant Ancient City in the Valley of Mexico," *Science*, 170 (1970), 1077–1082.

6. D.H. Lawrence, *Selected Literary Criticism* (New York: Viking, 1956), 162.

7. Snyder, op. cit., 87.

8. Quoted in Robert Coles, "Measure of Man," *The New Yorker*, 46 (1970), 77.

9. Ralph Waldo Emerson, *Representative Men* (Boston: Houghton Mifflin, 1893), 29.

10. See Alfred North Whitehead, *Science and the Modern World* (New York: Macmillan, 1925) and Harvey Cox, *The Secular City* (New York: Macmillan, 1966).

11. René Dubos, *So Human an Animal* (New York: Charles Scribner's Sons, 1968).

4. *INDIVIDUALITY, PERSONALITY, AND COLLECTIVITY*

1. Miguel de Unamuno, *Tragic Sense of Life* (New York: Dover, 1954), 1.

2. Irenaus Eibl-Eibesfeldt, *Ethology: The Biology of Behavior* (New York: Holt, Rinehart & Winston, 1970), 416, 420.

3. Quoted in Robert Coles, "Measure of Man," *The New Yorker*, 40 (1970), 89–90.

4. René Dubos, *So Human an Animal* (New York: Charles Scribner's Sons, 1968), 133.

5. Quoted in Robert Coles, *Erik Erikson, The Growth of His Work* (Boston: Little, Brown, 1970), 169.

6. Albert Camus, *La Chute* (Paris: Pleiade, 1962), 1502.

7. George Orwell, *The Collected Essays, Journalism and Letters. IV. In Front of Your Nose 1945–1950*, edited by Sonia Orwell and Ian Angus (New York: Harcourt, Brace & World, 1968), 515. See

also the statement "A man of fifty is responsible for his face," attributed to Edwin M. Stanton in H.L. Mencken, *A New Dictionary of Quotations* (New York: Knopf, 1942), 375.

8. Quoted in Herbert Blau, "The Future of the Humanities," *Daedalus*, 98 (1969), 663.

9. Quoted in Philip Hallie, *The Scar of Montaigne* (Middletown, Conn.: Wesleyan University Press, 1966), 42.

10. Michel de Montaigne, *The Complete Essays*, translated by D. Frame (Palo Alto, Calif.: Stanford University Press, 1958), 615.

11. José Ortega y Gasset, *The Dehumanization of Art and Other Writings on Art and Culture*, translated by Helene Weyl (Garden City, N.Y.: Doubleday, 1956), 153.

12. André Gide, *Les Nourritures Terrestres* (Paris: Mercure de France, 1897), Envoi (quotation translated by René Dubos).

13. Paul Tillich, *The Courage to Be* (New Haven: Yale University Press, 1952), 113.

14. Feodor Dostoevski, *Notes from Underground*, in *The Short Novels of Dostoevsky*, translated by Constance Garnett (New York: Dial Press, 1945), 145, 149.

15. Quoted in Philip Hallie, op. cit., 45.

5. OF PLACES, PERSONS, AND NATIONS

1. Feodor Dostoevski, *Notes from Underground*, in *The Short Novels of Dostoevsky*, translated by Constance Garnett (New York: Dial Press, 1945), 145, 149.

2. A.R. Luria, *The Mind of a Mnemonist*, translated by Lynn Solotaroff (New York: Basic Books, 1968).

3. Lawrence Durrell, *Spirit of Place* (New York: Dutton, 1969), 157, 163.

4. C.D. Darlington, *The Evolution of Man and Society* (London: George Allen and Unwin, 1969), 611.

5. D. Carleton Gajdusek, "Physiological and Psychological Characteristics of Stone Age Man," *Engineering and Science*, 33 (1970), 62.

6. Quoted in ibid., 62.

7. J.M. Thoday, "Geneticism and Environmentalism," in J.E. Meade and A.S. Parkes (eds.), *Biological Aspects of Social Problems* (London: Oliver and Boyd, 1965).

8. Gary Snyder, *Earth House Hold* (New York: New Directions, 1969), 40.

9. Hippocrates, *Of Airs, Waters, and Places*, translated by W. Jones (London: Heinemann, 1931).

10. James Baldwin, *Notes of a Native Son* (New York: Dial Press, 1963), 26, 25, 20.

11. Ibid., 28, 125, 34.

12. Martin Buber, *Israel and the World* (New York: Schocken, 1948).

13. Nochman Krochmal (1785–1840), quoted in ibid., 197.

14. Ernest Renan, *Qu'est ce qu'une nation?* (Paris: R. Helleu, 1934).

15. George Orwell, *The Collected Essays, Journalism and Letters. III. As I Please, 1943–1945*, edited by Sonia Orwell and Ian Angus (New York: Harcourt, Brace and World, 1968), 6.

16. Max Lerner, "Images of America and Man," *Graduate Journal*, III (1960), 22.

17. Orwell, op. cit., 6.

18. Thomas Sprat, *History of the Royal Society of London* (London: 1667).

19. Quoted in Terry Coleman, "History—Yes; Charity—No," *New Society*, 14 (1969), 733.

20. James Bryce, *Social Institutions of the United States* (New York: Chautauqua Press, 1891), 176–179. See also *Bulletin of New York Academy of Medicine*, 46 (1970), 291.

21. Quoted in Arthur Tourtellot, *The Charles* (New York: Farrar & Rinehart, 1941), 229.

22. Emil Lengyel, "America from the Lecture Platform," in

B.P. Adams (ed.), *You Americans* (New York: Funk & Wagnalls, 1939), 249–261.

23. Michel-Guillaume Jean de Crèvecoeur, *Journey into Northern Pennsylvania and the State of New York,* translated by C. Bostelmann (Ann Arbor, Mich.: University of Michigan Press, 1964), 493.

24. Francis J. Grund, *The Americans in Their Moral, Social, and Political Relations* (London, 1837), vol. 2, 263–264. See also David Lowenthal, "The American Scene," *The Geographical Review,* 58 (1968), 75.

25. Quoted in John A. Kouwenhoven, "What's American About America?" in Charles Muscatine and Marlene Griffith (eds.), *The Borzoi College Reader* (New York: Knopf, 1966), 184.

26. Henry Shapiro and Zane Miller (eds.), *Physician to the West: Selected Writings of Daniel Drake on Science and Society* (Lexington, Ky.: University Press of Kentucky, 1970), 313.

27. Ralph Waldo Emerson, *English Traits,* in *The Selected Writings of Ralph Waldo Emerson* (New York: Modern Library, 1950), 548.

28. Quoted in David Lowenthal, "The American Scene," op. cit., 76, 85.

29. Octavio Paz, "A Literature of Foundations," *TriQuarterly,* 13/14 (1968/69), 8.

30. Ibid., 9.

31. Quoted in Van Wyck Brooks and O.L. Bettmann, *Our Literary Heritage* (New York: Dutton, 1956), 237.

32. Quoted in ibid., 224.

33. Quoted in ibid., 237.

34. D.H. Lawrence, *Selected Literary Criticism* (New York: Viking, 1956), 257.

35. Quoted in E.H. Spicer, *Cycles of Conquest: The Impact of Spain, Mexico and the United States on Indians of the Southwest 1533–1960* (Tucson: University of Arizona Press, 1962), 581–582.

36. Quoted in Kouwenhoven, "What's American About America?" op. cit., 184.

37. Courtesy of Dr. Irven DeVore, Education Development Center, 15 Mifflin Place, Cambridge, Mass. 02138.

6. PERSISTENCE OF PLACE

1. V. Gordon Childe, *Man Makes Himself* (London: Watts, 1965), 107.

2. George Perkins Marsh, *The Earth as Modified by Human Action: A New Edition of "Man and Nature"* (New York: Scribner, Armstrong & Co., 1874).

3. Quoted in David Lowenthal, *George Perkins Marsh, Versatile Vermonter* (New York: Columbia University Press, 1958), 270.

4. Quoted in Clarence J. Glacken, "Changing Ideas of the Habitable World," in William L. Thomas, Jr. (ed.), *Man's Role in Changing the Face of the Earth* (Chicago: University of Chicago Press, 1956), 70.

5. Jacquetta Hawkes, *A Land* (New York: Random House, 1951).

6. Sir Cyril Fox, *The Personality of Britain* (Cardiff, Wales: National Museum of Wales, 1952).

7. Hermann Schreiber, *Merchants, Pilgrims and Highwaymen* (New York: Putnam, 1961).

8. J. Todd Snow, "The New Road in the United States," *Landscape*, 17 (1967), 13.

9. Vincent Scully, *The Earth, the Temple and the Gods* (New York: Praeger, 1962).

10. Robert M. Newcomb, "Monuments Three Millennia Old—The Persistence of Place," *Landscape*, 17 (1967), 24.

11. Nina Jidejian, *Byblos Through the Ages* (Beirut: Dar El Machreq, 1968).

12. Quoted in John Kirtland Wright, *The Geographical Lore of the Time of the Crusades* (New York: Dover, 1965), 331–332.

13. Quoted in ibid., 341–42.

14. William Murray, "The Porn Capital of America," *The New York Times Magazine*, January 3, 1971, 8. See also Kenneth Rexroth, *An Autobiographical Novel* (New York: Doubleday, 1966), 366–67.

15. D.H. Lawrence, *Studies in Classic American Literature* (London: Heinemann, 1964), 5–6.

16. D.H. Lawrence, *Phoenix* (New York: Viking, 1936), 46, 142.

17. R.J. Wurtman, "Good Light and Bad," *New England Journal of Medicine* 282 (1970), 394–95.

18. Rory Fonseca, "The Walled City of Old Delhi," *Landscape*, 18 (1969), 13–25.

19. Ralph Waldo Emerson, *Representative Men*, in *The Selected Writings . . .* (New York: Modern Library, 1950), 21.

20. Lawrence Durrell, *Spirit of Place* (New York: Dutton, 1969), 159.

21. Sigfried Giedion, *Space, Time and Architecture* (Cambridge, Mass.: Harvard University Press, 1967), 716, 755.

22. Stephen Vincent Benét, *Western Star* (New York: Farrar & Rinehart, 1943), Prelude, line 12.

23. See Ian McHarg, *Design with Nature* (New York: Natural History Press, 1969), 181.

7. HUMANIZED NATURE

1. Eric Julber, "A Nature Purist No Longer," *The Milwaukee Journal*, December 16, 1970, 23.

2. Claude Lévi-Strauss, *Tristes Tropiques*, translated by John Russell (New York: Atheneum, 1969), 98–99.

3. Leo Marx, *The Machine in the Garden* (New York: Oxford University Press, 1964).

4. Quoted in Arthur A. Ekirch, Jr., *Man and Nature in America* (New York: Columbia University Press, 1963), 12.

5. Quoted in E.T. Carlson and P.C. Novel, "Stress and Behavior in the Founding Pilgrims," *Bulletin of New York Academy of Medicine*, 47 (1971), 149.

6. V. Gordon Childe, *Man Makes Himself* (London: Watts, 1965), 107.

7. Quoted in Clarence J. Glacken, *Traces on the Rhodian Shore* (Richmond, Calif.: University of California Press, 1967), xxix.

8. I.G. Simmons, "Britannia Deserta," *Landscape*, 15 (1965–66), 27–29: "Environment and Early Man on Dartmoor, Devon, England," *Proceedings of the Prehistoric Society*, 35 (1969), 203–219.

9. Marjorie Hope Nicolson, *Mountain Gloom and Mountain Glory* (Ithaca, N.Y.: Cornell University Press, 1959), 2.

10. Quoted in David Lowenthal, "Daniel Boone is Dead," *Natural History*, 77 (1968), 16.

11. Massachusetts Institute of Technology, *Man's Impact on the Global Environment: Report of the Study of Critical Environmental Problems* (Cambridge, Mass.: M.I.T. Press, 1970).

12. Samuel R. Ogden (ed.), *America the Vanishing: Rural Life and the Price of Progress* (Brattleboro, Vt.: Stephen Greene Press, 1969).

13. René Dubos, *Reason Awake! Science for Man* (New York: Columbia University Press, 1970), xvii.

8. FRANCISCAN CONSERVATION VERSUS BENEDICTINE STEWARDSHIP

1. Paul B. Sears, "Climate and Civilization," in H. Shapley (ed.), *Climatic Change* (Cambridge, Mass.: Harvard University Press, 1953), 44.

2. Quoted in Raymond Nace, "Arrogance Toward the Landscape: A Problem in Water Planning," *Bulletin of the Atomic Scientists*, 25 (1969), 14.

3. Carl O. Sauer, *Land and Life* (Berkeley, Calif.: University of California Press, 1963), 148.

4. George P. Marsh, *The Earth as Modified by Human Action: A New Edition of "Man and Nature"* (New York: Scribner, Armstrong & Co., 1874).

5. Aldo Leopold, *A Sand County Almanac and Sketches Here and There* (New York: Oxford University Press, 1949).

6. Clarence J. Glacken, *Traces on the Rhodian Shore* (Richmond, Calif.: University of California Press, 1967), 494.

7. Lynn White, Jr., "The Historical Roots of Our Ecologic Crisis," *Science*, 155 (1967), 1203–1207.

8. Ibid., 1207.

9. See John D. Buffington, "Predation, Competition, and Pleistocene Megafauna Extinction," *BioScience*, 21 (1971), 167–170; Robert Gordis, "Judaism and the Spoliation of Nature," *Congress Bi-Weekly*, April 2, 1971, 9–12; Daniel A. Guthrie, "Primitive Man's Relationship to Nature," *BioScience*, 21 (1971), 721–723; Joe Ben Wheat, "A Paleo-Indian Bison Kill," *Scientific American*, 216 (1967), 44–52; Richard T. Wright, "Responsibility for the Ecological Crisis," *BioScience*, 21 (1970), 851–853; and "Here We Go Again," *Scientific American*, 224 (1971), 59.

10. Joseph Needham, *Science and Civilisation in China*, 4 vols. (Cambridge: Cambridge University Press, 1954–1962).

11. Yi-Fu Tuan, "Our Treatment of the Environment in Ideal and Actuality," *American Scientist*, 58 (1970), 248.

12. Nina Jidejian, *Byblos Through the Ages* (Beirut: Dar El Machreq, 1968).

13. Arthur O. Lovejoy, *The Great Chain of Being* (Cambridge, Mass.: Harvard University Press, 1936).

14. Anthony Smith, *The Seasons: Life and Its Rhythms* (New York: Harcourt, Brace, Jovanovich, 1970), 162, 166.

15. Carl O. Sauer, *Agricultural Origins and Dispersals: The Domestication of Animals and Foodstuffs* (Cambridge, Mass.: M.I.T. Press, 1969), 15.

16. Quoted in Max Nicholson, *The Environmental Revolution* (New York: McGraw-Hill, 1970), 168.

17. David Ehrenfeld, *Biological Conservation* (New York: Holt, Rinehart and Winston, 1970).

18. Quoted in Paul Fleischman, "Conservation: The Biological Fallacy," *Landscape*, 18 (1969), 26.

19. Fleischman, op. cit.

20. Lynn White, Jr., *Machina ex Deo* (Cambridge, Mass.: M.I.T. Press, 1968), 65.

21. Quoted in Glacken, op. cit., 214.

22. Clarence Glacken, op. cit., 213.

23. White, *Machina ex Deo*, 67.

24. Wolfgang Braunfels, "Institutions and Their Corresponding Ideals," in *The Quality of Man's Environment* (Washington, D.C.: Smithsonian Institution Press, 1968).

9. *FITNESS, CHANGE, AND DESIGN*

1. Peter Kalm, *Travels in North America* (London: Lowndes, 1772), quoted in R. Hill, M. Hoyt, and W. Hard, Jr., *Vermont, A Special World* (Montpelier: *Vermont Life*, 1968), 53.

2. Gilbert White, *The Natural History and Antiquities of Selborne, in the County of Southampton* (London: Bensley, 1789; reprint, London: The Cresset Press, 1947).

3. Nan Fairbrother, *New Lives, New Landscapes* (New York: Knopf, 1970), 20–21.

4. Quoted in ibid., 22.

5. Roger Agache, "Dévastation du paysage picard," *Médecine de France*, 214 (1970), 39.

6. René Dubos, *So Human an Animal* (New York: Charles Scribner's Sons, 1968), 77–95.

7. Louis LeRoy, *De la Vicissitude ou varieté des choses en l'uni-*

vers, et concurrence des armes et des lettres par les premieres et plus illustres nations du monde, depuis le temps ou a commencé la civilité & memoire humaine iusques à present (Paris: Pierre L'Huillier, 1575); see also Werner L. Gundersheimer, *The Life and Works of Louis LeRoy* (Geneva: Librairie Droz, 1966).

8. Alfred Russel Wallace, *The Wonderful Century, Its Successes and Its Failures* (New York: Dodd, Mead, 1899).

9. Alvin Toffler, *Future Shock* (New York: Random House, 1970).

10. Quoted in Ralph B. Perry (ed.), *The Thought and Character of William James*, (Boston: Little, Brown, 1936), vol. II, 255.

11. May Theilgaard Watts, "The Trees and Roofs of France," in Paul Shepard and Daniel McKinley (eds.), *The Subversive Science* (Boston: Houghton Mifflin, 1969), 168–175.

12. Louis Pasteur, *Oeuvres Complètes* (Paris: Masson, 1933–1939), VII, 233.

13. Hippocrates, *Humours*, translated by W. Jones (London: Heinemann, 1931), 89.

14. Herbert Read, *High Noon and Darkest Night*, Monday Evening Papers Number 3 (Middletown, Conn.: Wesleyan University Press, May 11, 1964).

15. F. Fraser Darling, "The Ecological Approach to the Social Science," in Shepard and McKinley, op. cit., 15.

16. Ian McHarg, *Design with Nature* (New York: Natural History Press, 1969).

17. I. W. U. Chase (ed.), *Horace Walpole: Gardenist* (Princeton, N.J.: Princeton University Press, 1943), 214.

18. Alexander Pope, "Epistle IV, to Richard Boyle, Earl of Burlington, on the Use of Riches," *Works*, edited by W. Elwin and W.J. Courthope (London: 1881), vol. 3, 176.

19. William H. Whyte, *The Last Landscape* (Garden City: Doubleday, 1968), 181.

10. A DEMON WITHIN

1. See Sir Kenneth Clark, *Civilisation* (New York: Harper & Row, 1969).

2. John Nef, "Civilization, Industrial Society, and Love," *Occasional Paper* (Santa Barbara: The Center for the Study of Democratic Institutions, 1961). See also Lucien Febvre, *Civilisation, le mot et l'idée* (Paris: Centre International de Synthèse, 1930).

3. John Kenneth Galbraith, *The Affluent Society* (Boston: Houghton Mifflin, 1958).

4. Lewis Mumford, *The Myth of the Machine: Technics and Human Development* (New York: Harcourt, Brace & World, 1967); *The Myth of the Machine: The Pentagon of Power* (New York: Harcourt, Brace & Jovanovich, 1970).

5. René Dubos, *Reason Awake! Science for Man*, (New York: Columbia University Press, 1970), 43–52.

6. Albert H. Smyth (ed.), *The Writings of Benjamin Franklin* (New York: Macmillan, 1905–1907), VIII, 10.

7. E.M. Forster, *The Collected Tales* (New York: Knopf, 1959), 176.

8. Max Born, *My Life and My Views* (New York: Charles Scribner's Sons, 1968); Norbert Wiener, "The Monkey's Paw," in J. Burke (ed.), *The New Technology and Human Values* (Belmont: Wadsworth, 1966), 130–134; Dennis Gabor, *Innovations: Scientific, Technological and Social* (New York: Oxford University Press, 1971).

9. Jay W. Forrester, "Counterintuitive Behavior of Social Systems," *Technology Review*, 73 (1971), 1–16. See also Jay W. Forrester, *World Dynamics* (Cambridge, Mass.: Wright-Allen Press, 1971), and D. H. Meadows *et al.*, *The Limits to Growth* (New York: Universe Books, 1972).

10. Jacques Ellul, *The Technological Society*, translated by John Wilkinson (New York: Knopf, 1965).

11. John Kenneth Galbraith, *The New Industrial State* (Boston: Houghton Mifflin, 1967).

12. Henry Adams, *The Education of Henry Adams* (Boston: Houghton Mifflin, 1918), 379–390.

13. Chicago Century of Progress International Exposition, *Official Guidebook of the Fair* (Chicago: A Century of Progress, Inc., 1933). See also Lowell Tozer, "A Century of Progress, 1833–1933: Technology's Triumph Over Man," *American Quarterly*, 4 (1952), 78–81.

14. Pica della Mirandola, quoted in E. Cassirer, *The Renaissance Philosophy of Man* (Chicago: University of Chicago Press, 1948), 224–225.

11. INDUSTRIAL SOCIETY AND HUMANE CIVILIZATION

1. Ray Brosseau, *Looking Forward* (New York: American Heritage, 1970).

2. Herman Kahn and Anthony Wiener, *The Year 2000: A Framework for Speculation on the Next 33 Years* (New York: Macmillan, 1968).

3. R. Buckminster Fuller, "Planetary Planning," *The American Scholar*, 40 (1970–71), 29–63 and 285–304; Philip Handler, "Can Man Shape His Future?" *Perspectives in Biology and Medicine*, 14 (1971), 207–227.

4. H.G. Wells, *Mind at the End of Its Tether* (New York: Didier, 1946).

5. Henry Adams, *The Education of Henry Adams* (Boston: Houghton Mifflin, 1918), 380.

6. Professor LaMont Cole, Department of Ecology, Cornell Uni-

versity, Ithaca, New York, personal communications to the author. See also Bruce Wallace, *Essays in Social Biology. I. People, Their Needs, Environment, Ecology* (Englewood Cliffs, N. J.: Prentice-Hall, 1972), 81.

7. Paul Chabrol, "La Desertification de l'Espagne est-elle historique ou climatique?" *Mémoires de l'Académie des Sciences de Toulouse* (Toulouse: 1969), 77.

8. Herman E. Daly, "Toward a Stationary-State Economy," in John Harte and R.H. Socolow (eds.), *Patient Earth* (New York: Holt, Rinehart, Winston, 1971). See also Paul B. Sears, "The Steady-State: Physical Law and Moral Choice," *The Key Reporter*, 24 (1959), 2–3, 8.

9. Stephen Vincent Bénet, *Western Star* (New York: Farrar & Rinehart, 1943).

10. Fred Smith, *America Is a Growing Country* (New York: privately printed, 1971).

11. Jean Cocteau, "J'ai traversé tant d'événements extraordinaires," preface to *L'Evénement: Les Peintres Témoins de Leur Temps* (Paris: Maison des Artistes, 1963).

12. Charles Luce, in Frank Herbert (ed.), *New World or No World* (New York: Ace Books, 1970), 65.

13. Dennis Gabor, *Innovations: Scientific, Technological and Social* (New York: Oxford University Press, 1971).

12. ON BEING HUMAN

1. Lewis Thomas, "Notes of a Biology-Watcher," *New England Journal of Medicine*, 285 (1971), 101–102.

2. J.M. Ziman, "Information, Communication, Knowledge," *Nature*, 224 (1969), 318–324.

3. Lord Ritchie-Calder, *The Center Magazine*, Santa Barbara, California, 4 (1971), 5–6.

4. Benjamin Barondess, *Three Lincoln Masterpieces* (Charleston, West Va.: Education Foundation of West Virginia, 1954), 3.

5. William James, *The Will to Believe* (New York: Longmans Green, 1907), 259.

6. Joanna Richardson, "Romantic Bohemia," *History Today*, 19 (1969), 460–467.

7. Claude Bernard, *Experimental Medicine*, translated by H.C. Greene (New York: Macmillan, 1927), viii.

8. F. Grande and M. Visscher (eds.), *Claude Bernard and Experimental Medicine* (Cambridge, Mass.: Schenkman, 1967), 27–30.

9. W.B. Cannon, *The Wisdom of the Body* (New York: Norton, 1939).

10. Norbert Wiener, *I am a Mathematician* (Garden City: Doubleday, 1956).

11. Talcott Parsons (ed.), *American Sociology* (New York: Basic Books, 1968).

12. Otto Mayr, "The Origins of Feedback Control," *Scientific American*, 223 (1970), 110–118.

13. D.W. Richards, "Homeostasis: Its Dislocations and Perturbations," *Perspectives in Biology and Medicine*, 3 (1960), 238–251.

14. René Dubos, *So Human an Animal* (New York: Charles Scribner's Sons, 1968), 63–106.

15. John Dewey, *Creative Intelligence* (New York: Holt, 1917), 36.

16. Henri Bergson, *Creative Evolution*, translated by A. Mitchell (New York: Holt, 1911).

17. Frederick Jackson Turner, *The Frontier in American History* (New York: Holt, Rinehart & Winston, 1962).

18. Vannevar Bush, *Science the Endless Frontier* (Washington, D.C.: National Science Foundation, 1960).

19. Walter Pater, "A Study of Dionysus," *Greek Studies* (London: Macmillan, 1925), 9–52; see also E.R. Dodds, *The Greeks and The Irrational* (Berkeley: University of California Press, 1951).

20. John W. Bennett, "Cultural Integrity and Personal Identity: The Communitarian Response," paper presented at the Smithsonian

Institution's Fourth International Symposium, The Cultural Drama, 1970; a shorter version, "The Challenge of Communes," was published in *Dialogue*, 4 (1971), 68–75.

21. Alfred North Whitehead, *Science and the Modern World* (New York: Macmillan, 1925), 252–269.

13. ARCADIAN LIFE VERSUS FAUSTIAN CIVILIZATION

1. Harry Levin, *The Myth of the Golden Age in the Renaissance* (Bloomington, Ind.: Indiana University Press, 1969).

2. Hesiod, *The Works and Days*, translated by Richmond Lattimore (Ann Arbor, Mich.: University of Michigan Press, 1959), 31.

3. Erwin Panofsky, "*Et in Arcadia Ego*, Poussin and the Elegiac Tradition," in *Meaning of the Visual Arts* (Garden City, N.Y.: Doubleday, 1955), 295–320.

4. Ralph Solecki, *Shanidar* (New York: Knopf, 1971).

5. Quoted in ibid.

6. Clarence J. Glacken, *Traces on the Rhodian Shore* (Richmond, Calif.: University of California Press, 1967), 214.

7. Bernard Rudofsky, *Architecture without Architects* (Garden City, N.Y.: Doubleday, 1969).

8. A. Whitridge, "Bougainville and Tahiti," *History Today*, 19 (1969), 815–822.

9. Quoted in David Lowenthal, "Is Wilderness Enow?," *Columbia University Forum*, Spring 1964, 37.

10. Chauncey Starr, "Energy and Power," *Scientific American*, 225 (1971), 37–49.

11. Manson Benedict, "Electric Power from Nuclear Fission," *Bulletin of the Atomic Scientists*, 27 (1971), 8–16.

12. International Chamber of Commerce, "The Vienna Pa-

pers," United States Council participation in ICC XXIII, "Technology and Society: A Challenge to Private Enterprise," 1971.

13. Gérard Hubert, "Château de Malmaison," *Médecine de France*, 224 (1971), 25–40.

14. René Dubos, *Reason Awake! Science for Man* (New York: Columbia University Press, 1970), 64, 125.

15. Don K. Price, "Purists and Politicians," *Science*, 163 (1969), 25–31.

16. See Kenneth Boulding, *Beyond Economics* (Ann Arbor, Mich.: University of Michigan Press, 1968); Nigel Calder, *Technopolis* (London: MacGibbon and Kee, 1969); E. Jantsch (ed.), *Perspectives of Planning* (Paris: OECD, 1969); Bertrand de Jouvenel, *The Art of Conjecture*, translated by N. Lary (New York: Basic Books, 1967); Robert Jungk and Johan Galtung, *Mankind 2000* (London: Allen and Unwin, 1969); Herman Kahn and Anthony Wiener, *The Year 2000: A Framework for Speculation on the Next 33 Years* (New York: Macmillan, 1968); Emmanuel G. Mesthene, "How Technology Will Shape the Future," *Science*, 161 (1968), 135–43; Donald N. Michael, *The Unprepared Society* (New York: Basic Books, 1968); John Platt, "How Men Can Shape Their Future," *Futures*, March 1971, 32–47.

17. Lars Emmelin, "Restoring Damaged Lakes," *Environment Planning and Conservation in Sweden*, Swedish Information Service Newsletter No. 10, November 1970.

18. Aldo Leopold, *A Sand Country Almanac and Sketches Here and There* (New York: Oxford University Press, 1949), 205.

19. H.W. Higman and E.J. Larrison, *Union Bay: The Life of a City Marsh* (Seattle: University of Washington Press, 1951).

20. *The Environment Monthly*, September 1970.

21. Dennis Gabor, *Inventing the Future* (New York: Knopf, 1964).

22. T.S. Eliot, *Four Quartets* (New York: Harcourt, Brace & World, 1943), 39.

23. See Barry Commoner, *The Closing Circle* (New York:

Knopf, 1971); Paul R. Ehrlich, *The Population Bomb* (New York: Ballantine, 1968); Paul R. Ehrlich and A.H. Ehrlich, *Population, Resources, and Environment* (San Francisco: Freeman, 1970); Noel Hinrichs, *Population, Environment and People* (New York: McGraw-Hill, 1971).

24. Peter Laslett, *The World We Have Lost* (New York: Charles Scribner's Sons, 1965).

25. Antony Jay, "Who Knows What Primitive Instincts Lurk in the Heart of Modern Corporation Man?" *New York*, 4 (1971), 29–35. See also Antony Jay, *Corporation Man* (New York: Random House, 1971).

26. Anthony Bailey, "The Village—1", *The New Yorker*, 47 (1971), 41. See also Anthony Bailey, *In the Village* (New York: Knopf, 1971).

27. Jay Forrester, *World Dynamics* (Cambridge: Wright-Allen Press, 1971). See also D.H. Meadows *et al.*, *The Limits to Growth* (New York: University Books, 1972).

28. François Rabelais, *Gargantua and Pantagruel*, Book 3, chapter X.

29. Quoted in Sherman Paul, *The Shores of America: Thoreau's Inward Exploration* (Urbana, Ill.: University of Illinois Press, 1958), 154.

30. Joseph Wood Krutch, *The Best Nature Writing of Joseph Wood Krutch* (New York: William Morrow, 1969), 261–262.

ENVOI

1. Carl Sandburg, *The People, Yes* (New York: Harcourt, Brace, 1936), 43.

Selected Bibliography

BROOKS, VAN WYCK, and BETTMANN, O.L. *Our Literary Heritage.* New York: Dutton, 1956.

CHILDE, V. GORDON. *Man Makes Himself.* London: C.W. Watts, 1956.

______. *Social Evolution.* London: C.W. Watts, 1963.

COLVIN, BRENDA. *Land and Landscape.* London: John Murray, 1948.

COMMONER, BARRY. *The Closing Circle.* New York: Alfred Knopf, 1971.

DARLING, F. FRASER, and MILTON, JOHN P. (eds.). *Future Environments of North America.* Garden City, N.Y.: Natural History Press, 1966.

DODDS, E.R. *The Greeks and the Irrational.* Berkeley, Calif.: University of California Press, 1951.

DUBOS, RENÉ. *Mirage of Health.* New York: Harper and Brothers, 1959.

______. *Man Adapting.* New Haven, Conn.: Yale University Press, 1965.

______. *So Human an Animal.* New York: Charles Scribner's Sons, 1968.

EHRLICH, PAUL R., and EHRLICH, ANNE H. *Population, Resources, Environment.* San Francisco: W.H. Freeman, 1970.

GLACKEN, CLARENCE J. *Traces on the Rhodian Shore.* Richmond, Calif.: University of California Press, 1967.

HINRICHS, NOËL (ed.). *Population, Environment and People.* New York: McGraw-Hill, 1971.

JOUVENEL, BERTRAND DE *The Art of Conjecture.* Translated by N. Lary. New York: Basic Books, 1967.

LEE, RICHARD B., and DE VORE, IRVEN (eds.). *Man the Hunter.* Chicago: Aldine, 1968.

MC HARG, IAN. *Design with Nature.* Garden City, N.Y.: Natural History Press, 1969.

MARX, LEO. *The Machine in the Garden.* New York: Oxford University Press, 1964.

MASSACHUSETTS INSTITUTE OF TECHNOLOGY. *Man's Impact on the Global Environment: Report of the Study of Critical Environmental Problems.* Cambridge, Mass.: The M.I.T. Press, 1970.

MEDAWAR, P.B. *The Future of Man.* New York: Mentor Books, 1961.

MUMFORD, LEWIS. *The Myth of the Machine: Technics and Human Development.* New York: Harcourt, Brace & World, 1967.

———. *The Myth of the Machine: The Pentagon of Power.* New York: Harcourt, Brace & Jovanovich, 1970.

PLATT, JOHN. *The Step to Man.* New York: Wiley, 1966.

SAUER, CARL O. *Land and Life.* Berkeley, Calif.: University of California Press, 1963.

———. *Agricultural Origins and Dispersals.* Cambridge, Mass.: The M.I.T. Press, 1969.

SCULLY, VINCENT. *The Earth, the Temple and the Gods.* New York: Praeger, 1962.

SHEPARD, PAUL. *Man in the Landscape.* New York: Alfred Knopf, 1967.

SHEPARD, PAUL, and MC KINLEY, DANIEL (eds.). *The Subversive Science: Essays Toward an Ecology of Man.* Boston: Houghton Mifflin, 1969.

THOMAS, WILLIAM L. (ed.). *Man's Role in Changing the Face of the Earth.* Chicago: University of Chicago Press, 1956.

WHITE, LYNN, JR. *Medieval Technology and Social Change.* Oxford: The Clarendon Press, 1962.

———. *Machina ex Deo.* Cambridge, Mass.: The M.I.T. Press, 1968.

WHITEHEAD, ALFRED NORTH. *Science and the Modern World.* New York: Macmillan, 1925.

Index

About the Author

RENÉ DUBOS, professor emeritus at The Rockefeller University in New York City, is a microbiologist and experimental pathologist who more than a quarter of a century ago was the first to demonstrate the feasibility of obtaining germ-fighting drugs from microbes. For his scientific contributions, Dr. Dubos has received many awards; most recently he was the recipient of the first Institut de la Vie prize for his work devoted to environmental problems. He is well known as an author and lecturer as well as a scientific investigator; his books include *So Human an Animal* (1969 Pulitzer Prize winner), *Reason Awake! Science for Man*, *Only One Earth* (with Barbara Ward), *Louis Pasteur—Free Lance of Science*, *The Torch of Life*, *The Unseen World*, *The Dreams of Reason*, *The White Plague* (with Jean Dubos), *The Mirage of Health*, and *Man Adapting*.

LAWRENCE MOBERG